Beethoven

Beethoven

A Life in Nine Pieces

LAURA TUNBRIDGE

VIKING
an imprint of
PENGUIN BOOKS

For Richard

VIKING

UK | USA | Canada | Ireland | Australia
India | New Zealand | South Africa

Viking is part of the Penguin Random House group of companies
whose addresses can be found at global.penguinrandomhouse.com.

First published 2020
001

Copyright © Laura Tunbridge, 2020

The moral right of the author has been asserted

Set in 12/14.75 pt Bembo Book MT Std
Typeset by Jouve (UK), Milton Keynes
Printed and bound in Great Britain by Clays Ltd, Elcograf S.p.A.

A CIP catalogue record for this book is available from the British Library

ISBN: 978-0-241-41427-9

Contents

List of Illustrations   vi

A Note on Beethoven's Finances   ix

A Note on Musical Terms   xi

Introduction: Beginnings   1

1. Success: Septet, op. 20 (1800)   19

2. Friends: Violin Sonata no. 9, op. 47, the 'Kreutzer' (1803)   43

3. Heroism: Symphony no. 3, op. 55, the 'Eroica' (1804)   69

4. Ambition: Choral Fantasy, op. 80 (1808)   90

5. Love: 'An die Geliebte', WoO 140 (1812)   111

6. Liberty: *Fidelio*, op. 72 (1814)   138

7. Family: Piano Sonata no. 29, op. 106, the
   'Hammerklavier' (1818)   162

8. Spirit: *Missa solemnis*, op. 123 (1823)   183

9. Endings: String Quartet, op. 130, and the 'Grosse Fuge',
   op. 133 (1826)   204

Coda   226

Further Reading   232

Acknowledgements   237

Notes   238

Index   261

List of Illustrations

i.1 The unveiling of the Beethoven monument in 1845
(*Illustrated London News*, 23 August 1845). 2

i.2 Map of the Habsburg Empire (public domain). 6

i.3 Frontispiece for Beethoven's op. 1 (public domain). 7

1.1 Poster for Beethoven's academy in the Burgtheater on
2 April 1800 (© Beethoven-Haus Bonn). 26

1.2 Sketch for Beethoven's op. 131. British Library Add
MS 38070 [f. 51r] (public domain). 39

2.1 Christian Horneman's portrait of Beethoven, given
by the composer to Stephan von Breuning (Heritage
Image Partnership Ltd/Alamy Stock Photo). 46

2.2 Map of Vienna (from the collections of the Ira F.
Brilliant Center for Beethoven Studies, San José State
University) (public domain). 50

2.3 Schuppanzigh caricature (© Gesellschaft der
Musikfreunde). 53

2.4 Changing bow shapes in the eighteenth century.
Photograph courtesy of Richard Gwilt. 66

3.1 The title page of the fair copy of the Third Symphony
owned by Beethoven (public domain). 80

3.2 Antonio Rizzi, *Beethoven: Sinfonia Eroica – II Tempo*.
NOVISSIMA. Albo d'arti e lettere, (Milan, 1903)
(By permission of the Biblioteca comunale dell'
Archiginnasio, Bologna). 87

4.1 Interior of the Theater an der Wien. Stalls and boxes. Vienna, Historisches Museum der Stadt Wien (History Museum) (Photo by DeAgostini/Getty Images).   91

4.2 Map of Europe in 1810 (public domain).   107

5.1 Ludwig van Beethoven's life mask, made in 1812 by Franz Klein (Lebrecht Music & Arts/Alamy Stock Photo).   132

5.2 Ludwig van Beethoven, bronze bust by Franz Klein, 1812 (reproduced 1890). (Beethoven-Haus Bonn).   133

5.3 Ear trumpets (Chronicle/Alamy Stock Photo).   135

6.1 Ball at the Imperial Riding School during the Congress of Vienna, by Johann Nepomuk Hoechle, 1815. (Austrian National Library/Interfoto/ Alamy Stock Photo).   139

6.2 Dungeon scene from *Fidelio*, Act II. *Wiener Hoftheater-Taschenbuch* (1815) (Lebrecht Music & Arts/Alamy Stock Photo).   153

7.1 Karl van Beethoven, miniature portrait, 25 June 1825 (public domain).   166

7.2 An illustration of the different ranges of the instruments Beethoven owned, shown in comparison to today's standard eighty-eight keys.   169

8.1 A nineteenth-century print depicting the first perform-ance of Beethoven's Ninth Symphony, with Beethoven drawn in the middle of his orchestra (History and Art Collection/Alamy Stock Photo).   195

9.1 A sketch of Beethoven by Johann Peter Theodor Lyser, originally published in the journal *Cäcilia* in 1833 (FALKENSTEINFOTO/Alamy Stock Photo).   205

9.2 First edition of the score of the String Quartet in F Major, op. 135 (Schlesinger: Paris/Berlin, 1827).   207

9.3 Landscape made out of Beethoven's hair (© Beethoven-Haus Bonn). 224

C.1 Bonn, Germany. 17 May 2019. Seven hundred Ludwig van Beethoven sculptures stand on Bonn's Münsterplatz. The sculptures were created by Prof. Dr Ottmar Hörl (dpa picture alliance/Alamy Stock Photo). 230

A Note on Beethoven's Finances

Reference is made throughout this book to the sums Beethoven earned. These are especially difficult to compare to today's currency because of the unstable economic situation of Austria during the Napoleonic Wars (1803–15). There were also several types of currency in circulation. There were 60 kreuzer in a gulden or florin; two gulden made a taler. A ducat was 4 gulden 30 kreuzer of Konventionsmünze (literally, 'convention coin'), the silver standard that had been agreed towards the end of the Seven Years War. Twenty gulden made a Kölner mark (Cologne mark), the Prussian currency. Paper currency, the Bancozettel, had been introduced in Austria in 1762 and was supposed to be equivalent to metal coinage. As the government printed more money in an attempt to fund its war efforts, however, its value plummeted. By 1811, the Bancozettel had been devalued to a fifth of its face value and a *Finanzpatent* was instituted that replaced it with a new Viennese currency (Wiener Währung) that, in turn, failed to bring about the stability the government hoped for. Inflation peaked again in 1817, after the Austrians bore the brunt of the costs of the Congress of Vienna: it has been reckoned that between 1795 and 1816 hyperinflation caused a fortyfold reduction in the purchasing power of Beethoven's income. The financial situation in Vienna stabilized only in 1820, the year in which Beethoven assumed responsibility as the legal guardian of his nephew Karl after a five-year battle in the courts.

Food prices fluctuated according to inflation – sometimes rising and falling within a day – and in response to shortages caused by war and the failure of crops (1815–16 was a particularly bad year in that regard). The average Vienna resident in the early nineteenth century spent about 40 per cent of their income on food, 20 per cent on clothing, and only about 15 per cent on rent, the price of which was set twice a year. When Beethoven arrived in Vienna in 1792 his monthly rent was 14 florins and a month's worth of meals with wine was 16 florins. From 1800, Prince Lichnowsky gave Beethoven 600 florins per year as well as lodgings in his palace. Four years later, an article by writer and librarian Johann Pezzl stated that a middle-class single man could subsist adequately on 967 florins per annum and comfortably – including entertainments such as going to the theatre – on 1,200 florins. The annual stipend of 4,000 florins bestowed on Beethoven in 1809 was generous, but because it was paid in Bancozettel it was almost immediately devalued by the financial crisis.

Perhaps the best way to illustrate the fluctuating cost of living is through the price of Beethoven's beloved coffee. By the end of the eighteenth century, coffee had replaced beer and wine as the breakfast drink for most Viennese, but it was relatively expensive and the lower classes resorted to substitute drinks made from acorns, dried fruit or chicory. The first coffeehouse in Vienna opened in 1685; a century later, there were more than fifty in the city. For those who could afford to frequent them, the price of coffee rose rapidly. In 1797, a cup of black coffee cost 4 kreuzer; by 1804, 7 kreuzer; by 1810, 24 kreuzer. Making coffee at home – as Beethoven did – required expensive machinery, and buying coffee by the *Wiener Pfund* (an ample 'Vienna pound') was also costly: it doubled within a decade at the end of the century (from 45 to 90 kreuzer). In terms of the relative prices of different items, by 1810 it was more expensive to buy two cups of coffee than it was to buy a *Wiener Pfund* of beef. Beethoven counted out his coffee beans not only in pursuit of the perfect cup but also out of economic concern, and the same observation might be extended to his dealings with publishers and concert promoters.

A Note on Musical Terms

On the whole, musical terms are defined as they come up in discussion. However, a brief explanation of some that recur might be helpful. In Beethoven's instrumental pieces – symphonies, sonatas and quartets – he followed the convention of using Italian terms as the titles of movements to indicate the tempo, or pace, of the music. Typically, the first movement is marked *allegro* ('lively'), which might be reinforced, for example, to *allegro assai* ('very lively'), or modified, for example, to *allegro con brio* (with zest or vigour) or *risoluto* ('determinedly'). The second movement is often *andante*, literally 'going', and often interpreted as 'at a walking pace'; or it may be *adagio*, 'slow'. These terms could be refined in many ways. *Cantabile* suggests a singing quality while *sostenuto* means 'sustained'. Diminutives like *andantino* could be interpreted as 'a little faster or a little slower than *andante*'; for Beethoven, it was more likely to mean 'more quickly', but he complained in a letter to George Thomson in 1813 about the ambiguity: 'that word, like many others in music, is of such imprecise meaning that on one occasion *andantino* can be close to *allegro* and on another almost like *adagio*'. Superlatives could stretch a meaning to its ultimate, such as *adagissimo* ('very slow'). Third movements often had their origins in dance music, most commonly the minuet, which was as much an indicator of character as tempo. Alternatively, the third movement could be a *scherzo*: a jest. The fourth and final movement is typically an *allegro* and sometimes a *presto*, which prioritizes speed. During the course of

Beethoven's career, his tempo indications became more elaborate and he was an early adoptor of the metronome, which specified the number of beats per minute. As nationalist sentiment intensified around 1815, he briefly used German rather than Italian terms: *allegro* became *Lebhaft* and *adagio* became *Langsam*.

Introduction: Beginnings

In the year after Beethoven's death in 1827, a campaign was launched to build a monument to him at his birthplace in Bonn. The habit of erecting statues to great men was not then established. Famous writers and musicians rallied behind the idea of doing so for Beethoven. Two of the age's most celebrated pianists, Frédéric Chopin and Franz Liszt, gave concerts together in Paris in April 1841, contributing the proceeds to the Bonn Association for the Beethoven Monument. It was increasingly rare for Chopin to perform in public, demonstrating his commitment to the cause. Liszt, one of the project's most fervent supporters, not only contributed generously but had come out of retirement for the concerts. Progress was slow, however, and the unveiling of the monument was delayed until 1845, when it formed part of a three-day Beethovenfest of fireworks, concerts (including Liszt's cantata for the inauguration, as well as new works by Felix Mendelssohn and Robert Schumann) and a banquet at which the Irish-born 'Spanish' dancer Lola Montez allegedly caused such a ruckus that Liszt was not invited to Bonn for the centenary of Beethoven's birth in 1870.

Meanwhile, two of Beethoven's childhood friends, the physician Franz Gerhard Wegeler and the teacher Carl Moritz Kneisel, claimed to have identified his birthplace. Beethoven's parents had moved into rooms at Bonngasse 20 shortly after their marriage in 1767; his grandfather lived across the hallway. Ludwig van Beethoven was their second child, baptized on 17 December 1770. The building housed several families, most of whom, like the Beethovens, worked for the court. The Beethoven family stayed there

Fig. i.i The unveiling of the Beethoven monument in 1845.

until 1774, when they moved into an apartment not far away. Had it not been for Wegeler and Kneisel's revelation, the building would have remained anonymous and would probably have been demolished. Aware of the potential to cash in on the composer's fame, however, nearly a century after the Beethoven family had left, the building's new owner opened a restaurant on the ground floor which he named Beethoven's Geburtshaus ('birthplace'). A beer and concert hall was added five years later. The building was saved from demolition in 1889, when it was taken over by the Beethoven House Association, which converted it into a museum that opened in 1893, later expanding into neighbouring properties. In 1927, the centenary of Beethoven's death, the newly founded Beethoven Archive moved in. Bomb damage from the Second World War was repaired in the 1950s and today the Beethoven-Haus owns the largest archival collection dedicated to the composer.

From beer hall to museum: it seems fitting for Beethoven, whose life did not always match the elevated sphere accorded him and his music by history. Music was his family's business, but alcohol also played an important role. His grandfather, god-father and namesake, Ludwig van Beethoven, was both director of court music and a wine merchant; his father, Johann van Beethoven, was a court singer and an alcoholic. Beethoven was one of only three surviving children from the seven borne by his mother, Maria. While he revered his grandfather, who died when he was only three, Beethoven had a difficult relationship with his father. Johann's ambitions for his son to be a child prodigy in the manner of Mozart made him a hard taskmaster, and he could be verbally and physically abusive. Tensions increased as Beethoven's musical career escalated and his father was left in his shadow.

Bonn provided formative musical experiences and, crucially, introduced the young Beethoven to nobility who would become long-term patrons. The city's situation in the Rhineland made it relatively Francophile and outward-looking and thus a cultural hub for the region. Although Beethoven's general education was limited, he was particularly lucky in teachers such as Christian Gottlob Neefe, who provided him with a solid musical grounding and some Enlightenment ethics. The Protestant Neefe espoused a puritanism and dedication to ethical betterment which, biographer Maynard Solomon speculates, were a welcome counterbalance to Beethoven's dissolute father.[1] More than that, Neefe imbued in his student a heady mix of Enlightenment ideals drawn from French and German philosophers such as Voltaire and Immanuel Kant. Neefe, like many of Beethoven's early supporters in Bonn – including Nikolaus Simrock, who became a music publisher, and violinist Franz Ries, father of composer Ferdinand – was active in the Order of Illuminati, a radical branch of the Freemasons. Their activities came under increased surveillance in the 1780s, and eventually they disbanded, forming in its place the *Lesegesellschaft* (Reading Society), comprised of 'friends of literature' that soon encompassed several of Beethoven's acquaintances. Among them was Count Ferdinand Waldstein, confidant to the Elector of Cologne, Archduke Maximilian Franz, youngest son of Holy Roman Empress Maria Theresa. The count and the archduke were Beethoven's most powerful patrons in Bonn. Beethoven was employed by the court as a substitute organist aged thirteen, just after Maximilian had become Elector. This was not an unusual position for someone from a musician's family to take up; it also reflected the fact that economic savings were being made at the court – a youngster was cheaper to hire than someone with more experience. No matter: Beethoven made good use of the opportunity, soon joining Maximilian's chamber music ensemble as a pianist and viola player. His first compositions thus were for piano quartet (violin, viola, cello, keyboard), with a prominent role given to the viola, which happened to be Maximilian's instrument; this also promoted Beethoven's skills to the electoral orchestra, an ensemble he joined when the court theatre reopened in 1789.

Bonn may have been small but, under Maximilian's rule, its musical life flourished. The Elector supported Beethoven's first visit to Vienna, in 1786, when the young musician's keyboard improvisation briefly captured the attention of the not easily impressed Mozart. The trip was curtailed, however, when Beethoven learned that his mother was gravely ill; her death intensified Beethoven's responsibilities for his younger siblings, especially as his father became more difficult. Beethoven's second journey to Vienna, in November 1792, was made ostensibly to study with Haydn, who had recently visited Bonn (Mozart had died the previous year). Maximilian had agreed to continue to pay Beethoven's salary, with a bonus, for the duration of his studies. A year later, Haydn wrote to Maximilian, enclosing some of Beethoven's compositions and commenting: 'On the basis of these pieces, expert and amateur alike cannot but admit that Beethoven will in time become one of the greatest musical artists in Europe, and I shall be proud to call myself his teacher. I only wish that he would be able to remain here with me for considerably longer.'[2] The problem – as always – was money. Haydn had been forced to make a loan to Beethoven, assuring Maximilian that this was not because the young man was profligate; 'for his art, he is capable of sacrificing everything without compulsion'. Maximilian was not persuaded: he recognized the compositions as music Beethoven had already produced in Bonn and predicted that – as on his first Viennese visit – he would 'bring back nothing but debts'.

In the end, Beethoven did not return to Bonn at all. In 1794, Napoleon's troops took over the city and the court was disbanded. Beethoven's stipend was discontinued. Despite occasionally considering other options, and retaining strong personal ties to his hometown, he would spend the rest of his life in Vienna. This archetypally German musician, then, resided abroad for most of his career. This is something often overlooked by those keen to claim Beethoven as their own, or to celebrate or berate him as the greatest German composer. It also serves as a reminder that continental Europe was configured differently at the turn of the nineteenth century. Germany as we know it did not yet exist. Until its annexation by France, Bonn belonged to the Electorate of Cologne, one of several separate states that later would be gathered together to form the German Confederation and, eventually, the German Empire. The most powerful of these was the Kingdom of Prussia, which included the city of Berlin. German-speaking areas were also encompassed by the ancient Habsburg Empire, which became the Austrian Empire in 1804. Two years later, the Habsburgs gave up their claim to

Fig. i.2 Map showing the changing boundaries of the Habsburg Empire. Bonn is 15 miles south-east of Cologne.

the title of Holy Roman Emperor. The configuration of 'Austrian' territories changed through the centuries but included what is now Austria, stretching down through north-east Italian states to the port of Trieste and into south-west Germany, the Netherlands, the Czech Republic (Bohemia), Poland (Silesia), Slovenia, Croatia, Bosnia and parts of Hungary (fig. i.2). Vienna's position as a gateway between central and south-eastern Europe made it an intriguing, occasionally exotic urban centre. So far as court culture was concerned, however, France loomed large. French was the language used for official communications, including the front pages of the first editions of Beethoven's music (see fig. i.3). Revolutionary France and the Napoleonic Wars shaped and reshaped Europe throughout the composer's lifetime, and at least for the first decades of his career he planned trips to Paris.

The move to Vienna was undeniably important for Beethoven, personally and professionally. It marked a detachment from his family, although his brother Kaspar Karl arrived after

Fig. i.3 The first edition of Beethoven's Piano Trios, op. 1, the title page of which is given in French, including the composer's name.

him. It also prevented Beethoven from following in his grand-father's and father's footsteps by taking up a permanent position in court. Most musicians before him had depended on such connections – Haydn was in the long-term employ of the Hungarian Esterházy family, serving as Kapellmeister, or director of music, for four successive princes – or on commissions from the aristocracy or royalty. Beethoven similarly accepted commissions and earned money through performances and teaching. He continued to benefit from aristocratic patronage – in this regard, his experience and connections from Bonn served him well – but he also benefitted throughout his life from new models of support and from being in a city that valued music highly.

Vienna was acutely aware of its musical heritage and of the cultural kudos that composers such as Christoph Gluck, Mozart and Haydn had brought to its salons and opera houses. At the turn of the nineteenth century, it was becoming known as a centre for music printing and piano building and its flourishing performance scene. One alternative means of income for Beethoven was publishing his music. Until the turn of the century, most music circulated in handwritten copies, and this circulation was inevitably limited to courts or to individuals wealthy or lucky enough to get hold of them. Printed music could be disseminated more widely and more cheaply. For a composer like Beethoven, it promised not only a way of making money but also of making his name known. He devoted a great deal of time and energy to negotiations with publishers in Vienna and around Europe. Concerts were riskier ventures, as they were important for raising the composer's profile but could be expensive. In the volatile financial situation of the period, Beethoven yearned for the stability of a regular stipend. Later in his career, in response to him threatening to leave Vienna, some of his well-heeled admirers clubbed together to provide him with financial support on an annual basis. He was not thereby indentured to them but rather granted greater freedom to live and work as suited him. Beethoven's willingness to experiment musically was partly a result of this arrangement; he did not have to worry that he would not be paid because a work did not please his employer.

This was something of a relief for all involved. Even when he first arrived in Vienna, Beethoven was unwilling to kowtow to anyone. In 1794, he protested that Artaria had published his virtuosic Variations on Mozart's 'Se vuol ballare' as his opus 1. No matter that Artaria were the most successful music publishing house in Vienna, holding the rights to scores by Mozart and Haydn and not typically disposed to support twenty-four-year-old newcomers; Beethoven wanted to exert control over which pieces of his music were printed, and how and when they appeared. It had become common practice for composers to publish sets of music – piano sonatas or string quartets – with an opus number (abbreviated as op.); this marked them as works that had entered the public sphere. Beethoven strengthened the significance of this labelling by keeping opus numbers for his most serious works in order to establish a particular professional trajectory: one that built on the past masters and demonstrated his command of a variety of genres. The Variations on 'Se vuol ballare' was not the type of music Beethoven wanted to be his opus 1 and he insisted that Artaria demote them to 'no. 1' instead. He then persuaded them to publish an alternative opus 1, a set of three piano trios (shown in fig. i.3), for which an unusual marketing strategy was adopted: subscribers were invited to purchase – at no small cost – copies in advance, creating something of a buzz. The list of aristocratic subscribers, printed on the piano part, included names who would provide long-term support to the composer in Vienna, including Count and Countess von Browne, Count Erdődy, Prince Lobkowitz, Count and Countess Razumovsky and Countess von Thun. Prince Lichnowksy bought twenty copies for himself and another nine for his family; he also quietly paid for the engraving. Prince Nikolaus Esterházy and Baron van Swieten bought three copies each. Beethoven had persuaded Artaria to allow him to sell up to 450 copies before they retailed them at a lower price. Thanks to Lichnowsky's efforts behind the scenes, Beethoven sold 244 copies in advance and made a profit of more than 880 gulden (see Note on Beethoven's Finances). He would not make as much money from a publication for decades.

Beethoven's artistic savvy is also apparent in his choice of work: piano trios. Whereas Mozart and Haydn had spent most of their careers composing for the harpsichord and then, in their later years, the fortepiano, Beethoven came of age as the fortepiano was transformed into the pianoforte. Unlike the harpsichord, the fortepiano had its strings struck rather than plucked, which made it more dynamically expressive. Yet it had a far lighter touch and a wider variety of tone between its low, middle and high registers than the later pianoforte, whose metal frame and heavier hammers produced a more consistent and brighter tone. In the course of his career, the keyboards Beethoven played extended so he could compose for a greater number of notes, reaching lower and higher than had previously been possible. Developments in musical technologies, in other words, expanded what could be done creatively and, in this regard, it was important for Beethoven that Vienna was a significant centre for instrument-building, because it encouraged him to experiment with new sound-worlds. His opus 1 is an early example of just that. The piano trio, as an ensemble, had grown out of the sonata for piano and violin, with a cello being added to support the bass line. Beethoven, though, treated each member of the trio more individually, allowing the cello to break away from its doubling role and so opening up the potential for more complex interplay between instruments. The great German writer Johann Wolfgang von Goethe had likened listening to a string quartet to hearing a conversation between four intelligent people, and a similar sense of communication among equals might be felt in Beethoven's recasting of the instruments' roles.

The fact that there were far fewer works for piano trio than there were for string quartets was also significant because it meant that Beethoven did not have to compete directly with Mozart and Haydn. At the same time, they were similar enough to the quartet in terms of their musical layout for Beethoven to be able to show his command of Viennese classical style. By the end of the eighteenth century, a series of conventions for instrumental genres had become established: for example, a string quartet typically had four movements (perhaps best compared to acts of a play), which fell into a fast–slow–dance–fast pattern and would normally subscribe to certain formal expectations, much as a poem can be in the form of, for example, a sonnet or an ode. The outer movements would often be in a sonata form, which presents two contrasting themes in a lively dialogue (see Chapter 3). The slow movement would be variations on a theme or have the shape of an arch, and the dance would be a minuet or a scherzo with a contrasting trio section in the middle. The work would begin in and return to a home key or harmonic area with the middle movements providing some – but not too much – harmonic contrast. The titles of movements generally indicated the tempo or speed at which they were to be performed, as explained in the Note on Musical Terms.

The principles of Viennese classical style, as exemplified by the music of Mozart and Haydn, were to do, then, with balanced proportions. That Mozart, and particularly Haydn, delighted in threatening to upset that balance and then cleverly reinstating it is testament both to their ingenuity and to how stable the principles were. An indication of the less serious status of the piano trio was that it tended to have only three movements, not four. By following instead the four-movement pattern of the string quartet and pursuing similar forms, Beethoven implied that he, too, had mastered classicism – but from a fresh angle.

The Three Piano Trios, op. 1, were played to Haydn on his return to Vienna, after a successful tour to London in August 1794. He admired the first two works of the set but thought that the last, in C minor, should not have been published, because the public would not understand it. Beethoven, incensed, refused to include the expected acknowledgement that he had been a pupil of Haydn on the cover of the score (see fig. i.3). History books take this moment as a significant early sign of Beethoven the rebel. He was prepared to disavow father figures (Haydn was colloquially known as 'Papa') and to lead sympathetic listeners on a journey beyond their wildest dreams. That the objectionable work was in C minor also matters; it would be the key of some of his moodiest and – perhaps partly for that reason – most celebrated works, including the 'Pathétique' Piano Sonata, op. 13, and the Fifth Symphony, op. 67. The real Beethoven, it seems, emerged triumphant as performers and audiences took up op. 1, no. 3 with enthusiasm.

Of course, the story was more complicated. Beethoven may well have been angry, but he was sensible enough to realize that he should not break ties with Haydn altogether and dedicated the Piano Sonatas, op. 2, to him shortly afterwards. While op. 1, no. 3 may be more intense, even more visceral than the previous two piano trios, it still functions within classical expectations. It is a question of the degree and type of experimentation. Haydn is often described as a 'witty' composer – unsettling players and listeners by undermining their sense of when things should happen (such as in the 'Joke' Quartet, which teases you into thinking that it is about to end and then doesn't). Beethoven's humour is not dissimilar, but it is more heavy handed. In the Piano Trio, op. 1, no. 3, it is most obvious in the interplay between instruments. For instance, in the third movement, piano and strings initially are at cross-purposes. A minuet is a type of dance, but Beethoven constantly wrongfoots the players; the regularity of the piano's melody is undermined by the strings' emphasis of the off-beats. The sense of the instruments being in competition intensifies in the central Trio section, when the piano's impressive runs seem like a challenge to the strings to keep up. The next, final movement begins with a sense of urgency: the trio rush through chords in the home key of C minor and then the violin introduces a remarkably simple main theme, hurried along by the busy accompaniment. This is, it seems, Beethoven the obsessive: while there are diversions, the theme constantly resurfaces, either in its full form or as fragments. There is then a surprise. When the theme returns at the very end it is not asserted aggressively, but gently. The strings slow to long-held chords and the piano's runs of notes dwindle in energy. It is as if a rushing stream has suddenly been released into a calm lake. The coda – a kind of bookend to a movement, which confirms its sense of ending – would, in Beethoven's hands, assume ever-greater weight: from the repeated chords at the end of the Fifth Symphony to the 'Ode to Joy' in the Ninth. In his opus 1, however, the coda suggests less closure, more the start of something new.

We only ever know pieces of someone else's life. Even as famous a figure as Ludwig van Beethoven, whose biography has been pored over again and again, manages to keep certain things secret. Speculation and stories fill in some gaps and, as they are repeated and the metaphorical mortar hardens, it can seem as if there is nothing further to say. Yet the image of Beethoven glowering from merchandise is only one aspect of the composer, and the music that dominates concert programmes today is only a small portion of his output. Of the nine symphonies, the Third, Fifth and Ninth are heard most often; of the thirty-two mature piano sonatas and sixteen string quartets, those from later in his life – five of each – feature more prominently than the earlier pieces that were more highly regarded in his day. His greatest commercial successes – the Septet, op. 20, or *Wellingtons Sieg* (*Wellington's Victory*) – are now presented as historical curiosities, if played at all. The complete *Missa solemnis* was not performed in Vienna until after Beethoven's death. His only completed opera, *Fidelio*, received fewer than twenty performances in Vienna in his lifetime: there were more performances than that scheduled for the year 2020 in the United Kingdom, not to mention the rest of the world. The symphonies, sonatas and quartets that seem archetypal became so over centuries of changing tastes, tenets and technologies.

Nine is a magic number for Beethoven: he completed as many symphonies, with the Ninth a musical mountain subsequent composers had to overcome. The power of three has been written about as a masonic or religious symbol in his works. His career has been divided into three periods: early, middle, late. Nine here is simply a number of pieces by Beethoven that introduce significant aspects of his music and the world in which he moved. They represent the range of Beethoven's music, from celebrated large-scale symphonies and Masses to popular septets and experimental string quartets, song to opera, piano improvisations to sonatas. Each piece is tied to a theme that sheds light on the historical context in which he lived, and on his personality.

My starting point, instead of the composer's childhood, which has been amply covered by other biographies, is Beethoven's first success, the Septet, op. 20. Although little known today, this work was the one played most often during his lifetime, revealing much about Viennese tastes in the early nineteenth century. Discussion then moves on to the 'Kreutzer' Violin Sonata, op. 47. Beethoven is usually thought of as a loner. Friendship and collaboration with other musicians, however, was of fundamental importance to him creatively and personally, as is demonstrated in the story of how the 'Kreutzer' came into being. Developments in instrument-building in this second chapter and elsewhere are also shown to have influenced the way in which Beethoven composed.

The third piece is the Third Symphony, the 'Eroica'. Beethoven's evocation of the heroic in this unprecedentedly long and complex work is situated within the back-and-forth of the Napoleonic Wars. This period of Beethoven's life also reflects what might be thought of as his personal heroism, expressed in the 'Heiligenstadt Testament', one of two unsent letters discovered after his death. The gradual deterioration of his hearing impacted his professional activities and, eventually, his reputation. Beethoven made his name in Vienna as a pianist as well as a composer. His skills as an improviser are displayed in the fourth piece, the Choral Fantasy, premiered alongside the Fifth and Sixth symphonies at a mammoth concert Beethoven gave in 1808. The Choral Fantasy is now remembered chiefly for containing a kernel of the Ninth Symphony's 'Ode to Joy'. Its first, chaotic performance illustrates the difficulties that faced Beethoven on trying to get his music heard in public.

The second unsent letter discovered among Beethoven's effects was to the 'Immortal Beloved' (*Unsterbliche Geliebte*). Debates still rage over who might have been the object of the composer's affections. In exploring the fifth piece, the song 'An die Geliebte', what seems clearer, through his choice of poetry to set to music, and his correspondence, is that Beethoven, increasingly isolated by deafness, was disappointed not to find a wife. Ironically, all this took place during the period of his greatest commercial success. The music he composed in the build-up to the Congress of Vienna, an assembly convened from November 1814 with the aim of bringing peace to Europe after the upheavals of the Napoleonic and French Revolutionary wars, tends to be dismissed as patriotic propaganda, even as the nadir of his output. Yet on the back of it he was able to revive his opera, *Fidelio*, the sixth piece discussed: a work that over the decade since its premiere reflected the changing political landscape from French revolutionary fervour to the defeat of Napoleon.

Vienna had always been a city ruled by censorship. Those

restrictions tightened under the regime of Klemens von Metternich, the Austrian Empire's Foreign Minister (and later
Chancellor), and public life became still more restrained. In the
aftermath of the Congress, Beethoven's focus turned inward, to
his family and his own health. Those years were dominated by
the protracted battle over custody of his nephew Karl. Beethoven's rate of composition slowed and the pieces he produced
became still more elaborate and experimental. The seventh
piece, the 'Hammerklavier' Piano Sonata, op. 106, pushed the
limits of the genre and the instrument to breaking point. In it,
Beethoven deepened his engagement with music from the previous century, particularly the fugal writing of Johann Sebastian
Bach, which would bear further fruit in the eighth piece, the
Missa solemnis, and the ninth, the String Quartet, op. 130, with
its original finale, the 'Grosse Fuge'. Beethoven's last, 'late'
pieces are now heralded as masterworks. While they had some
supporters, when they were first heard many in the audience were left perplexed, and it took time for them to be fully
embraced.

Beethoven's works often had alternative endings, determined
by publishers and critics as much as by the composer. Beethoven's life is no different. Looking again at the premieres of his
pieces and taking on board recent research into Vienna's music
scene, it becomes clear that there is still much to be discovered
about the composer. Biographies of Beethoven – like those of
most great men – habitually present him in near-isolation, as if
his genius sprang forth without the assistance or support of family, friends, teachers and colleagues; in fact, they are more often
presented as hindrances. Unappreciative listeners to his music
are dismissed; those who recognize something in it are quoted
extensively. The revolutionary elements of his politics – and
music – are preferred to those that are more reactionary.[3] The
story of how Beethoven became Beethoven is inevitably more

complex and did not depend solely on the greatness of his music but also on the people around him.

Beethoven and his contemporaries self-consciously cultivated an image of the composer for posterity, demonstrating a new awareness that as his music circulated more widely and was played and discussed with greater skill, his name might last beyond their lifetimes. Implicit within that process was a desire to protect the reputation of the city of Vienna and the status of the nobility who had for so long ruled the roost. Beethoven both took advantage of aristocratic patrons and wanted to keep his independence, as is illustrated by a famous anecdote. In the summer of 1806, Beethoven and his long-term supporter Prince Lichnowsky visited Count von Oppersdorff's country estate for a performance of the Second Symphony, the count being one of the few aristocrats who still maintained a full orchestra. The pair fell out, apparently because Beethoven refused to play the piano for some guests. He wrote: 'Prince, what you are, you are by circumstance and birth, what I am, I am through myself; there are, and there always will be, thousands of princes; but there is only one Beethoven.'[4]

Such a dramatic declaration of autonomy was possible because, by this stage of Beethoven's career, Prince Lichnowsky was no longer his main source of income. He had built up a larger network of patrons and collaborators to mitigate against changing personal relationships, including more distant connections with publishers and performers abroad. 'Brand Beethoven', as it has been called, was already well established, and while subsequent generations have emphasized different aspects of his life and works according to their own predilections, often over historical accuracy, the brand has remained strong.[5]

The statue erected in Beethoven's honour in 1845 was the first of many around the world. A major anniversary is an opportunity to take stock and not only reassess what we think of an artist now but also to ask how and why we have come to think of them in certain ways and what other paths might have been taken. Through these nine pieces, then, a more complex and human portrait of Beethoven can be glimpsed: of a life that is as elusive as any other.

1.   Success: Septet, op. 20 (1800)

Eight years after Beethoven had first arrived in Vienna, at 6.30 p.m. on 2 April 1800, he gave his first *Akademie* at the imposing Burgtheater, the Royal Imperial Court Theatre. An academy was a public benefit concert organized by an artist to promote their name and, hopefully, to make some money. The artist bore the cost of the event but took home the receipts. Academies took place in the theatre's 'dark' periods, when they refrained from putting on dramatic entertainments out of respect for the religious observation of Advent and Lent. Permission to give such a concert had to be gained from the police and the director of the theatres, which explains why it had taken Beethoven a while to get to this stage. He had needed to ingratiate himself with the right people and to have proved his musical worth by playing at salons and other concerts.

Beethoven's academy was designed to showcase his abilities as a performer and as a composer in multiple genres. Alongside a Mozart symphony and an aria and duet from Haydn's *Creation*, the twenty-nine-year-old displayed his skill as a pianist in an improvisation and his First Piano Concerto, op. 15. He also presented two of his new works: the Septet, op. 20, and the First Symphony. The programme also suggested, through the inclusion of Mozart and Haydn, his indebtedness to his Viennese predecessors. That they were the only other composers included further implied that Beethoven was not content with being compared to lesser contemporaries; he should be considered equal to the best.

So great is Beethoven's fame today it is hard to believe that the premieres of works that are now so venerated could have been criticized or, worse still, ignored. Or, that works rarely heard today were celebrated then. It took time, though, for the composer to establish himself. Unlike the poet Byron, who, on the publication of *Childe Harold's Pilgrimage* in 1812, woke up famous, Beethoven's success was less sudden. Of the pieces performed at the academy, we might assume that it would have been the symphony and concerto that made his name. After all, it is for those genres that he is most celebrated now. But that was not the case. His skills as an improviser impressed audiences and the most warmly received piece was the Septet, which was played again and again around Vienna, for the rest of Beethoven's life. Its unfamiliarity today reflects changes in music-making and in Beethoven's compositional style, which became celebrated less for crowd-pleasing than for challenging its audiences.

Beethoven's April concert was 'truly the most interesting academy in a long time', according to a correspondent for the Leipzig-based music journal, the *Allgemeine musikalische Zeitung*, in a round-up of the season. Established in 1798 by the music publishing house Breitkopf und Härtel under the editorship of Friedrich Rochlitz, through its combination of articles on music-related topics and reviews and reports from around Europe, the *AmZ* quickly became the leading organ for determining 'middle class public opinion'. That its review of the April concert did not appear until October of that year is a reminder that communications were slower in those days.[1] No matter; it was an important journal which spawned several imitators and competitors, all of which helped to spread news of Beethoven's music beyond his immediate environs.

'Interesting' was not a neutral term for the *AmZ* to use; it marked Beethoven out as an important new player on the scene. He had integrated himself into Vienna's concert life by contributing to preceding academies as a performer. His willingness to participate was also a way to persuade other musicians to take part in his own concert. The season had already included an academy by Beethoven's long-term collaborator, the violinist Ignaz Schuppanzigh, and by the renowned Czech hornist Giovanni Punto, who premiered Beethoven's Horn Sonata that season. It had also featured a musician with whom Beethoven was in direct competition, namely virtuoso pianist Daniel Steibelt.

According to the *AmZ*, Beethoven's Piano Concerto contained 'many beauties', especially in its first two movements; his improvisation was 'masterly'; and the symphony had an abundance of 'novel artistic ideas'.[2] There were issues with the orchestra, who did not like Beethoven's choice of conductor from the court theatre, Paul Wranitzky, and so paid him little heed (they would have preferred the leader from the Italian opera house, Giacomo Conti). That mattered because the difficulty of Beethoven's music meant that the standard one rehearsal was insufficient for the orchestra to be able to perform the music without several mistakes. What's more, Beethoven's scoring was quite woodwind heavy, meaning that without careful handling the penetrating sound of those instruments risked swamping the rest of the orchestra. The *AmZ* ended its review by criticizing the academies in general: they were not well attended, as their quality was mixed and the costs to artists were off-putting, particularly if they did not have the protection of an affluent patron.

The one unmitigated success in Beethoven's first academy was the Septet: the *AmZ* said that it had been composed with taste and feeling (*Geschmack und Empfindung*), two terms that had a special resonance in late-eighteenth-century aesthetics, as did the term 'interesting' when describing the academy as a whole.

Writers emphasized the importance of personal feelings or 'sensibility', explored in novels by Samuel Richardson, Jean-Jacques Rousseau and Johann Wolfgang von Goethe. Yet that sensibility never went beyond the boundaries of good taste. A similar principle applied in music. Playwright, poet and philosopher Friedrich Schiller had claimed that emotions could not be represented but that music could give them form.[3] German composers, such as the most famous of Johann Sebastian Bach's many sons, Carl Philipp Emanuel Bach, were associated with a 'sensitive style' (*empfindsamer Stil*) which exploited music's ability to move the emotions by, for example, emulating sighs and through piquant chromatic harmony. The slow music of Beethoven's Septet is in a similar vein. The introduction, for example, is full of gently accented dissonances that add colour and maybe a sense of yearning, but no real torment. Its tentativeness is soon swept aside by a decidedly crowd-pleasing Allegro con brio, which has an easy melodiousness that would neither bore nor unduly shock listeners.

The success of the Septet, and the academy as a whole, was that Beethoven had steered a route that avoided tedium on the one side and cheap titillation on the other. Each movement has a different mood, speed and metre (the beat), and strings and winds alternate in taking the melodic lead. The aim, in good eighteenth-century fashion, was to be interesting; to provide details that attracted attention and made the music marketable. Yet there was already a tension between Beethoven's commercial ambitions – his desire to sell his music widely – and his artistic ambitions. In a letter to the publisher Franz Anton Hoffmeister in which Beethoven tries to persuade him to take on the Septet, the composer implies that the Leipzig critics – probably from the *AmZ* – are 'asses', who should not be taken seriously because an artist's immortality is decided not by their 'chatter' but by Apollo.[4] There is hubris, no doubt, in claiming to care only for the judgement of the gods, but it is the kind of rhetoric that helped to make his name.

One reason why Beethoven's Septet was well received in the early nineteenth century and why it is less familiar today is its instrumentation and overall form. Unlike a piano sonata, a quartet or even a symphony, which by 1800 usually had four movements, the Septet has six. Several of the Septet's movements are quite long. They are also, as was the norm, mostly in the same key of E flat major. Only the second and sixth movements shift to a different key, and they do not stray far: the Adagio cantabile is in A flat major and the Tema con variazioni ('Theme and variations') is in B flat major. The extended length of the Septet and its layout is more in keeping with the serenade or divertimento tradition, which could have more than four movements and was designed as light, entertaining music, often to be played outside; something also implied by the inclusion of clarinet, horn and bassoon in the ensemble, the sound of which carries better in larger spaces than that of the stringed instruments. Length and harmonic uniformity are less of an issue when one can walk around or chat rather than having to sit in attentive silence in a concert hall, as we tend to do now. Generally, silent listening was not common practice outside of church services; even silent reading was a relatively novel phenomenon in an era when reading aloud was a popular domestic entertainment.

The academy concert was not outside, of course. An early reviewer conceded that the Septet might be too long for a 'mixed public', presumably meaning an audience that included commoners as well as aristocratic connoisseurs. Indeed, the critic declared it a work beloved by educated listeners, full of spirit and new, daring and delicate ideas. Yet while it displayed a profound erudition, it never became overly gloomy, cold or difficult.[5] The Septet thereby managed the unusual feat of being able to cross between the light and the serious: it was both pleasant and interesting, deserving of being heard in a concert hall. In the academy programme, it prefaced the First Symphony, functioning as relief from the weightier works and as a transition between genres. As a sort of overgrown chamber ensemble, the Septet bridged the gap between the string quartet – a genre not represented on the academy programme but one to which Beethoven had recently dedicated a great deal of energy while composing the six quartets that make up op. 18 – and larger-scale music-making. This broadened the work's appeal: the Septet's orchestration for clarinet, horn and bassoon might have harked back to the serenade or divertimento, but none of the instruments were doubled; in other words, they were not that loud and could still be accommodated indoors. The Septet, then, could be played in a concert hall, an aristocrat's salon, a tavern or a modest home. Its versatility would be extended further when it came to publication, as will be explained later. First, though, a little more on the performance options open to Beethoven at this stage of his career.

The academy was not the world premiere of Beethoven's Septet. It had been heard at least once before, at a reception at the home of Prince Schwarzenberg on 20 December 1799. The prince's residence was no lowly dwelling but a palace in Vienna's Mehlmarkt (now Neuer Markt), where the first, private performance of Haydn's *Die Schöpfung* (*The Creation*) had taken place the previous year, before its public premiere at the Burgtheater. Apparently, the Septet was 'much admired' at the palace, with Beethoven exclaiming, 'That is my *Creation*'; presumably, he foresaw that his piece would be as successful as his former teacher's oratorio.[6]

The pattern of introducing a new piece in the Schwarzenberg palace, to invited guests, before presenting it to a broader audience, illustrates how members of the aristocracy extended their influence over the city's musical life. They were the first to hear new music and by giving it their seal of approval sanctioned its introduction to the public sphere. 'Soft power' may have been a term coined during the Cold War, but the practice of using the arts to assert cultural supremacy has been around for a long time. Viennese nobility around 1800 harnessed the city's musical prowess to display personal and civic wealth and strength. One of the reasons for Beethoven's success, it has been argued, was that he was supported by patrons who recognized that his music consolidated the glories of Vienna's past as well as promising much for its future.

Connoisseurs are not usually concerned with the masses, however, and the notion of what constituted a private event and what was a public concert needs to be handled carefully. A salon or reception held at a palace might have been for a dozen people or it might have been for two hundred. Admission to a concert ostensibly open to the public might have been by invitation only; if tickets were for sale, they would have been beyond the means of many. Unlike other European cities, concert series were not yet well established in Vienna, which lent a cottage-industry aspect to events such as Beethoven's academy: the press notice advertised tickets as being available either from the theatre's box-keeper or from the composer's lodgings on the third floor of the Greinersches Haus at Tiefer Graben, no. 241 (now no. 10 and embellished with a Beethoven mural). Price of admission was said to be 'as usual'. This was an event for those in the know, not music for the masses (see fig. 1.1).

Simply finding a venue was a challenge for musicians. The Tonkünstler Societät (Society of Musicians) ran four concerts per year, to raise money for their pension fund. Beethoven was not a member, but he made his debut with them on 29 March 1795.

Fig. 1.1 Poster for Beethoven's academy at the Burgtheater in Vienna on
2 April 1800.

Otherwise, musicians had to organize concerts themselves, for
their own benefit or for others. Beethoven nurtured support for
his own project by participating in concerts for the benefit of
Mozart's widow, Constanze, as well as for Haydn, the singers
Maria Bolla and Josefa Dušek, violinist Schuppanzigh, and singer
and impresario – and *Magic Flute* librettist – Emanuel Schikaneder.
Although the profits made at such events were not usually large,
they were worth the financial risk: a meagre 200–300 florins
was the annual salary of a court theatre musician.

In a series of gestures designed to give the people of Vienna
greater access to the city's recreation facilities, including its
parks, in 1776 Holy Roman Emperor Joseph II had ended the
court's monopoly over putting on entertainments. This enabled
the foundation of privately owned theatres, such as the Theater
in der Leopoldstadt and the Theater an der Wien. The latter was

opened in 1801 by Schikaneder and was renowned for its size and lavish stage scenery. In the 'dark' seasons of Advent and Lent these theatres, as well as the two court theatres, the Burgtheater and the Kärntnertortheater, were available as venues for concerts. As mentioned, permits granted by the police were required for any public gathering and events had to be approved by the director of the theatres, from August 1794 Baron Peter von Braun, a civil-servant-turned-silk-manufacturer who was mistrusted by many musicians. As Beethoven frequently complained, the application process could be a lot of paperwork, and even prominent musicians were refused. Braun had favourites: most opportunities were given to pianist Josepha Auernhammer, who had collaborated with (and been smitten by) Mozart and who, unusually for a married woman, continued her career as a performer. Beethoven's case might have been helped by his dedication of various works to Braun's wife, Josephine, herself an accomplished pianist: they included the Piano Sonatas, op. 14, in 1799 (and the arrangement for string quartet in 1802) and the Sonata in F major for piano and horn, op. 17, in 1801. Musical genius was not enough, in other words: even Beethoven had to rely on connections to eventually gain the opportunity to present a concert.

Connections were also crucial in assembling an orchestra from available musicians. As mentioned, concerts were typically given on one rehearsal, usually on the morning of the performance. Given that Beethoven programmed several new works in his concerts and that his music was hardly straightforward, standards were not high. Prince Lichnowsky apparently saved the day in 1803 – a concert at the Theater an der Wien incorporating the premieres of the oratorio *Christus am Ölberge* (*Christ on the Mount of Olives*), the Second Symphony, and the C minor Piano Concerto, for which the rehearsal began at 8 a.m. – by providing refreshments for the musicians as tempers were beginning to fray mid-afternoon. Before they resumed, the prince asked them to go through the oratorio once more, so that it might be 'presented to the public in a manner worthy of it'. The concert began at 6 p.m. and while *Christ on the Mount of Olives* was rendered successfully, other pieces were ditched because the concert overran.

In this context, the success of the Septet is understandable. Having already been performed at the Schwarzenberg palace, it was known to some members of the academy audience. It was also, more importantly, better known to the performers. The Septet is not easy music to play for it is full of soloistic flourishes that require proficiency and preparation. Beethoven emphasized to a prospective publisher that there were no inessential (*non obbligato*) instruments. This is music for equals: each instrument – save for the double bass, a traditional instrument in a serenade ensemble – has its moment in the spotlight. Beethoven's awareness that it suited professionals more than amateurs is apparent in a letter in which he tried to persuade Baron von Zmeskall, a keen cellist, to step in at the last minute for a performance of the Septet at the home of Prince Odescalchi. Unusually, he promised to send the score beforehand so that Zmeskall could look at the 'most difficult' part, the solo in the trio of the Minuet, in advance of the rehearsal the next morning.[7]

As it was, Beethoven had a crack ensemble for the academy, led by violinist Ignaz Schuppanzigh, already mentioned as one of his most enduring collaborators. Schuppanzigh gave Beethoven violin lessons in the 1790s; he also established a regular quartet for Prince Lichnowsky that was probably the first group to play Beethoven's op. 18. The following decade, Schuppanzigh formed what was in essence the first professional string quartet, which also premiered several works by Beethoven. On top of performing with various Viennese orchestras, Schuppanzigh ran a concert series. He was therefore in a position to recruit capable performers, who were even named on the poster (see fig. 1.1). They were viola player Anton Schreiber, who later joined Schuppanzigh's quartet; the Kärtnertortheater's lead cellist Philipp Schindlöcker; Johann Dietzel, 'the only good double bass player in Vienna', according to Haydn; acclaimed clarinettist Joseph Bähr (for whom Beethoven wrote most of his chamber music for clarinet); Bohemian virtuoso bassoonist Johann Matauschek; and, on horn, Mathias Nickel.

Beethoven's desire to ingratiate himself with influential figures as a means to further professional success is apparent also in the dedication of the Septet to Empress Maria Theresa. The second wife of Holy Roman Emperor Franz II was a keen singer and a supporter of music at court. Her lively and long-lived salon continued despite her multiple pregnancies and she was an important patron of composers. Haydn – the teacher Beethoven both emulated and defied – had dedicated his Mass in B flat major (the *Theresienmesse*) to her in 1799. Beethoven had not yet, though, curried favour with the empress; he had not been invited to perform at any of her concerts nor had he previously ventured to dedicate a work to her. There is no record of Maria Theresa's response to the Septet – which was not included in any of her subsequent concerts – and, on the whole, her relationship to Beethoven remained distant despite his best efforts. In this, her husband's distrust of Beethoven's music and what he perceived to be his revolutionary spirit might have played a part. Personality and politics could get in the way of Beethoven's ambitions, no matter how hard he tried to ingratiate himself. Maria Theresa supported but seemed not to like his ballet *Geschöpfe des Prometheus* (*The Creatures of Prometheus*) and may have been behind Beethoven's interest in Jean-Nicolas Bouilly's play as a source for the opera *Fidelio*. However, like many Viennese nobles, because of the Napoleonic occupation she did not attend the premiere. Beethoven's dedication of the Septet to her,

then, was an act of public homage that, unlike other examples,
did not necessarily indicate a close or even a particularly supportive relationship between composer and dedicatee.

Musicians, by contrast, were won over by the Septet. It
became a signature piece for Schuppanzigh, who, until he left
Vienna in 1816, programmed it at least once a season in his
chamber music concert series, despite the extra cost the larger
ensemble required. On his return – after a stint in St Petersburg –
his audience's loyalty continued; a concert on 25 January 1824,
which included the Septet alongside a Haydn string quartet, was
reported to have been so crowded that 'people had to stand in
front of the door'.[8] The performance of the Septet was interrupted by outbreaks of applause, especially for the horn solo and
some of the violin passages. Indeed, the Septet's appeal for
Schuppanzigh was probably that the violin is first among equals
in the texture. It has a prominent role, presenting and embel-
lishing melodies to a far greater extent than any of the other
instruments. Franz von Brunsvik, whose two sisters, Josephine
and Therese, were then being taught piano by Beethoven, was
reported to have been 'particularly enchanted by a Septet of
Beethoven's which he thought to be the ne plus ultra in composition as well as in execution'.[9] Beyond playing the Septet well,
the violinist took special care when programming it. Generally,
Schuppanzigh was a cannier concert organizer than Beethoven;
he always advertised – and mostly kept to – starting and ending
times. When he included the Septet, because of its relatively
extended length he usually included only one other piece rather
than the conventional two, so that the concert did not last more
than two hours. Moreover, he often put the Septet last, apparently to send his audience home happy; presumably they would
be high on the elan of the energetic finale, with its impressive
violin cadenza.[10]

The support of a musician such as Schuppanzigh was crucial

in helping Beethoven successfully establish his reputation. The number of times a piece appeared in concerts, especially those by other people, is the best – indeed, really the only – way to gauge its popularity before it was published. Hardly any records of concert receipts survive to give clear figures of how many people were in the audience of any of these events and, at any rate, they might have attended for social reasons rather than to hear a particular musical work. There were few extended reviews of concerts in the press unless they featured new pieces or a notable performer. During the first decade of the nineteenth century, Beethoven's music was played in Vienna roughly as frequently as Mozart's and slightly less often than Haydn's. His works outnumbered performances of instrumental pieces by Anton Salieri and his pianist rival Daniel Steibelt. This is not to say that Beethoven's music had already achieved the dominance over concert programmes that it has today, but he was on his way. The next step was conquering the domestic market.

Beethoven offered the Septet to the publisher Hoffmeister on 15 January 1801, explaining that the piece 'has been very popular'.[11] There were several unusual elements to his approach. First, he offered Hoffmeister a package of works, bundling together with the Septet the Second Symphony, the Piano Sonata in B flat, op. 22, and the First Piano Concerto, op. 21. Second, Beethoven proposed an unorthodox pricing scheme: he wanted 70 ducats for the whole lot. In his breakdown of the total he explained that he was asking 20 ducats each for the Septet, Symphony and Sonata, and 10 ducats for the Piano Concerto. Beethoven acknowledged that larger-scale pieces generally warranted higher prices; however, he reasoned, the concerto was not his best effort and, although the Septet was a chamber work, it was substantial, with multiple movements. There may have been some sleight of hand here: generally, there was less money to be made by publishers from orchestral music because so few people would buy such large scores (a further motivation behind arrangements for smaller ensembles, of which more shortly). Although it was helpful to have some time delay between the premiere of a piece and its publication, as it meant that the composer could continue to earn money by performing it before it appeared in print, after a certain point it became more beneficial for the work to be released into the public domain. Third, Beethoven asked to be paid in Viennese ducats, which he thought was a more stable currency than the florin; a useful reminder of the economic uncertainty of Vienna during the Napoleonic Wars.

Beethoven then made a striking admission: he found the business side of things distasteful and wished that instead of having to sell pieces individually there might be a worldwide single storehouse, or market, of art (*ein Magazin der Kunst*) to which artists could send their works and then be given what they needed. As it is, he complains, one has to be half business-man, 'and how can one be reconciled to that!' It is intriguing that he made this admission to a publisher: perhaps on the expectation that Hoffmeister might have been more sympathetic than most because he was also a composer, perhaps because he was trying to sell in bulk.

Although Beethoven might have dreamt of a different model for making a living from his music, he was alert to its financial potential. By the summer of 1801, he had to reassure Hoffmeister that the Septet would not be published anywhere else. He admitted that he had sent a copy of the score to Johann Peter Salomon in London, the Bonn-born musical impresario who had brought Haydn to England, to great acclaim. However, Beethoven had granted Salomon only performance, not publication, rights. As further proof of his fidelity to his commitment to Hoffmeister, he included with his letter the titles and dedications of the works to be published. These signal how well connected he was, or wanted to be seen to be, in Viennese society. As well as the Septet 'composed for and dedicated to' Her Imperial Majesty and Queen, the Second Symphony was for 'His Serene Highness Maximilian Franz, Royal Prince of Hungary and Bohemia and Elector of Cologne etc.', Beethoven's old boss in Bonn. Count Johann Georg von Browne, the dedicatee of the Piano Sonata, op. 22, with his wife, was one of Beethoven's earliest supporters in Vienna – in the dedication to him of the String Trios, op. 9, the composer referred to von Browne as the 'premier Mécène de sa Muse' ('first patron of his muse', with a nod to Maecenus, sponsor of the Augustan poets Horace and Virgil). The Second Piano Concerto, which Beethoven had admitted to Hoffmeister was not his finest work, was dedicated not to a member of the nobility but to Karl Nickl von Nickelsberg, a treasury official with a passion for music.

By April 1802, Beethoven was trying to hurry Hoffmeister along, expressing concern that publication might be pre-empted by another edition, perhaps by someone who had access to the music through the circles around Maria Theresa. Beethoven warned that 'the rabble is waiting for it [the Septet] – and, as you know, the Empress has it and there are scoundrels in the Imperial city as well as the Imperial court, I cannot offer you any guarantee in this matter, so make haste'. What's more, he suggested of the Septet that 'for more frequent use one could arrange the three wind instrument parts': the clarinet part could be adapted for violin, the horn for viola, and the bassoon for cello. Over the next eighteen months, as he waited impatiently for publication, he continued to emphasize to Hoffmeister the Septet's commercial potential. Beethoven suggested that, if arranged for piano, it would gain a 'wider distribution . . . to our greater profit'.

Arrangements and transcriptions of pieces for other instruments were the primary way most people came to know music before the advent of sound recording. An unusual grouping such as the Septet on the whole was not readily available so, for those who nevertheless wanted the chance to play or hear the music, versions were devised for different ensembles. Beethoven proposed to Hoffmeister a version for flute, claiming that 'This would satisfy the *lovers of the flute* who have already entreated me to do this and they would swarm around it and feed on it like insects.' In the end, he devised an arrangement for piano trio, op. 38 (1802–3, published 1805), which he dedicated to his doctor, Johann Adam Schmidt. The scoring for clarinet, cello and piano is the same as his op. 11 trio from 1797, but Beethoven suggested that the clarinet part could be played by violin or the cello by bassoon, according to what was available. Fragments remain of another version, seemingly by Beethoven, for wind ensemble.

Arrangements were also made by other people and Beethoven and his publishers were sometimes made uncomfortable by the appearance of unauthorized arrangements. These were not really pirate editions, in that copyright was not fully established. Authorship was respected, but more in the manner of today's Creative Commons licences, which allow works to be adapted so long as their original creator is credited. As indicated by Beethoven's discussions with Salomon in London, rights were not granted internationally; a composer had to negotiate terms with publishers in different countries.

All these arrangements point to a lucrative market in amateur music-making and, beyond that, a freer attitude towards what constituted an original work than we tend to hold now. The authority of the score was further diminished because of the compromises that had to be made to make the Septet's idiomatic instrumental writing suitable for other forces: what sounds good on one instrument might be less convincing or even impossible on another. Beethoven himself was remarkably faithful to the original score in his trio version of the Septet, but that caused some issues in that the violin's florid cadenza in the final movement is a real finger-twister on the piano. Other ensembles made the transformation more radical. For example, the Septet became a duo for strings or wind. It was recast for military band and several times over for what was always the most popular domestic ensemble: four-hand piano. Pianist and composer Johann Nepomuk Hummel gave flautists a flute, violin and cello trio to feast on. Hoffmeister issued a version for string quintet. In later years, Beethoven's student Carl Czerny's numerous arrangements – including of the Septet for six-part wind ensemble (*Harmonie*) – have been said to have made him the composer's 'posthumous domestic ambassador'.[12] Through his adaptations of Beethoven, Czerny was able to teach musical skills and values to the bourgeois market. Cheaper sheet music and more affordable pianos meant that playing this music in the home was no longer the preserve of the aristocracy.

Arrangements were not necessarily of the whole work; it was quite common for only popular or appropriate movements to be selected. For instance, the Adagio was transcribed as a stand-alone piece for piano and for organ. The florid violin-writing of the Theme and Variations was reconceived for two guitars. The most popular movement of the Septet for arrangements, unsurprisingly, was the most straightforward: the Minuet. Its nicely balanced melody, with tick-tock accompaniment, is easily imagined as a tune for music boxes or mechanical organ. (Although one might think that Beethoven would not have lowered himself to compose for such an instrument, bear in mind that he had composed a series of variations for mechanical organ – known in Vienna as a *Flötenuhr* – as a wedding present for Josephine Brunsvik in 1799.) The Minuet in fact was itself a reworking of an earlier piece, the second movement of Beethoven's Piano Sonata, op. 49, no. 2, which had been composed in 1795–6. The Sonata was a relatively simple piece, intended for children, which Beethoven had not seen fit to publish. His brother Kaspar Karl organized its release in 1805, perhaps because he saw a chance to capitalize further on the popularity of the Septet, Beethoven's trio arrangement of which had also appeared that year.

Establishing a hierarchy of different types of music was an important part of Beethoven's strategy for success. His reluctance to publish the Piano Sonata, op. 49, no. 2, for example, might have stemmed from his reuse of its melody in the Septet, at a time when his creative originality was beginning to be held at a premium. Composers frequently borrowed and manipulated ideas from their own – and others' – music, and Beethoven was no exception. In the Septet itself, the fourth movement's theme was said by Czerny to have been based on a folksong from Beethoven's native Rhineland, 'Ach Schiffer, lieber Schiffer' ('Ah, Boatman, Dear Boatman'). To be sure, such a song appears in collections published later in the nineteenth century, with a note that it was used in Beethoven's famous Septet.[13] Beethoven may well have remembered the melody from his childhood in Bonn, but there is no written source corroborating its existence at that time. It could have been the case, in other words, that the familiarity of the theme meant that it came to be thought of as a folksong; Beethoven was then borrowing his own invention.

By 1805, Beethoven might also have resisted the promotion of the Septet's charming melodies, which sat at odds with the fiercely dramatic music he was by then composing. A review in the *AmZ*, of an arrangement for clarinet or violin, cello and piano, explained that the original was known to be one of the 'most beautiful . . . agreeable and friendly' of the master's compositions, produced at a time when he was not averse to such qualities.[14] Along similar lines, a critic for the newspaper *Der Freymüthige*, reviewing the Third Symphony on 26 April 1805, wished that Beethoven had continued to produce music in a similar manner to his first two symphonies and 'the agreeable Septet'.[15] The composer's growing frustration with the continued popularity of the Septet was understandable. When Cipriani Potter, Principal of London's Royal Academy of Music, unwittingly praised the work in 1818, Beethoven retorted that 'In those days, I did not know how to compose. Now I believe I do.'[16] Czerny reported: 'He could not endure his Septet and grew angry because of the universal applause with which it was received.'[17] A gentler judgement was given to Karl Holz, to whom Beethoven acknowledged that there was much 'natural feeling' (*natürliche Empfindung*) in the Septet, but little art. The composer's annoyance that this early work overshadowed his later achievements perhaps should be taken less seriously than his explanation of the change in style away from the artless *Empfindsamkeit* ('sensibility') that had also been detected by the *AmZ* reviewer of the 1800 academy. Music was no longer to be merely an entertaining or interesting diversion but something more substantial.

The success of Beethoven's Septet can be judged in a variety of ways. It was warmly received on its first performances and became popular, in that it was performed often and its score and arrangements sold well. Although the Septet was hardly Beethoven's most radical music, it was appreciated by connoisseurs as well as the less well educated and continued to be played throughout the nineteenth century. Arrangements of the Septet kept a foothold in domestic music-making until the practice of playing the piano at home began to wane in favour of listening to recordings and radio broadcasts in the 1920s. In the professional sphere, large-scale chamber ensembles such as the

Septet began to be overlooked: Beethoven's symphonies and concertos were preferred in concert. Such changes in the attitudes of performers help explain why the Septet was performed less frequently in the twentieth century. It is less clear why it doesn't feature more prominently in accounts of Beethoven's life and works.

Around 1800, there was a growing perception among philosophers and a new breed – music critics – that composition was something that should be taken more seriously as an artform instead of as entertainment. Kant had advocated a more elevated kind of artistic contemplation that held back from considering art commercially; that did not invest monetarily but aesthetically.[18] Art may be interesting and full of feeling, but the observer should keep a critical distance: they should be disinterested, the better to appreciate its formal qualities. Kant, famously, was dismissive of music's intellectual properties; he considered it an art of sensation. However, other philosophers and critics argued that music need not be mere ephemera. Certain works by Mozart, Haydn and Beethoven were held up as examples of pieces that would stand the test of time; that would last beyond their generation to constitute a museum of musical works. Beethoven's own working practices suggest that he, too, had posterity in mind or, at the very least, that he had plans for the upkeep of his own reputation.

Around the time of the Septet's composition, Beethoven had begun a new way of working that can also be taken as a signal of his transition from creating music of 'feeling' to 'art'. Beethoven was an inveterate sketcher, noting down musical ideas as they came to him. From 1798, his method of organizing those initial ideas became more systematic. Instead of using loose leaves of paper he began to use sketchbooks that enabled him to plan works on a larger scale (fig. 1.2). It also meant that he could make preliminary notes for other projects as he went, returning to

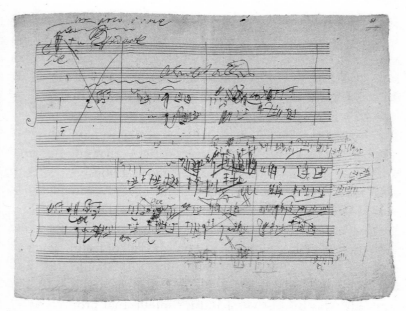

Fig. 1.2 Sketch for the String Quartet, op. 131, in the composer's hand.

pieces on other pages of the sketchbook as necessary. This more systematic way of working was important as Beethoven became busier professionally. It also facilitated his more ambitious and unusual musical structures. Some scholars believe that he began to use sketchbooks only while he was composing the complex textures of the Six String Quartets, op. 18, but it seems that he used similar plans for the Septet.

Beethoven kept hold of these sketchbooks throughout his life, and many have survived, providing a treasure trove for music-ologists eager to trace how his compositions came together. After his death, though, some were given away or sold off as individual pages, scattering their contents around the world. That was the fate of the first two sketchbooks, now known after their owner as Grasnick 1 and Grasnick 2, portions of which eventually were found in Bonn, Paris, Stockholm and Washington DC. They have since been reassembled. Amid refinements to the Piano Sonata, op. 14, no.1, and sketches for the String Quartet in D major, op. 18 (the first to be composed but the third in the published set), a cadenza for the First Piano Concerto, a couple of songs ('Der Kuss' ('The Kiss') and 'Opferlied' ('Sacrificial Hymn')) and the G major Rondo, op. 51, no. 2, are some ideas for the Septet. There may have been an earlier sketchbook, which would have contained more Septet material, as well as ideas for the First Symphony, which has since been lost. A page containing a plan for a work in E flat that might have been an early sketch for the Septet is in another collection.[19]

The sketchbooks are attractive sources because they seem like a diary of works in progress, giving a glimpse into Beethoven's creative process. While other composers such as Mozart and Schubert might have gone through similar stages, they did not leave behind such an extensive paper trail, giving the probably erroneous impression that their musical inspiration flowed more easily. By contrast, Beethoven's sketchbooks and manuscripts are heavily annotated, full of revisions and abandoned ideas. It has been claimed that Beethoven put so much effort into his sketches because they represented a kind of order that was increasingly hard to maintain in his personal life. At the same time, they demonstrate the greatness of his endeavour: his music grew from hard graft – it was work and, increasingly, conceived as a work of art. It is important to recognize that his serious purpose began relatively early in his career, with a work like the Septet which, because of its popularity and graceful style, might seem not to have required much forethought.

A more studious approach to music was further encouraged by the expansion of the publishing industry, which made available more scores, more affordably. A series of changes in copyright law were also significant. In the 1770s, Johann Christian Bach – the youngest of Johann Sebastian Bach's eleven sons, four of whom were musicians – had won a court case in which he argued that copyright laws for books should be extended to musical scores, so that the author of a text held rights over it rather than the publisher. By the turn of the century, as Beethoven's correspondence with publishers and his discomfort over the numerous arrangements of the Septet shows, the notion of intellectual property was gaining ground. So, too, was a determination among composers to control the quality of publications: Beethoven's extensive correspondence over corrections to editions, as well as his ever-expanding instructions to performers in expression and tempo markings, reveals his concern to make sure his music was presented as he intended. On one occasion, he complained that, in an edition of the op. 18 string quartets, mistakes 'wriggle about like little fish in water'.[20] This mattered because, whereas manuscripts had mostly travelled with their creator or members of their circle, who could then assert some control over how a manuscript was performed, printed music circulated more freely. The published score, as a physical artefact, began to be considered the musical work as much as, if not in place of, a performance.[21]

Printed music inevitably had a longer shelf-life than its creators, and whereas, previously, programmers had concentrated on music of the present, music from the past was now being accorded greater respect. Vienna, in particular, was a city keen to capitalize on its musical heritage. Formerly, music tended not to last beyond the lifetime of a composer. There was a growing interest among aristocrats in collecting manuscripts from earlier generations. Baron Gottfried van Swieten, for instance, was an enthusiast for the music of Handel and, more unusually for the time, of Johann Sebastian Bach. He introduced Mozart, Haydn and eventually Beethoven to his collection of keyboard music and organized performances of some of Handel's choral works. The growing awareness of music's history influenced attitudes to the present. Mozart's and Haydn's glory reflected well on the city of Vienna. Critics had been writing about 'Mozart, Haydn &', as if waiting to see who could complete their triumvirate.[22] The real success of Beethoven's 1800 academy was in showing that he was ready to take that third spot, by being able to bridge past and present and to suggest paths for the future. To be the creator of something new: that was how to become an artist.

2. Friends: Violin Sonata no. 9, op. 47, the 'Kreutzer' (1803)

'No man is an island', but Beethoven typically is shown alone. His reputation in later years, as he was increasingly isolated by family problems, deafness and his own recalcitrance, made Beethoven a model for the solitary artist, misunderstood by his time. But he was not incapable of making friends, and the more resilient among them stayed loyal to him throughout his life. Several were musicians; others were professionals, some of whom had been ennobled, who would help with practical matters, such as legal and health concerns. For, in truth, no composer can afford to be an island: however great, they need to work with others to have their pieces performed. The story behind the work discussed in this chapter, the Violin Sonata, op. 47, demonstrates particularly well that music, perhaps above all others, is a collaborative art.

Beethoven's friendships need to be considered in historical context. What it meant to be friends at the turn of the nineteenth century was different from what it means today, because society was much more tightly bound by class and etiquette. Yet this was a revolutionary era, when conventional hierarchies were being tested across Europe by republicanism and industrialization, and social relationships were inevitably reshaped in the process. Placing Beethoven within this broader milieu helps to explain both how much he was a man of his time and how he challenged its norms. Before introducing the Violin Sonata, which shows the way that such relationships shaped Beethoven's music, this chapter examines the constitution of the composer's friendship circles. Family, schoolmates, colleagues, patrons and their wives and daughters might all have considered themselves to be friends with Beethoven. Those circles rarely overlapped, however, and were quite easily broken.

Family relationships, as so often is the case, could be close and fractious. On her death, Beethoven referred to his mother as his best friend, although anecdotes reveal she certainly had a temper. His relationship with his father was made difficult by professional pressures, personal abuse and their fiery personalities. As a youth, Beethoven found that friends and their families could provide him with some of the stability that was lacking at home. When he was twelve or thirteen he met the slightly older Franz Gerhard Wegeler, who recommended him as a piano tutor to the von Breuning family; the mother, Helene, widow of the physician to the Elector Maximilian Franz, introduced Beethoven to a wider world of culture and society. The second son, Stephan von Breuning, became a lifelong friend: he trained as a lawyer and moved to Vienna in 1801, where he remained until his death in 1827, within three months of Beethoven's. Wegeler became a physician and married von Breuning's sister Eleanor; he spent two years in Vienna in the 1790s and then returned to Bonn, continuing to correspond with Beethoven. A sign of the closeness of these friendships is that it was to Wegeler that Beethoven confessed first that he was having trouble hearing and second when he was in love – and that he was concerned that von Breuning was overworking.[1] There was something almost fraternal about these friendships; all parties were prone to periods of argument and separation, with reconciliations sometimes brokered by other acquaintances, sometimes by Beethoven himself. After one spat, he wrote to Wegeler:

> No, Wegeler, dearest, best, O, venture again to throw yourself entirely into the arms of your B.; trust in the good qualities you

used to find in him; I will guarantee that the pure temple of sacred friendship which you erect shall remain firm forever; no accident, no storm shall ever shake its foundations—firm— forever—our friendship—pardon—oblivion—a new kindling of the dying, sinking friendship.[2]

Such over-the-top apologies may well have been sincere, but Beethoven wrote a lot of them. They signal that, however difficult or misanthropic he might have been, he recognized his need to keep sympathetic people around him and for that he was willing to sacrifice his pride on the altar of friendship.

Friendship as a state to be venerated or to aspire to was a concept that was being addressed directly by contemporary poets and philosophers. Enlightenment authors were reshaping the way in which more profound emotions were conceived and expressed. Immanuel Kant wrote about friendship as the 'maximum of mutual love', whereby two people think and feel with even greater equality than is possible between spouses (he never married). Friedrich Schiller, apparently inspired by his own friendship with jurist Christian Gottfried Körner, applauded those who succeeded in being 'a friend's friend' in his 1785 ode 'An die Freude' ('Ode to Joy'), the text which formed the basis for the choral finale of Beethoven's Ninth Symphony. Beyond the special relationship between individuals, there was a broader concern with cultivating a new sociability. Sympathy, previously defined as the attraction of two bodies to one another, or illustrated through the treatment of a wound by what had caused it, was reimagined as compassion for others. Or, as Beethoven put it in a letter complaining about an argument he'd had with Stephan von Breuning, 'A well-founded friendship demands the greatest affinity of heart and soul between two persons.'[3] When he and von Breuning reconciled, Beethoven sent as a gift Christian Horneman's portrait of him, for 'To whom else could I give it

Fig. 2.1 Christian Horneman's portrait of Beethoven, given by the composer to Stephan von Breuning.

with whole-hearted friendship but to you, my good, faithful, noble Steffen!' The ivory miniature depicts a stylishly attired Beethoven with a fashionable haircut: it is the kind of expensive keepsake shared by sweethearts, and Beethoven mentioned that it had been intended for another. His old friend was as deserving.

In this new world order, friendship could extend beyond the relationships of individuals to shared circles of intimates. There was a moral and political aspect to this idealization of friendship among equals that would feed into late-eighteenth-century revolutionary fervour. Being a 'friend of literature', in the manner of the *Lesegesellschaft* founded in 1780s Bonn, for example, might represent the impetus to self-improvement and instruction that was fundamental to the Germanic concept of *Bildung* (for want of a better way of putting it, a well-rounded education). It could also indicate political resistance: many of its members – several Beethoven's associates – had belonged to the Freemasons or Illuminati, then being carefully monitored, if not actively suppressed, by the authorities. In Vienna, by contrast, clubs and societies dedicated to philosophical or literary interests were not so much political hotbeds as bourgeois gatherings that seemed to reinforce social boundaries.

Vienna was a strictly hierarchical society and, while musicians as performers, composers and teachers could gain entrance to almost any circle, Beethoven positioned himself carefully. As mentioned in the previous chapter, his patrons in his first decades in Vienna were almost all aristocratic and that exclusivity was important in establishing his reputation. He made it clear that he was not a servant, as musicians tended to be thought of earlier in the eighteenth century. He also failed to correct those who thought that the Flemish 'van' in his name, acquired from his Belgian grandfather, was the equivalent of the German 'von' – in other words, that it indicated ennoblement – which caused problems in the custody battle for his nephew in 1818, of which more in Chapter 7. There were minor or 'sub' nobles with whom he was on friendly terms – Baron Nikolaus Zmeskall, for instance, or Count Moritz Lichnowsky, the younger brother of the prince – but Beethoven would never have presumed himself to be on the same social level as major noble patrons, for while they could be very supportive of artists their relationships were primarily professional rather than personal. The business end of patronage was also clear in the way Beethoven cut ties when the money ran out; for instance, when Prince Lobkowitz went bankrupt. An influx of cash could also smooth things over: in a letter to Wegeler from summer 1801, Beethoven admitted that he and Prince Lichnowsky 'had some slight misunderstandings, but these have only strengthened our friendship', which no doubt had been assisted by the 600 gulden the prince had just given him.

Women have not tended to have a prominent role in the history books of this era, as their lives were less well documented and typically not conducted in public. However, they played a significant part in the cultural and social life of Vienna. Friendship between men and women was not impossible in the early nineteenth century, but it was fraught with misunderstandings. On the one hand, a musician could have unprecedented access to upper-class women; on the other hand, they were kept in their place. Beethoven's closest female friends tended to be the wives and daughters of friends and patrons, women who ran their own salons or who were able musicians themselves and sometimes had lessons with Beethoven. The excellent pianist Countess Erdődy, for instance, was a confidante, while the intimidatingly monickered Princess Maria Theresia Hohenlohe-Waldenburg-Schillingsfürst, who was married to the banker Count Moritz Johann Christian Fries, made their extensive library available to Beethoven as well as providing him with accommodation for some months. Class remained an issue: the composer was quick to accuse the princess of treating him like a servant when he felt his status was undermined by her surreptitiously supplementing his servant's pay.

The endless speculation over Beethoven's romantic life has also meant that women who might simply have been friends have routinely been suspected of being something more. Piano students, inevitably, were a source of intrigue: the Brunsvik sisters and their cousin Giulietta Guicciardi were all proposed at one time or other as possible candidates for being Beethoven's 'Immortal Beloved'. And then there was Nanette Streicher, daughter of Mozart's favoured piano-maker Johann Stein and wife of piano-maker Anton Streicher, a capable businesswoman who assisted Beethoven with musical and family matters, who at one stage was rumoured to be inappropriately close to the composer. There were strict codes in play for appropriate behaviour between men and women, which musicians might seem to bypass or undermine, particularly if they were as inured to social convention as Beethoven. Moreover, suspicion of the emotional or sexual motives for making music with others, particularly in the close quarters of chamber music, lingered, as will be discussed later, with regard to the reception of the Violin Sonata, op. 47.

The renegotiation of public and private life, implicit to changing notions of friendship, occurred in the face of rapid urban expansion. Like many European cities, the population of Vienna was growing quickly; at the end of the eighteenth century there were around 250,000 inhabitants, which made it twice as big as Berlin but only half the size of Paris and a quarter the size of London. As Vienna grew, the spaces in which people lived, worked and socialized changed. Beethoven lived in more than sixty apartments during his thirty-five years in Vienna. It was not unusual for him to have more than one apartment at a time; the writer Bettina von Arnim reported, facetiously, that he could then hide in each one in turn. On occasion he lodged with patrons – such as at the Lichnowsky palace – and while he was commissioned to write an opera he had rooms adjoining the Theater an der Wien, though he seems to have used those mostly to receive visitors. Beethoven often spent his summers outside of the city, finding solace in the countryside around the village of Heiligenstadt, taking water cures in the spa town of Baden, or visiting friends such as Princess Marie Erdődy, who had a residence in Jedlesee. His Vienna apartments were not necessarily grand but usually had several rooms and had the benefit of being removed from street noise and dirt by being on the upper floors of buildings. Beethoven moved frequently because he often

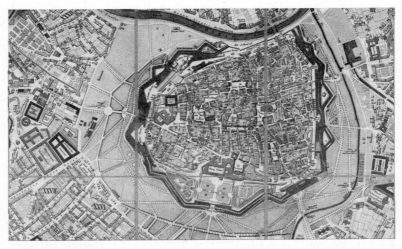

Fig. 2.2 Map of Vienna, 1824.

became restless and wanted to find a more amenable – and sometimes a more affordable – situation. It should also be acknowledged that he could be an inconsiderate tenant, prone to disturbing his neighbours with music and arguments with his servants, who he changed even more often than his address.

Social and cultural entertainments such as attending the theatre had primarily been the reserve of aristocrats. While they continued to host private events in their palaces and could keep to the safety of their boxes in the opera house, Emperor Joseph II instigated several reforms that opened up public life in the city. Theatre, opera and concert tickets went on sale to the public and promenading in the park was no longer a privilege of the nobility but available to all. By the end of the eighteenth century, there were more than eighty coffeehouses in Vienna, important social centres for men; respectable women kept to the home or, if aristocratic, to their salons. Coffee was expensive but a popular refreshment while smoking, reading newspapers, playing billiards and sometimes listening to musical entertainment: in 1797 Beethoven's quintet for wind and piano was played at one of his favourite haunts, Café Frauenhuber. According to his early biographer Anton Schindler, coffee was the one indispensable element of Beethoven's diet: each day began with a cup made carefully at home (he counted out sixty beans per cup, apparently) and it was always itemized in his budget of living costs. Coffee snobbery, much as today, was the height of fashion, and the essential part the stimulant and its pricey equipment played in Beethoven's lifestyle has sometimes been likened to his predilection for technical innovations in music, his new takes on old forms.[4] On a more everyday level, the presence of café culture within Vienna fostered friendship circles that provided Beethoven with professional and personal support from like-minded people.

Inevitably, friendship between men – particularly when alcohol and other stimulants were involved – was not always as noble as philosophers and essayists liked to make out. Jokes in Beethoven's letters suggest he had some rumbustious relationships. 'Barbarischer Freund!' ('Barbarian Friend!') began one brief letter that continued in scurrilous vein but was signed 'Dein Freund Beethoven' ('Your friend Beethoven').[5] Publishers had nicknames – Steiner was 'Lieutenant-General' and Tobias Haslinger 'Adjutant' – and received letters from 'Your Generalissimo'. The violinist Karl Holz was subjected to endless variations on his surname, which means 'wood': 'Best Chip!'; 'Best lignum crucis!'; and so on.[6] Nikolaus Zmeskall received, alongside summons to the pub, a musical setting of 'Graf, Graf, Graf . . . liebstes Graf/Schaf, bester Graf/Schaf' ('Baron, baron, baron . . . beloved baron/sheep, best baron/sheep').[7] These exchanges illustrate Beethoven's love of puns and his capacity for a more playful appreciation of different types of friendship which might mingle good-natured mockery with expressions of affection. Some of Beethoven's contemporaries gave as good as they got: at a soirée at the home of Count and Countess von Browne in 1803, at which his student Ferdinand Ries played Beethoven's Sonata, op. 23, the composer tapped Ries on the head when he missed a note. When it came to Beethoven's turn to play and his fingers slipped so that it sounded 'like a piano being cleaned', the countess rapped him several times on the head, explaining: 'If the pupil received one tap of the finger for one missed note, then the Master must be punished with a full hand for worse mistakes.'[8] Beethoven laughed and started again, playing incomparably well. However, the composer's jests could on occasion seem overly cruel and he frequently fell out with friends and family. His musical collaborations, as the story of op. 47 will illustrate, were often fraught, veering from joyful camaraderie to desertion or fragile truces.

One of the most long-suffering of Beethoven's friends and collaborators was the violinist Ignaz Schuppanzigh. The two men probably met at the Friday-morning informal quartet concerts that took place in Prince Lichnowsky's apartments in the 1790s, after which Beethoven received some violin lessons from him. Schuppanzigh was both a prominent performer and an innovative programmer; he was instrumental in giving the first public quartet concerts in Vienna and established new standards of performance through his carefully chosen and – just as importantly – relatively stable ensembles. Without access to musicians of such calibre, Beethoven would have had little chance of his works being played adequately, and Schuppanzigh took part in several important premieres, including that of the Septet, op. 20, discussed in the previous chapter, and most of the quartets; he was also leader and co-organizer of the concert at which the Ninth Symphony and parts of the *Missa solemnis* were first performed, of which more in Chapter 8. Beethoven may have respected Schuppanzigh's musical judgement, but the violinist had to endure constant ribbing about his weight:

Beethoven's nickname for him was Falstaff and he wrote him teasing pieces such as 'Lob auf den Dicken' ('In Praise of the Fat Man'), WoO 100 (1801), and 'Schuppanzigh ist ein Lump' ('Schuppanzigh is a Rogue'), WoO 184, a canon composed in 1823 for chorus and three solo male voices that heralded the violinist's return to Vienna after seven years in St Petersburg. (WoO is the abbreviation for 'Werke ohne Opuszahl', or 'work without opus number', which typically are pieces published after a composer's lifetime.) Humour does not necessarily translate across countries or centuries, but it should be said that Beethoven was not alone in mocking obesity: a pull-out cartoon from the time gave the violinist an expanding stomach, beer glass in hand (fig. 2.3).

Beethoven also composed eight sonatas for piano and violin with Schuppanzigh in mind. His ninth, though, was for another, and demonstrates the influence a performer could have over his musical imagination. The violinist George Polgreen Bridgetower arrived in Vienna in April 1803, with letters of introduction to aristocratic circles following his successful concerts in Dresden the previous year. The twenty-four-year-old had made his debut at Paris's Concert Spirituel at the age of ten, before moving to

Fig. 2.3 Caricature of Ignaz Schuppanzigh, *c.*1810

England, where he was marketed as an 'African Prince' (Bridgetower was unusual but not unique for the time in being a
musician of mixed race; born in Biala, Poland, his mother was
Austro-German and his father a West Indian who served as a
personal page for Haydn's patron Prince Esterházy). The Prince
of Wales became a prominent patron – Bridgetower was leader
of his private orchestra for many years – and the violinist made
frequent appearances as a soloist at prestigious concerts in London, including alongside Haydn.

The importance of Beethoven's network of friends and
patrons is apparent in how he met Bridgetower and in turn integrated him into his circle. Their first meeting likely took place in
Schuppanzigh's rooms. Count Lichnowsky, who eventually
financed their concert, probably made the official introduction,
but they had other well-placed mutual acquaintances who may
have done so, such as Count Dietrichstein, who supported many
musicians' ventures; as well as helping to organize concerts for
Beethoven, he was the dedicatee of Schubert's op. 1, the song
'Erlkönig' ('Elf king'). Dietrichstein instructed Bridgetower to
join him for breakfast at Lichnowsky's, explaining that he would
then take him to meet Beethoven. However they were introduced, Beethoven and Bridgetower quickly began collaborating:
the Bohemian doctor Johann Thomas Held recalled that on
16 April 1803 he and Count Prichowsky of Prague ran into
Beethoven in the street and were invited to a rehearsal at Schuppanzigh's of an arrangement of one of his piano sonatas (probably
op. 14, no. 1) for string quartet. One of the players was the newly
arrived Bridgetower. Beethoven in turn introduced the violinist
to others: for instance, he took him to a dinner hosted by Giulietta Guicciardi, dedicatee of the 'Moonlight' Sonata, who had
been his piano student and with whom he had been enamoured,
but who later that year married Count Wenzel Robert Gallenberg. Certainly, he would not have taken Bridgetower along

had he not thought his company would be acceptable, entertaining or in some other way useful.

Most importantly, Beethoven was impressed by the violinist's musicianship and tried to help him make professional connections. An interesting sign of the times was that those relationships were beginning to extend beyond the aristocracy. On 18 May 1803 he wrote to Alexander Wetzler, a keen patron who hosted musical evenings but whom he did not know personally. He asked for Bridgetower to be introduced to Wetzler's acquaintances, explaining that the violinist had already met Prince Lobkowitz, Count Moritz Johann Christian Fries and other 'distinguished [music] lovers', and describing him as 'a very capable virtuoso who has a complete command of his instrument'. Beethoven also suggested to Wetzler that Bridgetower might be invited to the home of another music enthusiast, Therese Schönfeld, whom he had heard often had guests. Both Wetzler and Schönfeld belonged to the wealthy middle classes and, while it would be some time before Beethoven directly made their acquaintance, his awareness of their growing influence within Viennese musical life is clear.

A further reason for trying to broaden Bridgetower's range of contacts in Vienna was that he was keen to organize an academy in the city for his own benefit. It was helpful to be well connected to gain access to the court theatres. Several patrons lent their support and Beethoven, who had recently had his own successful *Akademie*, no doubt helped by agreeing to write him a new sonata and to perform without a fee; something he did for other artists as well, in the hope that his own benefit concerts would be supported in the future. Being absorbed into Beethoven's network, then, had a practical, professional purpose for all involved, which – as will be seen in the case of Bridgetower – could supersede simple friendly support.

Public concerts were less common than the kinds of musical

events that took place in the salons discussed in the previous
chapter, partly because Vienna did not have a purpose-built
concert hall until 1831. One available venue was a hall in the
Augarten, a park that was opened to the general public by
Emperor Joseph II in 1775. Visitors could wander the gardens,
take all manner of refreshments (hot chocolate was the latest
novelty) and, among other entertainments (dancing, billiards),
enjoy regular, reasonably priced concerts. A summer subscription
series of weekly morning concerts had featured performances
by Mozart and, in the late 1790s, was taken over by Schuppanzigh, who directed orchestras mostly made up of accomplished
amateurs and later organized quartet concerts there. The Augarten was also a common venue for musicians making their debut,
including students of Schuppanzigh and Beethoven. It seemed
an obvious choice, then, for Bridgewater's inaugural *Akademie*
on 24 May 1803, at which he gave the first performance of
Beethoven's Ninth Sonata for piano and violin, op. 47, with the
composer at the piano.

The concert took place two days later than originally planned,
for reasons that were unspecified. It may simply have been
because the piece was not ready. Apparently, on the morning of
the concert, Beethoven roused Ferdinand Ries, who also served
as his secretary and copyist, before daybreak. He needed him to
prepare the violin part of the first movement from his autograph
score; in other words, Ries had to copy out the violin's melody
from Beethoven's manuscript, which included both the piano
and violin parts and would be too unwieldy for the violinist to
play from. There was not time to make a separate violin part for
the second movement and so Bridgetower had to read from the
autograph, presumably over Beethoven's shoulder. This was not
the only instance of Beethoven asking for Ries's help at the last
minute and the dead of night. One reason for the early start on
this occasion was that the concert itself seems to have taken

place in the morning. Ries records the start-time as 8 a.m., as for other Augarten concerts (the smell of sausages being cooked for breakfast could waft over the audience), but there is some disagreement. Some sources say that it probably was at the still earlier time of 7 a.m. However, Joseph Carl Rosenbaum, who worked as a secretary to the Esterházys and was a friend of Haydn, noted in his diary that the concert took place at midday and that 'It was not too crowded, a select company' with Prince Esterházy, Count Razumovsky and the British ambassador in the audience.[9] The scant evidence makes it hard to piece together precisely what happened at such concerts. Whatever time in the morning it took place, that it was to a small audience is unsurprising, for pretty much everyone bar aristocrats would be either at work or about to be.

Despite this first performance of the sonata being unrehearsed, it was reported to have been well received. Bridgetower added a flourish to the violin part to match, or perhaps compete, with the piano's cadenza; Beethoven, delighted, jumped up, exclaiming, 'Noch einmal, mein lieber Bursch!' ('Once more, my dear fellow!'). The slow movement was 'unanimously hailed' and repeated twice. Subsequently, Beethoven annotated one of his manuscripts with a dedication: 'Sonata mulattica, composta per il Mulatto Brischdauer, gran pazzo e compositore mulattico' (*Mulatto Sonata, composed by the mulatto Brischdauer* [*sic*], *great fool and mulatto composer*) and elsewhere called it 'Sonata per un mulattico lunatic' ('Sonata for a Mad Mulatto'). 'Mulatto', meaning someone of mixed race, is now a derogatory term, as, it might be said, is 'fool' or 'lunatic'; actually, they doubtless were then as well. But Beethoven's inscription, despite its repetition of the word 'mulatto', was not only about race or madness, or, if it was, it was not necessarily negative. It can be read as a spoof of the elaborate dedications composers often made to their patrons, the aggrandizing 'Mulatto Brischdauer' echoing, say, 'Count

Bridgetower'. Beethoven's misspelling of the violinist's name was probably not deliberate: he made many such errors and spoke neither English nor Italian, the latter being the common tongue for these kinds of dedications. However, referring to Bridgetower as a great fool or lunatic seems in keeping with the kinds of terms Beethoven reserved for his friends, especially his drinking buddies (such as Holz, 'Most Excellent Piece of Mahogany!').

There is a musical point to be made here, too, about the 'mixed' nature of the sonata Beethoven had composed. Op. 47 is often heard to reflect Bridgetower's technical prowess: it is a far more challenging violin sonata than previous ones. Yet not all the music was originally written for Bridgetower. Beethoven drafted the first and second movements early in 1803, probably in response to having met the violinist. The third movement, though, had originally been composed as the finale of the Violin Sonata, op. 30, no. 1, in A major, which had then been replaced by a more mild-mannered set of variations. The impetus for bringing the three movements together came from the opportunity to write something for Bridgetower's concert, and while it may well have been influenced by his playing, it was not music inspired by him alone. Moreover, the fact that the finale was already complete meant that he was able to use its musical materials to determine the shape of the first two movements and thereby craft a more coherent trajectory throughout the work. That emphasis on unifying constituent parts would become increasingly important in Beethoven's 'heroic', 'new way' of composing, said to begin with the symphony he started the same month, the 'Eroica'.

The 'mixed' aspect of the sonata might also be taken to refer to its stylistic hybridity. When the sonata was published in 1805, it had the subtitle 'Sonata, scritta in uno stilo concertante, quasi come d'un concerto' – 'Sonata, written in the concertante style, almost as if a concerto'. (Initially, Beethoven had also included the phrase 'un [*sic*] stilo brilliante molto concertante', but it was erased, perhaps because it was over-egging the pudding.) This was a radical blurring of genres. The sonata was chamber music, designed to be played in intimate spaces and normally accessible to amateurs; the concerto, by contrast, was a vehicle for virtuosic display. By writing parts for piano and violin that sounded more like a concerto, Beethoven was paying scant heed to convention. He was also attempting to transform a genre that might be characterized as introvert into an extrovert one. It was probably for these kinds of reasons that a contemporary reviewer described the sonata's subtitle as 'wunderlich, anmassend und prahlerisch' ('whimsical, presumptuous and ostentatious'). Beethoven's openness to combining sonata and concerto may have been because he was in the midst of composing several concertos: the Third and Fourth Piano concertos, the Violin Concerto and the Triple Concerto for violin, cello and piano. With concertos on his mind, it would be understandable for Beethoven to have allowed one mode of composing to seep into another. The layout of the sonata, though, is nothing like a conventional concerto, which would alternate between accompaniment and solo much more clearly. In this regard, another tiny grammatical change on the title page of op. 47 was also significant. Previously, all of Beethoven's sonatas had been for keyboard *with* (*mit*) another instrument; the violin, in other words, was an accompaniment or decoration for the piano, which typically introduced the main themes. The title page of op. 47, though, said for keyboard *and* (*und*) violin, suggesting a more equal relationship between the parts.

Perhaps as a consequence of encounters with performers of the quality of Bridgetower, then, Beethoven began to grant his musical partners a more powerful voice. In so doing, the status of the violin sonata was also elevated, to become something more suited to skilled professionals than to amateurs. There is also the question of scale: this sonata is longer than any of Beethoven's other sonatas for piano and violin, despite having only three movements. The movements themselves are outwardly conventional in form. The first has a slow introduction, which becomes a lively Presto in sonata form; the central, slow movement is an Andante con variazioni, or theme with variations; and the finale is another Presto, its recurring theme making it a rondo. Yet the first movement alone takes the same time to play as the whole of Sonata no. 8 in G major, op. 30, no. 3. Beethoven, in other words, is expanding the work from within, extending its musical content and demanding, on top of technical brilliance, quite some stamina on the part of the performers.

Nowhere is the violin's new status more apparent than at the sonata's start, described by early biographer Wilhelm von Lenz as 'a veritable declaration of war against the piano'.[10] It begins alone, carving out a melody from chords – a flamboyant gesture, thrown down like a gauntlet. It is much easier to play chords on a piano than on a violin, and the volume of the response is bruising. What's more, the violin's bright major-mode is abruptly made minor. Not to be deterred, the violin responds with a brief phrase that pushes the harmonies elsewhere; the piano responds in kind until the two instruments are no longer playing full, lumbering chords but teasing couplets, descending from their grandstanding to act like schoolchildren thumbing their nose at each other: na-na; na-na; na-na; na-na; na-na-na-na-na-na. Eventually, the violin seizes the couplet and forges it into the theme of the Presto, which confirms the move to the minor: na-NA!

The sonata continues to be a two-way exchange; the piece requires, an advert for the score later explained, 'two artists who are in very mighty command of their instruments, and who understand how to use them with meaning and with feeling. One finds here not just a random murmuring with notes, rather, one believes that one perceives a penetrating dialogue, relentlessly driven forward.'[11] The heightened importance of each individual part, begun in the Piano Trio, op. 1, no. 3, is pushed further here. Throughout the Presto of the first movement, violin and piano alternate ideas; there is little sense here of the earlier melody-and-accompaniment model. Instead, each is the other's equal. Similar challenges to those thrown down in the introduction are repeated in the Presto. The piano repeats the violin's opening theme and rips its concluding chord into a cadenza-like flourish; the gesture Bridgetower had copied at the premiere to Beethoven's delight. Interruptions of this kind occur frequently in the movement, contrasting with the busy passagework of the faster-moving sections, and unsettling the sonata-form principle of having two clearly delineated themes, which are developed and then recapitulated. The music's 'penetrating dialogue' in part, then, has to do with the multiple musical ideas which challenge expectations about what should happen next.

The sonata's compositional history suggests another way in which the different movements are in dialogue with one another. As mentioned, the finale was produced first, followed by the first movement and then the Andante. That order of events suggests that the finale is the source of material for the whole work and demonstrates Beethoven's intent to create coherence across the movements. There are both more blatant and other more subtle connections between them. The finale shares the first movement's fluctuations between major and minor, and the energy of its quicksilver Presto. There are also moments, as in the first movement, of something like reflection, when the music slows before plunging back into the relentless theme. Points of contact with the Andante are harder to detect because its speed and mood are so different from the energetic movements at its flanks, but it also features accented off-beat rhythms; the heavy ornamentation of the theme in its variations might link to the finale's many trills. Yet, however quickly put together, the sonata was not simply conceived backwards, nor was its unity conceptualized immediately. Beethoven tweaked the last movement to forge a link between new and old, adding the loud opening chord in the piano only as the whole piece went to be engraved. The addition provides a brief preface to the violin's theme, rather than leaving it to begin alone, as it had at the start of the sonata. This is helpful here because the violin's repeated pitches and jerky rhythm seem more like half an idea than a melody, even when the piano starts to imitate it. It also clarifies the underlying harmony. By the end of the sonata, violin and piano are no longer in combat or tailing one another but playing together: a consensus that suggests a mutual respect, a friendship, which is all the stronger for having been tested – as Beethoven had claimed of his relationship with Prince Lichnowsky.

The Violin Sonata, op. 47, is also in dialogue with new musical technologies. Beethoven's imagination was captured by innovations in instrument-building which allowed for greater dynamic range and more varied articulation. Érard had started selling its first series of grand pianos in 1797. They based their design on that of Broadwood from London. These instruments had a heavier touch than was fashionable in Vienna at the time; their articulation was less clear (on top of which, Viennese pianos had more responsive dampers, which halted the vibration of the strings when the finger was lifted from the key) and they were uneven across their range (tinkly up top, buzzy down below). But the Érard compensated for the weakness of its upper register with a sweet tone, and its middle and lower registers blended well to create a full-bodied singing quality. Moreover, it had a new pedal, the *una corda*, that facilitated greater dynamic control through a shift mechanism that allowed the performer to choose whether the hammers would hit all three, two or only one of the strings per pitch, becoming softer accordingly. There are not the kind of detailed pedal markings in the Violin Sonata, op. 47, that there would be in the later Piano Sonata, op. 101, where Beethoven instructs that the cadenza transition between movements three and four is marked to be played 'Nach und nach mehrere Saiten' ('with gradually more strings') and then 'Alle Saiten' ('all strings'). However, there are relatively frequent pedal marks in the piano part of op. 47, particularly on its characteristic flourishes and sustained chords, which suggest that he was already exploring its rhetorical effect.

Beethoven was fascinated by the Érard's sound-world, and in the autumn of 1802 had hinted to his friend Zmeskall that he was considering purchasing a piano from them. In the end, he may have been assisted in the transaction by other friends and colleagues, such as composer Anton Reicha, who he had known well in Bonn and was now based in Paris. By whatever means, an Érard arrived on 6 August 1803, seemingly as an unsolicited gift, and prompted Beethoven's composition of the 'Waldstein' and 'Appassionata' sonatas. Although he had already completed op. 47 by this time, the arrival of the piano had a bit-part to play in the piece's history. Sometime soon after its premiere, Beethoven and Bridgetower appear to have fallen out; no one seems certain of any details, but it has been suggested that they had a fight over a woman after a long bout of drinking. As a result, Beethoven withdrew the dedication to Bridgetower. Or perhaps he had a bigger name in mind, one that would promote his work in the important musical market of Paris, which Beethoven had yet to crack but planned to visit in 1805. Ferdinand Ries, writing on the composer's behalf to their old Bonn friend the publisher Nikolaus Simrock on 22 October 1803, offered them the sonata for 50 gulden, the same fee he had received from Breitkopf und Härtel for the String Quintet, op. 29, the year before. It was to be dedicated to Rodolphe Kreutzer and Jean-Louis Adam 'as first violinist and pianist in Paris, because Beethoven is indebted to Adam on account of the Paris piano'. The reference to 'first violinist and pianist' acknowledges the musicians' first-class standing at the Paris Conservatoire, where they both taught. Quite what Adam's role had been regarding what was presumably the newly arrived Érard is unclear and in the final publication he was not mentioned. Perhaps the pianist would have been more appreciative of the sonata: despite accepting the dedication, Kreutzer did not like Beethoven's music and never played it.

Beethoven's Érard was thought to be a gift from the Parisian firm until this century, when archival research revealed otherwise.[12] The firm's sales book from 5 August 1803 notes: 'Mr Beethoven, keyboardist in Vienna, owes 1500 francs for the sale of a grand piano, no. 133.' Not only does this refer to Beethoven as merely a 'keyboardist', not a composer (a reminder that at this stage of his career Beethoven did not have an established reputation in France), it indicates that the piano was no gift. But back in Vienna, friends and associates readily believed that it had been. After all, Haydn had been sent an Érard a couple of years previously, though admittedly his was much more elaborately decorated, as might be expected of a tribute to an esteemed master.

All of this demonstrates how the reputation of a historical figure, even one as famous and as often studied as Beethoven, can be built on misinformation and misunderstandings. The sonata for piano and violin, op. 47, is still known as the 'Kreutzer', despite Kreutzer having rejected the piece. Again, what Beethoven intended by the dedication is ambiguous. Although, following French conventions, Beethoven's dedication was to 'son ami' – 'his friend' – they did not know each other well. They had met in Vienna in 1798, when the violinist had visited as part of the retinue of the French ambassador General Bernadotte. Since then, Kreutzer's career had been reported assiduously in the Viennese press; he was also highly regarded as a composer. His Grande Sonate in A minor was published in Leipzig in 1802 and bears some striking similarities to Beethoven's op. 47 (it also suggests a link with Adam, a Romance by whom formed the basis of Kreutzer's second movement). The *Allgemeine musikalische Zeitung* described Kreutzer's Grande Sonate as having a 'spirited and fiery' first movement, which when played 'by swift and robust players creates an excellent effect'.[13] Its many embellishments and modulations notwithstanding, it was said to fit well under a violinist's fingers so was not too difficult to perform. Kreutzer was a tremendously influential teacher as well, producing studies and treatises which shaped violin-playing and pedagogy around Europe. Beethoven had studied the violin in Bonn and his teachers were advocates for the French school of playing represented by Kreutzer (and, incidentally, by Bridgetower), which makes it likely that Beethoven would have first-hand knowledge of the technical exercises in Kreutzer's 42 Études (1796), which foreshadow some of the chordal writing in Beethoven's Sonata, op. 47, as well as its extensive trills.

The changes in keyboard-making, which were expanding the types of sound and articulation available to pianists, had a counterpart in a new design for the violin bow. Previously, bows had been made in an arch shape with a pointed tip, which made them quite nimble and light but also meant that the sound naturally died off at either end. The Viotti or, more commonly, Tourte bow, by contrast, had a longer, stronger stick with a concave curve and a 'hatchet' or 'battle-axe' head, which allowed for a broader band of hair that, through a new tightening mechanism (the 'frog'), could be given more tension (see fig. 2.4). The

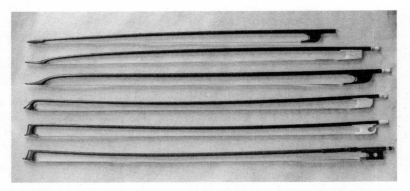

Fig. 2.4 Changing bow shapes in the eighteenth century, from early (*top*) to the Tourte bow (*bottom*).

result was a fuller tone from one end to the other, enabling longer and more lyrical, as well as louder, melodies, and a wider range of attacks. One such was a hammered, or martelé, stroke, played with force at the tip of the bow, which Beethoven may have had in mind for the repeated quick notes of the opening theme of the sonata's finale.

Kreutzer was closely associated with another bowing technique that may also be used in these opening bars, the *contre coup d'archet*, which reversed the usual association of strong beats with a down-bow (pulling away from the violin) and weaker beats with an up-bow (moving towards it). Such an unsettling gesture seems in keeping with Beethoven's compositional interest in rhythmic play; he often uses accents and dramatic changes of dynamic to go against the grain of the music's underlying metre. Beethoven's sensitivity to the rhythmic impetus of a bow stroke is also suggested by the dynamics at the very start of the sonata: the notes of the famous opening chords could easily be played evenly using an old-fashioned bow, but with a Tourte bow they more naturally split between the lower and the upper strings, a wrench that Beethoven seems to acknowledge by the *forte* marking on the first chord. It can sound like a struggle;

it is probably meant to. The concave shape to the Tourte bow enhanced its similarity to a sword or rapier, adding a sharp edge to the violin duels between virtuosi that were popular in the early nineteenth century, as were the piano duels in which Beethoven participated. In the Napoleonic era, for a German to adopt a French style of playing was also a political act, suggesting revolutionary sympathies (only after the accession of Louis-Philippe I as King of the French in 1830 did the Tourte style of bow become widely adopted in German-speaking countries).[14] Beethoven's attitude to Napoleon fluctuated between admiration and disdain, as we will see in the next chapter. Yet works such as the 'Kreutzer' Sonata and the opera *Fidelio* demonstrate his musical affinity with the French, which might amount to covert political insurrection.

The tensions between violin and piano in the 'Kreutzer' Sonata give the music much of its energy, to the extent that in Leo Tolstoy's 1889 novella of the same name Beethoven's piece is cited as a conduit for adulterous passion. The jealous husband complains:

> How can that first presto be played in a drawing-room among ladies in low-necked dresses? To hear that played, to clap a little, and then to eat ices and talk of the latest scandal? Such things should only be played on certain important significant occasions, and then only when certain actions answering to such music are wanted; play it then and do what the music has moved you to. Otherwise an awakening of energy and feeling unsuited both to the time and the place, to which no outlet is given, cannot but act harmfully.[15]

Making music in this way could lead even the most faithful of wives astray, the husband concludes: suspecting his of having an affair with her violinist friend, he stabs her to death. The association between Beethoven and murderous passion is in keeping with posthumous ideas of the composer's tumultuous inner life and was continued by Leoš Janáček, who borrowed the title of the Tolstoy for his first string quartet, composed in 1923, in which he said he had imagined 'a poor woman, tormented and ruined', as in the story. There is, though, a small detail in Tolstoy's novella, often overlooked, which indicates that it was not really the Beethoven that convinced the husband of his wife's infidelity, but rather what came next: 'I remember[ed] their faces that evening when, after playing the Kreutzer Sonata, they played some impassioned little piece, I don't remember by whom, impassioned to the point of obscenity.' The unnamed 'impassioned little piece' is the real vehicle for their love, even if it was unlocked by Beethoven. The tragedy of Tolstoy's novella is that it seems his wife was not having an affair; that the violinist was just a friend. The potential for men and women to be intimates socially was still doubted. Women were expected to be musically accomplished in order to attract a husband, but of course had to ensure they were alluring only to appropriate partners. In this context, Beethoven's 'Kreutzer' Sonata threatened to upset gender relations by presenting chamber music as a dialogue of equals, capable of virtuosic display – to be played by friends who, like the composer and Bridgetower, could spar together.

3. Heroism: Symphony no. 3, op. 55, the 'Eroica' (1804)

Beethoven's Third Symphony begins with two identical chords in quick succession. Too curt to be an introduction, they are more a call to attention: loud and for full orchestra. The theme that then emerges, however, is played not by a typical melodic instrument such as the violins or an oboe but by the cellos. Their tune is simple, quietly outlining the chord of E flat major the orchestra has just played. It would sound fanfare-like if it were played by brass and loudly; instead the cellos rumble gently to chugging accompaniment from violas and second violins. At the start it is unclear what metre the music is in, but it is swiftly evident that rather than being in duple time, which is more common for the first movement of a symphony, it is in triple time.

Suddenly the music goes off course. The cello melody slips away from the E flat chord to sink down towards a note foreign to the home key: C sharp. The first violins enter off the beat and the harmonic tension momentarily rises. It soon subsides, though, and the instruments of the orchestra adopt more familiar roles; the horns and woodwind take over the fanfare, the violins become more decorative, and the cellos and basses provide ballast. Scholars have written again and again about the beginning of Beethoven's Third Symphony, trying to explain the magical effect of that unexpected note and to rationalize it within common practice.[1] It is a revolutionary moment, musically speaking. Yet the revolution of this symphony is, for now, quiet and gone within less than a minute. Greater upset is still to come.

The 'Eroica' – as Beethoven's Symphony no. 3 in E flat major, op. 55, came to be known – has long been associated with revolutionary ideals. As this chapter explores, while some of those ideals are musical, others have to do with the work's biographical and political context. Beethoven began sketching a 'grand symphony' in the summer of 1802, which would use as its finale a piece he had already composed, the Variations and Fugue for Piano in E flat major, op. 35. Various projects intervened to delay its completion until October. Beethoven was then living in an apartment at the Theater an der Wien, as their 'in-house' composer, hatching operatic plans that would eventually become *Fidelio*. The 'Kreutzer' Sonata also took some time. Despite being different genres, there is some common ground between the Violin Sonata and the Third Symphony, showing that Beethoven was tussling with similar formal concerns in both. Each incorporated a finale from elsewhere. By already having that movement in place, Beethoven could aim towards it as his conclusion. Increasingly, he used sketches to conceptualize the structure of the whole work, not just individual movements. For the 'Eroica' he seemed less interested in making references across movements than in shifting the weight of the music towards its ending, which has encouraged listeners to think of narratives of victory or apotheosis.

The other similarity between the 'Kreutzer' Sonata and the 'Eroica' Symphony was their orientation towards France. As mentioned in the previous chapter, Beethoven had hoped to strengthen his association with French musicians through the sonata's dedication to the violinist Rodolphe Kreutzer, as a means, perhaps, to facilitate at least a trip to Paris. Had that come off, he might have intended to premiere the 'Eroica' there.[2] As it was, political circumstances transformed the Third Symphony from a work that looked towards France to one that firmly centred Beethoven in Vienna. The political beliefs of a historical figure are never easy to untangle, especially when they lived during an age of revolution when allegiances might switch according to circumstance. In the case of a composer, there is the further complicated question of whether their politics were reflected in their music, and if so how, especially in instrumental genres such as the symphony, which seem fundamentally abstract but could be freighted with extra-musical baggage by the addition of descriptive titles or programmes. The story of the 'Eroica' in and beyond Beethoven's lifetime illustrates the extent to which musical meaning can change. Every age has its own heroes; in the case of Beethoven's Third Symphony, each generation has made the music's hero in their preferred image.

Like many of his friends and associates, since his youth Beethoven had admired the French revolutionary spirit. The values of liberty, equality and fraternity were echoed in his statements about the importance of freedom and truth, no matter how elevated the society. However, in its earliest incarnation, the revolutionary motto had a sting in its tail: 'Liberté, égalité, fraternité, ou la mort'. The threat of death came ever closer as France declared war on the Habsburg Empire and Kingdom of Prussia in 1792. Bonn, in the Rhineland, was in a vulnerable position geographically and diplomatically, for it harboured refugees from the revolution. The Elector, Maximilian Franz, and his court fled to Münster and the soon to be twenty-two-year-old Beethoven was sent for a second time to Vienna, ostensibly to study with Haydn but also to be kept out of harm's way.

The capital of the Habsburg Empire had been Francophile – and its court Francophone – for much of the eighteenth century. The Queen of France, Marie Antoinette, was the sister of Austria's Leopold II, then Holy Roman Emperor, and Cologne's Elector, Maximilian Franz. Her execution and that of Louis

XVI had to be avenged. Yet war with the French was unpopular, especially after a series of defeats. Jacobin sympathizers, seeing a chance to unseat the Habsburg dynasty, were quickly quashed by the police, and either imprisoned or executed. Beethoven reported to Nikolaus Simrock back in Bonn that 'various important people have been locked up', that a curfew had been imposed and that the police were armed: 'You dare not raise your voice here.' But then, he reflected, 'so long as an Austrian can get his brown ale and his little brown sausages he is unlikely to revolt'.[3] Ultimately, Beethoven followed suit: in his professional engagements he remained on the side of his aristocratic Austrian patrons, composing patriotic songs and, at least at this stage of his career, rarely saying anything politically out of line. It was a sensible policy. Vienna was a city ruled by censorship, prohibiting not only political dissent but also artworks that might be subversive, such as plays by Friedrich Schiller or Paul Wranitzky's *Grande Sinfonie caractéristique pour la paix avec la République françoise* (1797), a battle symphony that controversially incorporated a funeral march for the death of Louis XVI while also celebrating the Peace Treaty of Campo Formio of that year.

Much of the rest of Beethoven's life took place against a backdrop of war and its related economic privations. When Elector Maximilian Franz curtailed his stipend it was less for artistic reasons than because of the financial burden of going into battle. The French Revolutionary Army was challenged by a series of loosely allied coalitions, often including Austria, and were led to victory after victory by a Corsican general, Napoleon Bonaparte. Beethoven was fascinated by the dashing figure of Napoleon, who seemed to have risen through the ranks on the basis of his strategic brilliance alone, and who espoused republican virtues. Following Campo Formio, Beethoven briefly befriended the French ambassador, General Bernadotte, who apparently tried to persuade him to compose a symphony in honour of Napoleon; the composer may even have attempted to meet the man himself.[4] The year in which Beethoven eventually began work on the symphony he would contemplate dedicating to Napoleon, 1803, was another period of relative calm, as Austria had remained neutral in recent skirmishes between France and Britain. Beethoven's disappointment at Napoleon declaring himself Emperor and the outbreak of further hostilities, including the French occupations of Vienna in 1805 and 1809, disillusioned him somewhat. Yet he continued to be intrigued by Napoleon and evidently felt they could be compared, as titans of their age. If only he understood the art of war as well as he did the art of music, Beethoven claimed with some chutzpah, he would conquer Napoleon.[5]

French musical influence over Beethoven proved more consistent than political allegiances. There was a vogue in Vienna for French operas by composers such as François-Joseph Gossec and Luigi Cherubini. Another significant genre, given that there were so many fallen heroes to be commemorated during this period, was the funeral march. Gossec's *Marche lugubre* was used for a string of revolutionary luminaries: the Count of Mirabeau, Voltaire, General Hoche and General Joubert. It was also popular sheet music in Vienna. Gossec's dramatic use of percussion, brass fanfares and silence, its minor key and dotted (unequal) rhythms, encapsulated conventions that Beethoven reproduced in his *Marcia funebre sulla morte d'un eroe*, a funeral march on the death of a hero, in the third movement of the A flat major Piano Sonata, op. 26 (1800). Beethoven reused that funeral march in 1815, in his incidental music for Johann Friedrich Duncker's play about German heroine Leonora Prohaska, who donned military garb to fight against Napoleon. According to Ferdinand Ries, who in addition to being his student and amanuensis would also be his biographer, when it came to the Third Symphony, Beethoven may also have had in mind an opera so admired by Napoleon that he persuaded the Italian composer to join his retinue: Ferdinando Paer's *Melodramma eroico* after Homer's *Iliad, Achille*. It had been premiered at the Kärtnertortheater in celebration of Marie Therese's birthday on 6 June 1801. Beethoven apparently liked one of its funeral marches so much he said 'he would have to compose it' (you will, Ludwig, you will, might be the Wildean response). In the end, the similarities between the funeral marches that recur in Paer's opera and the second movement of Beethoven's Third Symphony are more along the lines of family resemblance than outright borrowing, with the exception of the rumbling upbeats in the bass line that sound a little like muffled drums. The music's French heritage was important, though: a reminder that even a symphony that came to represent the German tradition had cosmopolitan ancestry.

The eventual title of the Third Symphony was determined by politics, patrons and publishers. The composer did not undertake all of the arrangements with publishers himself. This enabled him to play firms off against each other but could also cause friction and misunderstanding, especially if his brother Kaspar Karl was involved. Kaspar Karl had moved to Vienna in 1795 and worked part-time as Beethoven's agent. He was notorious for chasing after ever-higher fees, for passing off arrangements by other composers as being by Beethoven, and for going behind his brother's back by approaching other publishers to get a better deal. The siblings fought often but usually made up, to the frustration of Ferdinand Ries, who also represented Beethoven and thought little of the 'terribly rude' Kaspar Karl. It is apparent from how long it took to get the Third Symphony into print that the triangulated approach did not always work to Beethoven's advantage.

Kaspar Karl offered the Third Symphony to Breitkopf und

Härtel on 14 October 1803. A week later, Ries told Simrock that
the symphony had been completed and that Breitkopf und Härtel had already made a generous bid for it, with the 'Kreutzer'
Sonata thrown in. Beethoven was disinclined to accept, however, because he distrusted their arrangement with his brother.
Ries continued: Prince Joseph Lobkowitz had offered to pay
400 florins to own the work for six months. That was eventually
agreed, with the first performance of the symphony taking place
at Lobkowitz's palace at Eisenberg in Bohemia in August.[6]
Lobkowitz's support for Beethoven's Third Symphony was
important both financially and creatively. Having gained control of his family's considerable estate in 1799, the prince spent a
huge amount of money supporting musicians and concert series.
He took the novel step of converting the largest room in his
Vienna palace into a concert room, in which members of the
audience were seated on eighteen long upholstered benches with
back rests. On the other side of a dividing balustrade was a low
podium on which seats and cherry-wood music stands for his
in-house orchestra could fit. It was in this room that Beethoven
first rehearsed his Third Symphony, on 9 June 1804, which
means that it is now known as the Eroica-Saal, despite the fact
that both the Fourth Symphony (1807) and the Fifth Piano Concerto (1811) also had their premieres there. By today's concert-
hall standards, the Eroica-Saal is small – its audience capacity
was about thirty – and the ensemble used in the rehearsals was
modestly sized: only twenty-two players are listed in the financial records, who would probably have been supplemented by
extras.[7] However, use of the space was an invaluable opportunity for Beethoven to try out musical ideas. Haydn may have
enjoyed similar resources at the Esterházy court but had to pay
the price of servitude. Mozart never had such an ensemble to
hand. Prince Lobkowitz and Beethoven thereby tried a new,
more accommodating form of artistic patronage.

The first public performance of the Third Symphony took place at a benefit concert for the violinist Franz Clement at the Theater an der Wien on 7 April 1805.[8] Clement and Beethoven had known each other for some time and often worked together. Clement was music director of the Theater an der Wien and a renowned virtuoso (one of his tricks was playing his instrument upside down). He would in due course premiere Beethoven's Violin Concerto. Clement's own concerto began the programme that evening, and was fulsomely praised. As for Beethoven's Symphony, there was less consensus. A critic for *Der Freymüthige* described the audience as split into three: Beethoven's 'very special friends', who declared the work a masterpiece and who viewed those who did not understand its 'elevated beauties' as simply uneducated; those who thought it strained too hard for 'distinction and oddity' at the expense of the 'beautiful and sublime'; and those who found the symphony too long, difficult and disjointed but at the same time recognized that it had many 'beautiful qualities'.[9] The *Freymüthige* critic went on to predict that if Beethoven were to continue along this path it would be to the detriment of himself and the public. His music could quickly reach the point when those who do not understand its rules and enjoy its difficulties would find no pleasure in it. They would instead be overwhelmed and exhausted by its overabundance of ideas and 'continuous tumult'. Worse still, Beethoven was impolite: he did not even nod to those who did applaud.

Beethoven's ability to split his audience was noted by other reviewers. One complained that the symphony was 'so shrill and complicated that only those who worship the failings and merits of this composer with equal fire . . . could find pleasure in it'.[10] The pro- and contra-camps among Beethoven's early listeners forecast what have continued to be routine responses to concerts of challenging new music: some delight in radical experimentation; others dislike what they hear as being complexity for its own sake. Nineteenth-century listeners had a clearer sense, perhaps, of what constitutes beauty than we do today. Classical principles of balance, proportion and coherence were generally agreed. Beethoven's determination to test those aesthetic categories signalled that it was time to find new ways to construct music, which need no longer be considered merely entertainment. It was art, and the musician, as a result, was no longer an artisan but an artist. Why should he nod to his admirers?

After the April concert, Beethoven wrote again to Breitkopf und Härtel, insisting that the Third Symphony should be published immediately, as the delay was causing damage to his reputation, but they returned the score to him in June. They were still waiting for other works Beethoven had promised them – from *Christus am Ölberge* and the Triple Concerto, op. 56, to the 'Appassionata' Sonata, op. 57 – and in the turbulent political climate may have been wary of publishing a work the composer had at one stage suggested should be entitled 'Bonaparte'. The following year, a critic in the *Allgemeine musikalische Zeitung*, reviewing a piano arrangement of the Second Symphony, wished that the Third Symphony – 'one of the most original, most sublime, and most profound products' – would be published: 'Would it not be a shame if, perhaps due to lack of support or trust of a publisher, it should remain in the dark and not be brought out into the world?'[11] In the end, the orchestral parts of the Third Symphony were published in October 1806 by the Vienna-based Kunst- und Industrie-Comptoir, a small firm with the backing of some important creative voices in the city, including Joseph Sonnleithner, the original librettist of *Fidelio*. Although the firm usually concentrated on piano and chamber music, they had already published the Second Symphony and the Third Piano Concerto, and their willingness to take on the Third Symphony indicated that publishers were beginning to recognize that while larger-scale works might not make money as readily as smaller pieces, they had a cachet that would be lucrative in the longer term.

Dedicated to Prince Lobkowitz, who had paid an extra 80 ducats for the honour, the published title page of the Third Symphony read: 'Sinfonia eroica, composta per festeggiare il sovvenire di un grand uomo' ('Heroic Symphony, composed to celebrate the remembrance of a great man'). The composer had continued to resist advice from critics that if he shortened the symphony it would bring 'light, clarity, and unity to the whole'.[12] However, he did take the unusual step of printing a preface in the first violin part of the first edition which cautioned that because the symphony was 'purposefully written to be much longer than is usual', it should be performed near the start of a concert rather than at its end, so that the audience is not too tired to appreciate its affect. 'Near the start', Beethoven clarified, meant after an overture, an aria and a concerto; a reminder of the length of concert programmes during this era.

Notes were increasingly used to help audiences find a foothold in the piece. For example, for the Leipzig premiere in 1807 the programme announced the 'Eroica' as a 'Grand, heroic symphony' consisting of '[1] fiery, splendid Allegro; [2] lofty, solemn funeral march; [3] vehement Scherzando; [4] grand finale in part in the strict style'.[13] The chosen adjectives – 'fiery', 'lofty' and 'vehement', all associated with the Romantic sublime – seemed to have encouraged a more serious approach to the work. The Leipzig orchestra was reported to have volunteered to meet for extra rehearsals and, unusually, scores were made available to them so that they could 'penetrate the meaning and purpose of the composer'. And then:

> The most educated friends of art in the city were assembled in great numbers, a truly solemn attentiveness and deathlike silence reigned and was sustained not only throughout the

whole (as is well known, nearly hour-long) first performance, but also during the second and third, which, upon diverse requests, followed within a few weeks.[14]

Not all cities were willing to accord Beethoven's music the dedicated study granted by Leipzig audiences. However, gradually, the piece became better known through piano arrangements, and better prepared for performances. As a result, there were more favourable reviews: the Third Symphony began consistently to be heralded as 'the greatest, most original, most artistic and, at the same time, most interesting of all symphonies'.[15]

Despite freely attributing 'heroic' qualities to the Third Symphony, no direct reference was made to Napoleon in the initial concerts and reviews of the work. Politically, that was unsurprising: the Austrian and Russian armies had been routed at the Battle of Austerlitz in December 1805. Vienna's hospitals were full of injured soldiers from both sides, and while a peace treaty ended the occupation of the city there were financial penalties: taxes rose and food was scarce. Amid the vicissitudes of the Napoleonic era, there seems to have been no connection made publicly between Beethoven's *Eroica* and the French emperor. It was not until more than a decade after the composer's death, in 1838, when Ries published his biographical notes on Beethoven, that the symphony's initial dedication to Bonaparte was revealed. Ries relayed how, on hearing that Napoleon had been crowned Emperor on 2 December 1804, Beethoven exclaimed: 'Is he then, too, nothing more than an ordinary man! Now he will trample on all the rights of man and only indulge his ambition. He will exalt himself above all others and become a tyrant!' Annoyed, he ripped the manuscript in two. No autograph manuscript of the Third Symphony survives, so perhaps Ries's account holds true. On the title page of the fair copy owned by Beethoven, is written: 'Sinfonia grande/[illegible line]/del Sigr/Louis van

Fig. 3.1 The title page of the fair copy of the Third Symphony owned by Beethoven.

Beethoven' ('Grand symphony/[ ]/by Mr/Ludwig van Beethoven') (fig. 3.1). The missing line – 'intitolata Bonaparte' – has been scratched out so vehemently that there is a hole in the paper, while in pencil, in the composer's hand, is added 'geschrieben auf Bonaparte' ('written for Bonaparte'), along with instructions for tidying up the score and for how to incorporate the third horn. In the absence of Ries's explanation, and with access only to the published score, Beethoven's 'great man' was left unnamed. There were and have been proposals of other people who might have filled his boots: Prince Louis Ferdinand of Prussia, perhaps, or the Elector of Cologne.[16] Even if there were a real-life model for the hero, they have been abstracted and idealized, overlain with myth and, of course, music.

Heroism can take many forms. As a young man, Beethoven's fighting spirit was illustrated musically by the 'piano duels' in which he participated. These were salon entertainments at which two virtuosi, each sponsored by an aristocrat, would attempt to outperform the other. Beethoven's greatest challenger was Berliner Daniel Steibelt. The details of what was played at their contests, hosted in the palace of Count Moritz von Fries, vary between accounts. It is clear that each performed the other's works and improvised on themes they were given; and that, like other types of duelling, the contest was as much about honour as skill. The week after the premiere of Beethoven's Clarinet Trio, op. 11, Steibelt improvised on the theme of its variations. Beethoven took umbrage, apparently because the improvisation was prepared, but perhaps also because the theme itself, 'Pria ch'io l'impegno', was a popular tune taken from Joseph Weigl's comic opera *L'amor marinaro ossia Il corsaro*, the words of which run, 'Before I begin work, I must have something to eat'; hardly the most respectful of themes. Disinclined, perhaps, to have a taste of his own irreverent medicine, Beethoven, in return, placed his adversary's music upside down on the keyboard and hammered out the first four notes of its cello part with one finger, on which he then improvised at length, parodying the Berliner's famous 'storm' effects. Steibelt left before he had finished, saying he never wanted to be in the same room as Beethoven again. The anecdote illustrates one aspect of Beethoven's heroism; more importantly, it has been suggested that the four notes of Steibelt's theme reappear in the Third Symphony.[17]

The importance of improvisation to Beethoven's musical imagination is apparent in the painter Willibrod Joseph Mähler's reminiscence of the composer in late summer 1803, playing the finale of the Third Symphony on the piano and then continuing 'in free fantasia for two hours'.[18] The earliest-known sketchbook for the symphony also shows how Beethoven tried out ideas, returning to previous works and saving for future projects as he went. As mentioned, the finale was based on the op. 35 variations. Beethoven might have initially intended to use that music for the first movement, preceded by a slow introduction shaped a little like the eventual opening theme. He soon replaced the introduction with the two chords and moved the theme and variations to the final movement. But these were not the only migrations of the finale's music. The theme quotes the finale to Beethoven's ballet *Die Geschöpfe des Prometheus*, op. 43 (1801). He had already reused music from the ballet in *Twelve Contredanses*, WoO 14, designed for ballroom dancing; in the manuscript of one set, Beethoven couldn't resist a pun on the sponsor's name, Monsieur de Friederich being converted to Liederlich ('slovenly').[19] It was not unusual for a composer to quote or reuse music in multiple works. In fact, it was standard practice, especially in the operatic world. In the case of the 'Eroica', it led to the narrative of the ballet being overlain on to the symphony. As punishment for stealing fire to give to humankind, the mythical Prometheus was chained to a rock, where each day an eagle pecked out his liver. In Beethoven's ballet, Prometheus was a civilizing force who gave life to the arts and sciences.[20] The hero of the 'Eroica', it has been argued, was therefore no mere mortal but Prometheus.[21] There remained, however, an association with the present day, as the opening verse of the poem on which the ballet was based, Vincenzo Monti's *Il Prometeo* (1797), made a direct comparison between Prometheus and Napoleon. It is a reminder that one hero, whether mythical or human, can stand for or be combined with others.

The comparison of the 'Eroica' to classical figures and literature – Homer, or Plato's *Republic*, have been other suggestions – proved a crucial step in the critical assessment of the symphony. Early reviewers had criticized Beethoven's music for not having the beauty or sublimity of Mozart's or Haydn's; instead, it was 'glaring and bizarre', as well as too long. The first positive reviews took one of two approaches. They either delved into technical details, arguing that this was music that needed to be paid serious and sustained attention in order to be fully understood. One should not always expect to be entertained, it was pointed out.[22] Or, they waxed lyrical. In 1807, Berlin critic Heinrich Hermann (writing under the pseudonym Ernst Woldemar) wrote a review in the literary journal *Morgenblatt für gebildete Stände* that used overtly poetic language: 'we feel called forth . . . to an almost Shakespearean world of magic . . . In these extremes and in the frequent and abrupt exchanges of fearful, violent, percussive rebukes with the most ingratiating flowers of melody lies a great part of Beethoven's humour.'[23] By invoking Shakespeare, no less, and by attributing to the 'glaring and bizarre' aspects of Beethoven's music a sense of humour, Woldemar – and the critics who followed in his wake – suggested that such symphonies resembled great drama. Others found the noisiness of the symphony to evoke the tumult of the battlefield. For Wilhelm von Lenz, the opening chords were 'two blows from the heavy cavalry that split the orchestra like a turnip'.[24] By 1825, Adolf Bernhard Marx, reviewing the 'Eroica' Symphony for his new Berlin-based music journal, the *Berliner Allgemeine musikalische Zeitung*, felt able to describe the first movement as a battle from which the hero emerges victorious; the second as a walk through a corpse-strewn battlefield; the third as troops massing together; the fourth as the warriors returning home in peacetime. Beethoven, apparently, was pleased.[25]

The comparison A. B. Marx made between the individual movements of the Third Symphony and scenes from an imagined drama demonstrates how willingly nineteenth-century critics gave instrumental music poetic or extra-musical meaning. That depended not only on titles or descriptions provided by the composer, or imagined on his behalf, but also on the formal structures that underpin the music. The division of a symphony into movements might be compared to the division of a play into acts, although it is probably more accurate to liken them to tableaux. At the turn of the nineteenth century, the contrasting moods of the four movements – fast, slow, dance, fast – were more important than heading towards a dramatic conclusion. Or at least they were until Beethoven began to conceive of all four movements as constituting a whole, with a new emphasis on the finale as the climax of the work.

Within those individual movements there were, in Beethoven's day, tacitly agreed conventions for how the music should be structured. The most significant of these was sonata form, which guided most first movements and sometimes slow and final movements. Again, it is probably most easily explained dramatically. A movement in sonata form typically begins with a principal subject or protagonist. They start out from home – the 'home' key or harmony – and go on a journey that will take them to 'foreign' lands, or different harmonic areas. There, they will meet another subject, an antagonist, different in harmony and character. Here ends the first scene, or exposition. Next, the development, when the subjects have various adventures, and explore new harmonies and different ways to express themselves. Finally, they decide to return home together, first and second subjects now belonging to the same harmony in the recapitulation. There may be a coda, or epilogue, that affirms their arrival.

While Beethoven's music is often used to demonstrate sonata form, he typically honoured convention in the breach. In the first movement of the 'Eroica' Symphony, as described at the start of this chapter, the 'home' from where the principal subject starts is almost immediately abandoned with the melody's tenth note, the alien note of C sharp. While the principal subject is reaffirmed, it seems like the second subject might already have arrived with a new lilting phrase shared around the woodwind section; that turns out to be a bridge to another contrasting theme that alternates between wind and strings. These multiple thematic ideas and the constant peaks and troughs of energy contribute to the disjointedness of which some critics complained. Another point of contention – the 'continuous tumult' or noisiness of Beethoven's music – reaches a climax in the development with a series of repeated, dissonant chords, the whole orchestra shifting the pulse of the music to the off-beat. The tension is released only as the strings convert the chord into another endlessly circling little tune that gathers earlier melodic ideas to build towards another climax. Afterwards, the music again subsides, growing softer and softer until the violins are left alone, almost trembling on one note, a passage sometimes described as the 'cumulus'.[26] Suddenly, through the clouds, the third horn enters with the opening theme. Too soon! The full orchestra arrives moments after and begins the recapitulation proper. At the first rehearsal, Ferdinand Ries chastised the horn for entering early and Beethoven nearly boxed his ears for not understanding that their pre-emption was deliberate. Having blurred the boundary of one section, Beethoven then massively extends the coda. It begins by bouncing the opening theme down three harmonic steps (E flat, D flat, C) and is so substantial it seems almost like an extra development. Finally, there is a glorious, expansive version of the principal subject, in its original key of E flat major without that destabilizing C sharp: we're home, we're home, we're home.

Despite its extensive length, and the noisiness of its dissonances, Beethoven did not expand the orchestra for the 'Eroica' – with the exception of one addition: a third horn. As mentioned, it is a disruptive instrument in the first movement, entering too early. In the third movement, the three horns take control of the central Trio section, playing a four-square melody that harks back to the instrument's ancient association with hunting. By extension, horns evoke pastoral scenes, which some critics have heard as being the realm inhabited by the Third Symphony, rather than the military.[27] Towards the end of the finale, though, the horn-calls are fully part of the fray as the orchestra surges towards its joyous, possibly victorious, climax.

The Third Symphony gained other political inflections both in translation and as it moved around Europe. An 1809 edition printed in London by Cianchettini and Sperati was given the subtitle 'Sinfonia composta per celebrare la morte d'un Eroe'. Rather than being about remembering a hero, it thus became about celebrating his death. When news of Napoleon's actual death arrived in 1821, Beethoven reportedly said, 'I have already composed the music for that catastrophe,' but did not specify the piece. Whether or not it is associated with Napoleon, the bellicose aspects of the Third Symphony have been repeated, again and again. In 1903, the Italian artist Antonio Rizzi wrote out the opening music of the second movement beneath his depiction of a procession of military casket-bearers, with the ruins of the battlefield smouldering in the distance. Two skulls, with black turbans, glare out from the print's frame (fig. 3.2). The precise reference is uncertain, but Beethoven's march was well known in Italy and military defeats in Africa were still fresh memories. In the last months of the Second World War, German composer Richard Strauss composed *Metamorphosen* for twenty-three solo strings. Towards the end, as the cellos and double basses reveal that the source for the musical material was the opening of the theme of the funeral march from the 'Eroica', Strauss wrote in the manuscript, 'In memoriam!' It is unclear whether he was commemorating casualties of war, the bombing of his beloved Dresden and Munich opera houses, or the destruction of Germany more broadly. It has even been suggested, and refuted, that the fallen hero of *Metamorphosen* may have been Hitler, with a parallel being made between Beethoven's

Fig. 3.2 Antonio Rizzi, *Beethoven: Sinfonia Eroica – II Tempo.*

withdrawn dedication to Napoleon and Strauss's turn away from Nazi politics. For all that music can have stories laid upon it, this fundamentally abstract form of art is continually evasive, shedding and gaining meaning at every historical turn.

Heroes are not always to be found on the battleground or at the barricades, and Beethoven's real claim to heroism during this period was expressed more privately. In April 1802, on the advice of his doctor, Beethoven had taken up lodgings in the village of Heiligenstadt. It was a restful environment, good for his daily walks and close enough to Vienna that he could receive visitors, and it proved to be a tremendously productive period: the Second Symphony; the three Violin Sonatas, op. 30; the three Piano Sonatas, op. 31; and the opp. 34 and 35 Piano Variations were soon dispatched. In a letter to Breitkopf und Härtel,

Beethoven boasted that the variations were in a 'new manner'.[28] Sometimes referred to as the start of his 'heroic' period, sometimes as the start of the 'middle' period, both labels are too broad to be all that useful. However, it is worth noting that Beethoven thought of himself as pursuing a new direction at this time.

The summer in Heiligenstadt may have been productive creatively, but by the autumn it became clear that Beethoven's health was not improving. He wrote a long letter to his brothers, dated 6 October 1802, in which he explained why he might seem 'malevolent, stubborn or misanthropic': he was losing his hearing.

> Ah, how could I possibly admit an infirmity in the <u>one sense</u> which ought to be more perfect in me than in others, a sense which I once possessed in the highest perfection, a perfection such as few in my profession enjoy or ever have enjoyed. – Oh I cannot do it, therefore forgive me when you see me draw back when I would gladly have mingled with you. My misfortune is doubly painful to me because I am bound to be misunderstood; for me there can be no relaxation with my fellow-men, no refined conversations, no mutual exchange of ideas . . . I must live almost alone like an exile.[29]

It had seemed like life was not worth living, Beethoven continued: 'It was only <u>my art</u> that held me back. Oh, it seemed impossible to me to leave this world before I had produced all that I felt capable of producing, and so I prolonged this wretched existence.' The remainder of the letter constituted a will, and the whole document was sealed and marked not to be opened until after his death. Four days later, Beethoven wrote an addendum announcing his departure from Heiligenstadt and his hope that Providence would 'grant me at least but one day of <u>pure joy</u>'.

The discovery of this letter among Beethoven's effects and its publication as the 'Heiligenstadt Testament' after his death transformed perceptions of the composer. Although many people had been aware of his deafness, its effect on his personal life had not been considered sympathetically. Beethoven's deafness had been thought to have negatively impacted his ability to compose rather than to have been a tragic impediment he had miraculously found the strength to overcome. The 'Heiligenstadt Testament' also influenced interpretations of the Third Symphony, which Beethoven had begun to sketch ideas for around the same time. Beethoven became his music's hero; his defiant stance towards adversity – his struggle with deafness and resultant sense of exile from the world around him – painted a portrait of the artist that would endure for centuries.

4. Ambition: Choral Fantasy, op. 80 (1808)

Composer Johann Friedrich Reichardt visited Vienna in the winter of 1808. The theatres were closed for Advent, which presented him with a cornucopia of concerts to choose from. There were some frustrating clashes: 22 December was the first night of the Tonkünstler-Societät annual concerts in aid of widows and orphans. That year they broke with the tradition of alternating between Haydn's *Creation* and *The Seasons* for a performance of Haydn's first oratorio, *Ritorno di Tobia* (*The Return of Tobias*), at the Burgtheater, featuring two hundred of the city's finest performers. The same evening, at the Theater an der Wien (fig. 4.1), Beethoven held his long-anticipated third academy, which, unusually, was dedicated entirely to his own music. Reichardt felt he could not miss the opportunity to hear 'der brave Beethoven' and accepted Prince Lobkowitz's invitation to join him in his box. Unfortunately, he regretted going, reporting:

> There we sat, in the most bitter cold, from half past six until half past ten, and confirmed for ourselves the maxim that one may easily have too much of a good thing, still more of a loud one.[1]

On their publication the following year, Reichardt's letters, full of tales of high society when much of Europe was suffering wartime hardship, were criticized for being fatuous. Beethoven described them as 'silly twaddle'.[2] However, Reichardt's diaries read more closely reveal a critical mind, if one that was easily swayed by pretty girls and good breeding. Given that he did make some positive comments about Beethoven's piano-playing

K.K.P. THEATER AN DER WIEN . №68. THÉÂTRE I.R.P. À LA VIENNE.

Fig. 4.1 Vienna, nineteenth century. Interior of the Theater an der Wien.

and improvisation on that cold December evening, that he also dared to complain of the excesses of this particular concert indicates that in some respects it really was unbearable.

Beethoven's academy may have been long, but it was not terribly out of line with other concerts, which also mixed solo and orchestral works, choruses and arias. What was unusual was its focus on one composer and its emphasis on the symphony as a genre. This was clearly intended to be a display of the thirty-eight-year-old's major achievements in recent years; or, as the Viennese journal *Der Sammler* put it, 'the youngest offspring of his inexhaustible talents'.[3] It included four entirely new works and two pieces that had not yet been heard in public in Vienna. The programme began with the premiere of his Sixth Symphony, entitled 'A Recollection of Country Life' (which came to be known as the 'Pastoral'). It was followed by the concert aria

for solo soprano and orchestra, 'Ah! Perfido', the Gloria from
the Mass in C, and then the recently published Fourth Piano
Concerto, with Beethoven as soloist. After an interval came the
premiere of a symphony in C minor, the Fifth, the Sanctus from
the Mass in C, and a Fantasia improvised by Beethoven at the
piano. For a finale, Beethoven had composed a Choral Fantasy
that brought together all the musicians: vocal soloists, chorus,
solo piano and orchestra.

The academy presented what came to be some of Beethoven's
most celebrated works: namely, the Fifth and Sixth symphonies
and the Fourth Piano Concerto. It was the only occasion at
which Beethoven premiered two new symphonies in the same
concert and, however much the audience were impressed by his
achievements, it was a lot to take in at once. Although he is now
closely associated with the genre, Beethoven went somewhat
against the grain in producing so many substantial symphonies.
What sold, so far as publishers were concerned, were dances,
piano music and chamber music, while opera productions far
outstripped performances of orchestral music. Beethoven's
determination to compose ambitious symphonies has been
described as being in defiance of what he later called the 'sewer'
(*Kloacke*) of the Vienna music scene.[4] Critics sensed the greatness
of the Fifth Symphony but, as was often the case with Beethoven's more challenging pieces, predicted it would take
repeated listening before it would be fully appreciated. The peasants' dance and storm in the Sixth Symphony was admired,
though there were thought to be longueurs elsewhere.[5]

Imagery has played an important role in shifting critical
opinion of the two symphonies. The 'Pastoral' Symphony, with
its birdsong and burbling brook, was illustrative in the manner
of Paul Wranitzky's battle-themed *Symphonie caractéristique*. While
effective, it came across as a little old-fashioned. There was no
programme or descriptive title attached to the Fifth Symphony.

It was 'purely musical'. Visual imagery, though, was used to describe its mysterious power. In a seminal review of the published score of the Fifth Symphony, the German author and music critic E. T. A. Hoffmann explained the music's features in technical and poetic terms. Both approaches were unprecedented. On the one hand, he presented a blow-by-blow analysis of each movement, with music examples. Readers were evidently expected to be able to follow the intricacies of a score and to think about music abstractly. On the other hand, Hoffmann claimed:

> Beethoven's instrumental music unveils before us the realm of the mighty and the immeasurable. Here shining rays of light shoot through the darkness of night, and we become aware of giant shadows swaying back and forth, moving ever closer around us and destroying within us all feeling but the pain of infinite yearning, in which every desire, leaping up in sounds of exultation, sinks back and disappears.[6]

The sublime scenery and emotions evoked by Hoffmann explain his declaration that Beethoven is 'a purely romantic' composer. In his words, the Fifth Symphony 'unfolds Beethoven's romanticism, rising in a climax right to the end, more than any other of his works, and irresistibly sweeps the listener into the wonderful spirit realm of the infinite'. The connection made here between Beethoven's instrumental music and the ineffable became fundamental to Romantic musical aesthetics, which prized music's ability to say more than words, to access the spirit. However, recent scholarship has also pointed out that Hoffmann was a man of the theatre alongside all his other activities. He may then also have had in mind popular audiovisual entertainments such as the phantasmagoria, which raised ghosts with a little help from lights, smoke and mirrors.[7] This is not to demean Hoffmann or Beethoven but to emphasize the importance of the visual imagination in understanding how music worked.

Determining what Beethoven might have been yearning for in the Fifth Symphony became sport for biographers. Schindler claimed that the composer told him that the famous opening four-note motto was the sound of fate knocking at his door. It is an anecdote often dismissed, because it comes from Schindler's disreputable biography. Yet it is an anecdote as often retold, because of the alluring way it chimes with the composer's multiple references to defying fate.[8] The dominant image of Beethoven is of him railing against all that life threw at him. However, the music of the 1808 concert was not all as fist-shaking as the Fifth Symphony. The Fourth Piano Concerto, for example, represents a softer side of Beethoven the virtuoso: from its opening solo onwards, it has a lyricism and serenity at odds with the 'heroic' style.[9] An alternative history of the composer can begin to be constructed by recalling the expressive range of his works, the fictions put forward by biographers, and the fact that, sometimes, Beethoven was not triumphant.

The 1808 academy may have premiered several of what are Beethoven's most famous works. As a concert, however, it was a fiasco. The length of the programme and the frigid temperature drove away many members of the audience and the Choral Fantasy fell apart in performance. It is these latter, negative elements that this chapter explores, because within them hides the key to understanding Beethoven's musical ambitions. Attitudes towards concert behaviour were gradually changing as a result of more specialized programming and a realization that listeners and players needed to pay greater attention to the complexities of the music. Meanwhile, the experimental form of the Choral Fantasy paved the way for what is now considered one of Beethoven's masterpieces, the Ninth Symphony, with its climactic 'Ode to Joy'.

★

Inauspicious timing aside, quite why the 1808 *Akademie* went so badly is hard to pin down. It is clear that Beethoven had difficulties establishing a working relationship with the performers. He had somehow offended the house orchestra of the Theater an der Wien. While things were patched up with the help of concertmaster Franz Clement and Kapellmeister Ignaz von Seyfried, several people in the audience recognized that the ensemble was 'heterogeneous' or, more bluntly, cobbled together to an even greater extent than usual. Anna Milder, who had sung the title role in Beethoven's opera *Fidelio*, declined to sing 'Ah! Perfido' (biographer Alexander Wheelock Thayer claimed Beethoven had insulted her fiancé). She was replaced by Schuppanzigh's sister-in-law, Josephine Killitzky, who was under-confident and overstretched by the music's technical challenges. Although she 'has a very agreeable voice', one critic wrote, 'she nevertheless sang very few notes in tune and more often she actually sang wrong notes'.[10] Reichardt described her as shivering more than she sang, which was understandable as, even in their furs and greatcoats, he and Prince Lobkowitz were shivering too.

The ink was still wet on the parts for the Choral Fantasy, according to Seyfried. He explained that Beethoven forgot that at the 'hurried' rehearsal he had told the orchestra not to repeat the second variation in the performance. The resultant clash sounded 'not altogether edifying'; a polite way of saying that it was cacophonous. Having realized the mistake, Beethoven called out for the orchestra to stop and start again, with repeats. Apparently, he apologized heartily to the musicians afterwards.[11] The *AmZ* provided a less generous account: the clarinets had entered at the wrong place and Beethoven jumped up to stop them, which he could manage only by calling out 'Silence, silence, that will not do! Once again, once again! Carl Czerny recalled that Beethoven cried, 'Wrong, badly played, wrong, again!' while Czech composer Johann Emanuel Doležálek claimed that Beethoven had jumped up and run to the clarinets' desk to show them their error. Pianist Ignaz Moscheles, perched in a corner of the gallery, compared the performance to 'a runaway carriage going downhill – an overturn was inevitable'. At first Beethoven's instructions were not heard but 'after a moment's respectful silence on the part of the audience', the orchestra restarted and proceeded without any further hiccups. What had tripped Beethoven up, it seems, was his ambition to perform a difficult piece on very little rehearsal – that, and what must have been an exhausted orchestra playing in the cold by candlelight.

Practicalities aside, the other challenge for the audience was getting to grips with the music. A reporter for the *AmZ* complained: 'To judge all of these pieces after one and only one hearing, especially considering the language of Beethoven's works, in that so many were performed one after the other, and that most of them are so grand and long, is downright impossible.'[12] They would have to wait until they could study the printed scores. The previous summer an article in the same journal had declared: 'As is well known, one can rarely form a definite opinion about a Beethoven composition upon first hearing.'[13] They then demurred from passing judgement on the Triple Concerto, op. 56, until they had heard it several times. Similar criticisms of new works had not been made previously; reviewers had held forth on the meaning of Haydn's music, for instance, without hesitating.[14] There was evidently something about Beethoven's music that required deeper contemplation in order for it to be fully understood.

Deeper contemplation and more rehearsal. When we imagine the first performances of works by Beethoven, the sounds that come to mind are inevitably those of today: technically near-flawless renditions by professional ensembles with centuries of experience of interpreting his music. Yet it is clear from the premiere of the Choral Fantasy that what was heard in 1808 was rather rougher. There were famous virtuosi in the city whose skills were unparalleled. The standards of ensemble performances, however, could be low because, as I have mentioned, there were so few rehearsals for concerts: typically one, sometimes none, rarely two. Instruments were configured differently as well: strings were made of gut, horns were natural, timpani were tuned by individual screws, and the clarinet was a recent invention. Tuning was unreliable and the sounds early-nineteenth-century instruments produced were generally less predictable than their steel-stringed, keyed or pedal-tuned modern equivalents. Historical accounts reveal that the speed of pieces fluctuated widely, that many singers and string players slid between notes (the resultant swoops are called *glissandi*) instead of moving cleanly from one to the next, and that it was fairly common for performers to add embellishments to ornament melodies – even when they were playing in an orchestra. These performance traits reflected style and taste, not poor execution. What might seem alien and awkward to many twenty-first-century ears was the norm for the time.

Vienna may have had a reputation as a great musical city, but in the early nineteenth century many people complained about the low quality of its orchestral players. Outside of the private ensembles sponsored by wealthy patrons (such as Prince Lobkowitz), orchestras were attached to theatres, performing for plays and operas. There was no fully professional concert orchestra in Vienna in Beethoven's lifetime. Music societies often supported orchestras that habitually filled out their ranks with dilettantes: proficient but amateur musicians of varying degrees of skill and commitment. The fact that most members of the orchestra earned their living by other means was probably one reason why rehearsals were so limited. Lacklustre performances by professionals, meanwhile, were thought partly to be because of the dire economic situation; pay was so paltry there was little incentive to do anything more than the minimum. Motivation for reading difficult music like Beethoven's had to have been aesthetic rather than monetary.

The orchestra of the Theater an der Wien, which played in Beethoven's 1808 *Akademie*, was a medium-sized ensemble; exact numbers are hard to come by, but that meant around six first violins, six second violins, four violas, two cellos and two basses, with a complement of single wind (one flute, one oboe, one clarinet, one bassoon), brass and timpani.[15] Beethoven's orchestral works often were not only longer and more challenging to execute than most others, they could also require, or benefit from, extra instruments. A performance of the Fourth Symphony he conducted at a new concert series at the Mehlgrube in 1808 had twice as many string instruments as the mid-sized ensemble of the 'Eroica', while the premieres of the Seventh and Eighth symphonies at the Redoutensaal in 1813–14 had eighteen-person-strong violin sections, fourteen violas, twelve cellos, seven basses and doubled woodwind. The numbers were made up by amateurs – at the Mehlgrube, only eighteen of the fifty-five-strong orchestra were professionals – which became standard practice for larger-scale concerts.

Unlike later, when the string section would be segmented in a fan around the conductor, with the first violins on the conductor's left, second violins and violas in the middle, and cellos on the right, with the double basses behind them, in Beethoven's day the two violin sections faced each other and the lower strings were often behind the firsts. The chorus typically stood in front of the orchestra, as was the case at the premiere of the Ninth Symphony. The role of conductor was not yet properly established. Instead, the duty of leading the ensemble in concert was taken by the principal violinist, known as the concertmaster, who sat at the front of the section. It was a difficult task, espe-cially in under-rehearsed circumstances, and concertmasters were often criticized for being overemphatic in their gestures and expressions, or for stamping their foot or even hitting the stand to keep time. Sometimes – especially if a chorus was involved, who would not be able to see the orchestra behind them – there was also someone who beat out the pulse and gave them cues.

Had he belonged to a previous generation, which incorpor-ated a keyboard part in instrumental music (known as a *continuo*), Beethoven might have directed a performance from the harpsi-chord. He had studied the violin but had never led an orchestra and preferred to direct from a separate music desk. He did not use a baton, the stick that the concertmaster and composer Louis Spohr began to substitute around 1820 for his violin bow. While contemporaries referred to Beethoven as conducting concerts, it seems that he was concerned primarily with expression. Appar-ently, he would hide below his desk for quiet passages and leap around wildly when the music should be louder. Seyfried recalled that Beethoven 'was very particular about expression, the delicate nuances, the equable distribution of light and shade as well as an effective tempo rubato', the last term meaning being willing to take, or literally steal, time over or from phrases.[16] Such matters he would discuss with individual play-ers. Even before he fully lost his hearing, it seems, Beethoven's conducting fit no established pattern. It may, though, have set a precedent for the more extravagant gestures of subsequent con-ductors and in this way at least encouraged performers to craft an interpretation of his works. His wild gestures scattered the seeds of ambition.

Beethoven's free approach to conducting helps explain why the Choral Fantasy might have fallen apart. It begins with a lengthy

and virtuosic prelude for solo piano – improvised by Beethoven
on the night – and the pianist plays almost continually throughout the twenty-minute piece, giving little chance to look up
from the keyboard to give other instruments their cues. On top
of that, the piece itself has an unorthodox construction, in keeping with the expectations of the fantasy as a genre. After the
piano prelude, instruments from the orchestra are gradually
introduced, starting with the lowest strings and gradually working upwards, the piano interjecting lyrical phrases, almost as if
trying to delay the onset of the finale proper. Eventually,
though, it is the piano that presents the theme on which there
will be a set of variations featuring each of the instrument
groups in turn: flute, oboe, those poor clarinets, strings. Then
the low strings begin their creeping ascent once again, this time
with more florid piano interjections, before the theme is reintroduced, now sung by four solo voices, who are soon joined by the
full chorus. The free structure of the Choral Fantasy is thus
combined with the piano's concerto-like virtuosic solo display,
while the inclusion of vocal soloists and chorus suggests the genre
of the oratorio.

The main theme of the Choral Fantasy was drawn from the
second of a pair of songs Beethoven had composed in the mid-
1790s, 'Seufzer eines Ungeliebten – Gegenliebe' ('Sighs of One
Unloved – Love Requited'), WoO 118. The poem 'Gegenliebe',
by Gottfried August Bürger, predicts the joys of the titular reciprocated love. Beethoven's undulating melody was in keeping
with simple folkish settings, such as those by musician Johann
Abraham Peter Schulz, and also resembles a theme from Mozart's
'Misericordias Domini', K222. He now explored the melody's
potential to be reworked into something more substantial. The
composer Ignaz Pleyel had been impressed, around the time of
the 1808 *Akademie*, by Beethoven's ability to improvise on 'trivial
notes' and 'Gegenliebe' seems ripe for embellishment.[17]

Improvisation had played an important role in Beethoven's music-making since his youth. He had triumphed at piano duels against visiting virtuosi such as Daniel Steibelt, and it seems that his compositional process was often shaped by experimenting at the keyboard. The solo Fantasia he devised for the *Akademie*, as well as his extemporization on the Fourth Piano Concerto, was further testament to his skills; Reichardt declared that it 'showed all his mastery'. Beethoven noted on one sketch from around this time that there should be no holding back when playing in public: 'Real improvisation comes only when we are unconcerned [with] what we play, so – if we want to improvise in the best, truest manner in public – we should give ourselves over freely to what comes to mind.'[18] It was perhaps inevitable, then, that to produce a work in haste Beethoven should in effect improvise on pre-existing material and depend on his pianistic abilities. However, combining piano improvisation with orchestral music and then, on top of that, choral singing was untested. The other performers would have had little sense of what to expect.

The words sung in the Choral Fantasy are about peace and joy, the magic of music, and how beautiful art can please the gods. The author of the three-verse poem is debated; it was probably Christoph Kuffner, a civil servant who wrote and translated plays and poetry as well as composed.[19] Beethoven was not particularly beholden to the text, offering to change it if the publishers deemed it necessary.[20] However, there was one word that he insisted should be kept or replaced by something with the same import: *Kraft* ('strength' or 'power'). There may have been significance in the meaning of the word itself, but it also constituted a high point in the musical setting: on the phrase 'Wenn sich Lieb' und Kraft vermählen' ('If love and strength are wedded'), 'und Kraft' is repeated three times, rising towards a loud, sustained chord that has added chromatic crunch. It is a sonority that, perhaps more than the main melody itself, and even more than the uplifting text, looks forward to the choral writing of Beethoven's Ninth Symphony – specifically to the line 'Und der Cherub steht vor Gott' ('And the cherub stands before God') in the 'Ode to Joy', which repeats 'vor Gott' thrice and ends with a similar sense of harmonic anticipation.

Czerny, in his 'Anekdoten und Notizen über Beethoven' ('Anecdotes and Notes on Beethoven', 1852), grouped the Choral Fantasy and the finale of the Ninth Symphony together as representatives of Beethoven's 'free-variation form'. Beethoven had acknowledged that the Ninth's finale was 'in the style of my fantasia for piano and chorus but on a far grander scale'.[21] Aside from the obvious similarities of their tunes, the two works share an experimental aspect. They are both generic hybrids: the Choral Fantasy melds concerto with oratorio, the Ninth Symphony orchestra and voices. They also have similar trajectories: each has an episodic structure that heads towards an almighty, communal climax. The 'grander scale' of the Ninth Symphony was not just a question of size but to do with the quality of its text, by Friedrich Schiller, which Beethoven described as the 'immortal and famous song *An die Freude*'.[22] Why Beethoven did not use Schiller's 'Ode to Joy' for the Choral Fantasy in 1808, instead of those rather blandly joyous verses, is unclear, unless the rush in which it was composed caused him to overlook it – which seems unlikely for a poem he had returned to repeatedly since the 1790s – or because he was saving it for something special.

The other connection between the Choral Fantasy and the Ninth Symphony, which seems surprising today, is that neither was entirely successful on its first outing (details of the premiere of the Ninth are given in Chapter 8). That was true, though, of Beethoven's academies in general: although they were useful ways of getting his name into the public domain, encouraging his music to be reviewed in the press, they were risky ventures that rarely made the composer much money. Practical arrangements might have been against him, such as scheduling and the weather. So, too, was the scale of his musical ambition, which needed more resources in terms of players and rehearsals in order to be realized.

The 1808 academy may not have been a success in itself, but it marked a significant turning point in Beethoven's fortunes. The Leipzig-based publisher Gottfried Christoph Härtel had visited him in Vienna over the summer and his firm eventually agreed to take on the Fifth and Sixth symphonies, the A major Cello Sonata, and the Two Piano Trios, op. 70, along with the Mass in C, op. 86. Breitkopf und Härtel had previously published the String Quintet, op. 29, and the Piano Variations, opp. 34 and 35, but they had been cautious about investing further in Beethoven because he and his brother Kaspar Karl had often indulged in double-dealing with other firms behind their backs in an attempt to drive up prices. The Leipzig publishers had been reluctant to accept the Mass in C, arguing that the market for sacred works was small, but Beethoven was persistent, throwing it in 'for free' (his total fee was 600 gulden, negotiated down from 900) and arguing that it could be translated into German and then performed in concert halls (the excerpts from the Mass performed at the academy had been advertised as hymns because of the prohibition on the Latin liturgy being performed in secular venues, as would happen again with the *Missa solemnis*). Beethoven had attempted to sell his works in bulk before, as per his package that included the Septet, op. 20, for Hoffmeister. This time he also wanted to continue the practice of allowing the person who had commissioned the piece to have exclusive rights to it for six months, before the composer did with it what they wanted. He thus offered Breitkopf und Härtel the Fifth and

Sixth symphonies on the understanding that they would not publish them for six months, Beethoven having made the usual promise to a nobleman – in this instance, Count Oppersdorff – that he could own the rights to the work for half a year before it was published. Oppersdorff had paid a deposit for the Fifth Symphony (the agreed fee was 500 ducats), but the composer then changed his mind. It seems the Fifth and Sixth symphonies instead were performed at one of Prince Lobkowitz's residences in the autumn.[23] There was an interesting double standard here: Beethoven was prepared to annoy a nobleman such as Count Oppersdorff in favour of his long-term supporter Prince Lobkowitz. However, he later objected to Breitkopf und Härtel dedicating the Choral Fantasy to King Maximilian Joseph of Bavaria without consultation. If they thought the king would send him a gift in gratitude, that was one thing, Beethoven wrote. If that wasn't the intention, then they should be aware that 'one is not supposed to dedicate anything to kings without their permission'.[24] He was alert to the fact that, while he was prepared to take advantage of all opportunities, the potential for misunderstandings between the old and new ways of doing business was great.

Around the time of the *Akademie*, Beethoven also received and accepted a position as Kapellmeister in Kassel, offered to him by the King of Westphalia, Jérôme Bonaparte, brother of Napoleon.[25] He told Breitkopf und Härtel that his salary was to be 600 gold ducats and that he was leaving Vienna because of 'intrigues, schemes and underhandedness'.[26] He was evidently hurt by the reports in the *AmZ* of him stopping the performance of the Choral Fantasy. He emphasized that, despite the mistakes, which were beyond his control, the audience had applauded enthusiastically. Beethoven pointed out that it was not unusual for performances to be stopped: in a production of Gaspare Spontini's 'easy' opera *Milton*, put on at the Kärntnertortheater the day before (in fact, it was on 27 December), 'the orchestra had fallen apart so much that the conductor and director were literally shipwrecked'.[27] Beyond that, Beethoven blamed the poor quality of the available musicians on the clash with the charity concert at the Burgtheater. Presumably, he would have known in advance when that annual event was scheduled to take place. He claimed that, ultimately, he was thwarted by the Tonkünstler-Societät vice-president, Antonio Salieri, who had, as a 'prank', threatened members with expulsion if they did not take part in the Haydn oratorio.[28]

Beethoven frequently complained that he was not well represented in public concerts in Vienna. He had made his debut as a pianist and composer with the Tonkünstler-Societät in 1795 and shortly afterwards, in recognition of his contributions, was made an honorary member, as was Haydn. Despite the director of the Tonkünstler-Societät, Paul Wranitzky, being keen to promote Beethoven's music, it was generally thought to be difficult to perform and to comprehend. The few works of his that were programmed tended to be in a lighter vein, such as the variations on Mozart's 'Là ci darem la mano', WoO 28, for two oboes and cor anglais. Wranitsky's sudden death in September 1808, a few months before the *Akademie*, did not help matters, especially as the new director, Salieri, was less sympathetic towards Beethoven's music, despite having once been his teacher. Yet the Tonkünstler-Societät concert that year did include some Beethoven: his Piano Concerto in C minor, no. 3, was played by Carl Friedrich Stein.[29] Beethoven had initially hoped that Ferdinand Ries would perform the Fourth Piano Concerto instead, but that proved too much for Ries, or his substitute, Stein, to take on.

Beethoven was also represented on the programmes of the winter-season subscription concerts known, among other names, as the Liebhaber Concerte ('amateur concerts'). The orchestra, which was open to skilled dilettantes, aimed at higher artistic standards by holding the customary one rehearsal no more than two days before the concert and even holding a second rehearsal for more challenging works. The programmes emphasized music by Mozart, Haydn and, tellingly, Beethoven, whose first three symphonies and his *Coriolan* Overture were performed twice in the inaugural season of spring 1808. Reichardt, in attendance, claimed that he was 'almost split asunder by the mighty strokes and blows each player made with all his strength' in a room too small for the 'gigantic and overwhelming' *Coriolan* Overture. The orchestra at the Liebhaber Concerte was large for the time – it numbered around fifty-five players – and its concerts mostly took place in the hall of the university, a resonant room with a high ceiling that could seat up to 1,300 people; if that was too small for the *Coriolan* Overture, it must have been a mighty din. Beethoven was also there, and Reichardt observed that this 'sensitive, irritable and suspicious' artist needed sympathetic admirers who could see past his gloomy countenance and 'not be shocked by any of his external peculiarities and his raw edges'.[30] Had the Liebhaber Concerte continued, they might have managed to secure a regular spot for Beethoven's symphonies in Vienna.

Ultimately, it seems that Beethoven's music was performed regularly around Vienna during his lifetime, if not as frequently as he might have liked. The timing of the *Akademie* was unfortunate and the clash with the Tonkünstler-Societät concert proved to be detrimental to both events: each had a smaller audience and made less money than expected (the Tonkünstler-Societät took 2,400 florins, when in other years it made closer to 4,000 florins). Haydn's *Il ritorno*, dismissed as 'an antiquated potboiler', was never performed in the series again.[31] Nor, from this point onwards, was any other Italian oratorio. Instead, exclusively German-language works were presented. It was a sign of the political times. As the Napoleonic Wars continued,

Austrian patriotism was gaining ground. At this stage in hostilities, cultural activities that rallied support for the newly founded empire were proving more successful than military action. Following a series of humiliating defeats for the Third Coalition, including the French occupation of Vienna in 1805 and of the Rhineland, Berlin and Warsaw the following year, expressions of Austrian patriotism had gained intensity. The emperor finally agreed to the formation of a *Landwehr*, a people's army, which supplemented existing reserves by the conscription of able-bodied men. The Fifth Coalition of Austria and the United Kingdom declared war against the French in April 1809, leading to another occupation of Vienna — Beethoven hid from the shelling in his brother Kaspar Karl's basement, holding pillows over his ears — and another bloody rout at the Battle of Wagram. In the ensuing Treaty of Schönbrunn the Austrian Empire conceded lands and about a fifth of its population.

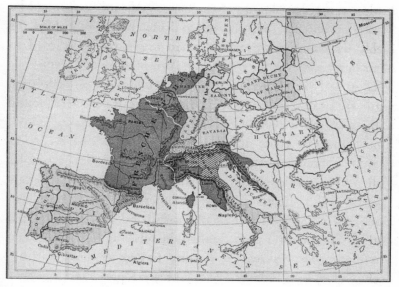

Fig. 4.2 Map of Europe in 1810.

Currency devaluation and rampant inflation rocked the city. Food and rent prices escalated rapidly; by 1814, the cost of living was more than five times greater than it had been in 1809. Many aristocrats cut back on their musical sponsorship. The young Countess Thürheim complained in her diary: 'Everything is finished, no more balls, no more festivities; no more joy. Nothing is heard but "the War, the War".'[32] Reichardt thought that Beethoven's *Akademie* represented the composer's only source of income that year, which was an exaggeration. Nonetheless, between holding an unsuccessful concert for his own benefit, frustration at the lack of other opportunities to perform his music, financial instability and impending war, the offer from Kassel – even if it meant living in the occupied territories – must have been attractive.

News that Beethoven was planning to leave Vienna, however, pushed some of his aristocratic patrons into action. Archduke Rudolph, Prince Lobkowitz and Prince Kinsky, probably at the behest of the Countess Erdődy, with whom the composer was then lodging, tried to find a way to persuade him to stay. He lay down his terms with characteristic ambition: he wanted an annuity of 4,000 florins for the remainder of his life, even if he were to stop composing. The sum was not quite as generous as the Kassel offer, but further perks were requested that would make it worth his while. Beethoven wanted to be free to travel for work; to have the title of Imperial Music Director; and to hold an academy for his benefit at the Theater an der Wien each year. The idea of an annuity in itself was not unheard of. Prince Lichnowsky had given Beethoven 600 florins per annum from 1800 until they fell out in 1806. After that, Beethoven had unsuccessfully proposed himself to the Royal Court Theatre as their house composer, asking for an annual salary of 2,400 florins – twice that of Kapellmeister Salieri, which might have explained his antipathy to the younger composer – as well as the right to hold a yearly benefit concert.

Negotiations this time were handled by Baron Ignaz von Gleichenstein. He had previously witnessed Beethoven's lucrative contract with Muzio Clementi to publish several of his works – the three 'Razumovsky' Quartets, op. 59, the Fourth Symphony, the *Coriolan* Overture, the Violin Concerto and its piano arrangement, and the Fourth Piano Concerto – in British territories. He now served as Beethoven's guarantor, receiving the dedication of the op. 69 Cello Sonata in return. The Countess Erdődy, for her part, received the dedication of the Piano Trios, op. 70. The three noblemen split the annuity unevenly between them; Archduke Rudolph gave 1,500 florins; Prince Lobkowitz 700 florins (a fraction of the 8,000 florins he spent a year on copying music); Prince Kinsky 1,800 florins. In return, Archduke Rudolph had the dedication of the Fourth Piano Concerto, and Prince Lobkowitz the Fifth and Sixth symphonies, jointly with Count Razumovsky; Prince Kinsky, the person least well known to Beethoven, would later be given the dedication of the Mass in C.

The contract that was eventually agreed was unprecedented, reflecting the belief of the composer's supporters in his ambitions even in the face of unsuccessful performances such as the premiere of the Choral Fantasy. It provided Beethoven with the sum he asked for, with just one stipulation: that he would remain in Vienna or its close environs and travel for work only with their consent. This arrangement had been made in recognition, the contract states, of Beethoven's 'extraordinary talents and genius as musician and composer . . . the necessities of life should not cause him embarrassment or clog his powerful genius'.[33] Payments would be made twice yearly until Beethoven received an appointment of equivalent worth or, failing that, for life.

Beethoven could supplement his earnings with commissions, publications and students. With this contract, Beethoven was promised unexpected financial stability and creative freedom, at a time when the deterioration in his hearing was making it clear that he would not be able to sustain a career as a performer. Although it was not without hitches – only the archduke proved to be reliable when it came to paying his dues – the security with which Beethoven could now contemplate his future was invaluable. He turned down the post in Kassel, declared his 'patriotic feelings for his second fatherland' of Austria,[34] and even wrote to Gleichenstein asking for help to find a wife.

5. Love: 'An die Geliebte', WoO 140 (1812)

What's in a song? The combination of music and words has been one of the most common forms of expression and entertainment for centuries. Songs take many shapes: they can be for almost any forces, from solo voice to having elaborate accompaniments, and their texts might be new or old. Songs can be in the vernacular and represent folk traditions, popular culture or political movements, or they might be foreign or challengingly modern. Songs can seem to be outpourings from the heart. They can also help emotional experiences to be shared and imagined.

In eighteenth-century aristocratic homes and salons poetry was often read aloud. Recitations sometimes included musical accompaniments – typically played on a keyboard instrument or a guitar – as a way to make the verses more memorable. Music could also add interest and drama but, in the opinion of prominent figures such as Goethe, should not distract too much from the words. Strophic songs, in which simple melodies were repeated for each verse of poetry, were Goethe's preference. This type of song composition suited poems with regular rhymes and metre. However, if the poem were more irregularly structured or if there was, say, a disruptive revelation in a later verse, the repeated music might be an expressive straitjacket. The musical restriction of strophic song placed more emphasis on the expressive abilities of the singer to make the poem engaging. Beethoven's teachers, Neefe and Haydn, began to grant the vocal part still more independence by writing it on a separate stave, which meant that it did not simply double the melodic line of the keyboard. Their most famous student continued the trend, composing songs in diverse forms, from folk-song arrangements to elaborate Italianate multi-part pieces. The bulk of his output was what are commonly referred to as *Lieder* or, if grander in conception, *Gesänge*, German words for 'song' that have come to represent in the English-speaking sphere songs that belong primarily to the classical-concert world, even if they would not necessarily have been performed on stage during Beethoven's lifetime.

Apparently, Beethoven admitted that he did not particularly enjoy composing songs.[1] Of the nearly ninety he nevertheless produced, few were published with an opus number, suggesting that he did not consider them particularly weighty. Among those that were, the majority were to poems by Goethe. There is nothing surprising in Beethoven's admiration for Goethe, whose cultural dominance was so profound German historians have named his lifespan (1749–1832) the *Goethezeit*, or Age of Goethe. Beethoven read his novels and planned an opera on *Faust*; he also composed incidental music for a production of the drama *Egmont*. A marker of Beethoven's standing was that Goethe came to admire his music in return, although with some reservations.

The two men met in the Bohemian spa town of Teplitz (now Teplice in the Czech Republic) in the summer of 1812. They had a few meetings over the following weeks, including one evening when Beethoven played the piano. Goethe reported:

> I got to know Beethoven in Töplitz. His talent leaves me in a state of amazement; he is, however, a completely intractable personality, who may not be wrong in finding the world detestable, but who surely does not thereby make it more pleasant, either for himself or for others. On the other hand, he may be forgiven this, and is to be pitied, for his hearing deserts him – a factor which perhasp afflicts the musical part of his being less than the social. He, who is already of laconic nature, now becomes doubly so through this loss.[2]

Beethoven, for his part, complained that Goethe was 'more fond of the court atmosphere than is seemly for a poet'.[3] Despite their respect for each other's work, then, Goethe and Beethoven had little appreciation of each other's temperaments. Critics often ascribe their differences to Goethe belonging to an earlier generation that was beholden to eighteenth-century social hierarchies, in contrast to the republican, revolutionary Beethoven. Yet Goethe arguably had paved the way for the type of 'uncontrolled' behaviour of which he disapproved. His immensely popular novel *The Sorrows of Young Werther* (1774), written when Goethe himself was only twenty-five and supposedly drawing on his own life experiences (a love triangle, a friend's suicide), confesses through letters a tragic tale of unrequited love and was notorious for having inspired copy-cat suicides. In less extreme terms, it also provided a stylistic model for how young men should express their passions – a model that Beethoven seems to have taken fully on board in his own communications. For instance, his friend Wegeler referred to one of Beethoven's youthful infatuations (with a 'beautiful and gracious mannered Fräulein v. W.') as a 'Werther love'.[4] As will be seen, Beethoven's own love letters reveal a Wertherian imprint; they are rife with dashes, exclamation marks and grand statements. When it came to romance, even Beethoven sometimes relied on convention.

Beethoven had trained as a musician, not as a man of letters, and from his first meetings with the Wegeler and von Breuning families in Bonn made a determined effort to improve his knowledge of literature. He borrowed books from friends and patrons, solicited copies from authors and publishers, scoured literary journals and almanacs for new poems, and gradually assembled his own small but diverse library, full of well-thumbed tomes, which often had exclamation marks or an approving *Ja!* written in the margins. He liked to pepper his letters with quotations, noting down significant passages he encountered in his diaries. Beethoven read and admired classical literature, including Homer and Euripides, and contemporaries such as Friedrich Schiller (author of the 'Ode to Joy'), poet Friedrich Klopstock, novelist and playwright Christoph Martin Wieland, and the faux-bard Ossian (a pseudonym for the Scottish poet James Macpherson). He also read philosophy and developed an interest in world religions and mysticism. Yet, aside from Goethe, the poets Beethoven chose to set to music typically were local rather than well-known names. One such was Austrian Army veteran Christian Ludwig Reissig, who solicited musical settings of his poetry; Beethoven admitted that he wrote them 'as a favour, out of friendship, because he was an invalid'. A somewhat different type of inspiration came from the folk songs – from Britain and around Europe – sent by the Scottish publisher George Thomson, of which Beethoven produced almost two hundred arrangements.

Songs, then, were another way in which collaboration bore fruit for Beethoven compositionally and in performance. He went through phases of hosting singing parties in his rooms, at which friends would gather to get to know new repertoire. Beethoven complained to Gottfried Härtel that the Napoleonic invasion of Vienna, with its 'drums, cannons, and human misery in every form', had put a stop to those weekly events, on top of all else.[5] It was not until the winter of 1811 that he began hosting them again. The singing parties were a kind of music-making more associated with his younger Viennese contemporary Franz Schubert and are a useful reminder that, whether or not he ranked them as highly as his other works, songs were an important part of Beethoven's creative life. Through their sociable aspects and sometimes their poetic themes, they also played a significant role in his personal life.

★

In December 1811, Beethoven composed a song entitled 'An die Geliebte' ('To the Beloved'), WoO 140. The poem is simply structured, consisting of two four-line verses with an alternating rhyme scheme, and its conceit is well worn: the protagonist wishes they could kiss the tears from their beloved's cheeks, to share their pain. Beethoven's music for the singer stays within a modest vocal and harmonic range, gaining urgency as they contemplate the welling tears, a poetic symbol of sympathy, excess emotion and, occasionally, of sexual desire.[6] Music can be used to add subtext to the reading of a poem: in this song, the opening melody returns at the line about their kiss, suggesting that idea had already been planted. Only then does Beethoven start to repeat words and lines of the poem, as if overcome. Having begun with a short piano prelude, there is no postlude: instead, the poem's perfunctory 'mine' is repeated more fervently, implying that the couple have other things to do than sing.

> O daß ich dir vom stillen Auge
> In seinem liebevollen Schein,
> Die Thräne von der Wange sauge,
> Eh' sie die Erde trinket ein.
>
> Wohl hält sie zögernd auf der Wange,
> Und will sich heiß der Treue weihn;
> Nun ich sie so im Kuß empfange,
> Nun sind auch deine Schmerzen mein.
>
> (Oh, if only from your quiet eye
> in its love-filled gleam
> I might drink the tears from your cheek,
> before the earth drinks them in.

Well do they hesitate on your cheeks,
as if to sanctify warmly its fidelity.
Now I receive it in this kiss;
now are your pains mine.)[7]

The author of these verses, Joseph Ludwig Stoll, had been appointed resident dramatist at Vienna's Burgtheater in 1807, having previously written comic plays for the Weimar court theatre. He and Beethoven became friends; they were seen together in coffeehouses and may have planned to collaborate on an opera. Stoll proved to be a tricky character, particularly when it came to money. His father, a renowned physician, had left his young and sickly son a large fortune, which Stoll duly squandered on travel and other exuberances, subsequently having to support himself by his wits and his writing. On the basis of his father's reputation he had wangled himself a pension from Napoleon during the occupation of Vienna, but that vanished with the departure of the emperor from the city. The remainder of Stoll's career was a series of peaks and troughs, from the successful comedy *Die Schnecken* (*The Snails*) to an advance for a biography of Schiller which was accepted although the manuscript was never delivered. Poets such as Justinus Kerner, Friedrich Schlegel and Ludwig Uhland admired Stoll: Uhland wrote 'Auf einen verhungerten Dichter' ('To a Starved Poet') in his memory. But Beethoven on occasion risked the wrath of other friends, such as the banker Franz Oliva, by acting as Stoll's guarantor. Oliva had complained so often about how Stoll had cheated him and tried to rupture his friendship with Beethoven that when the composer vouched for the poet with Oliva's employers, the banking firm Offenheimer, he asked them not to tell Oliva.[8]

Another reason for counselling Beethoven to be cautious in his dealings with Stoll was Beethoven's own precarious financial situation. In March 1811, the problem of escalating inflation was addressed by the *Finanzpatent*, a national currency devaluation. For five of the old Bankozettel returned, one paper Wiener Währung gulden was received. Those who held cash assets, and salaried employees and pensioners, found that their incomes were drastically diminished. Beethoven was among them. Of his annuity, Prince Kinsky's contribution of 1,800 florins, for example, was replaced first by 360 florins in Wiener Währung, and then by 726 florins.

Because aristocrats' wealth mostly resided in land and property, their financial situation was generally more stable. Beethoven appealed to his patrons that his annuity should be paid in the new currency at the original figure. A court decree adjusted the sums accordingly, but two of his sponsors caused further problems. In fact, Prince Kinsky had already delayed his payments. Despite assurances that he would rectify the situation, he died, in November 1812 – from injuries sustained in a horse-riding accident – before he had done so. Beethoven entered into lengthy legal proceedings with the prince's widow, which were not settled until 1815, when it was agreed that the composer would receive 1,500 florins per annum and outstanding arrears (in gratitude, Beethoven dedicated the revised song, 'An die Hoffnung', op. 94, to Princess Kinsky). The profligate Prince Lobkowitz paid the annuity until 31 August 1811, but then stopped because of his own debts and expenses, which had also been exacerbated by the *Finanzpatent*. Again, Beethoven went to the courts to demand that the prince pay what was owed in the new currency. The case was eventually decided in Beethoven's favour, and from April 1815 Prince Lobkowitz recommenced the annuity and paid the arrears. It was, again, in song that Beethoven expressed his gratitude, though the prince died before the publication of the song cycle dedicated to him, *An die ferne Geliebte* ('To the Distant Beloved'), in 1816.[9] Nonetheless, his son

continued the payments until the composer's death. Of the three
princes, then, only Archduke Rudolph honoured their agreement with Beethoven, so the composer was not in a terribly
secure financial position when he agreed to act as guarantor for
Stoll.

Beethoven also supported Stoll by accepting a commission
to compose four songs, to poems by Goethe, for Stoll's new
literary journal, which had the promisingly Beethovenian
title *Prometheus*. However, only one song, 'Sehnsucht', appeared
in print, in May 1808, as the journal had shut down by September because of the prospect of war.[10] In 1811, the first part
of Stoll's *Poetische Schriften* (*Poetical Writings*) was published.[11]
The poem 'An die Geliebte' was not included in the collection.
It seems from a note on one of Beethoven's sketches for the song,
recommending the addition of another couple of verses 'to make
it even more beautiful', that it may have been given to him
by Stoll.[12] If that was the case, perhaps the intention, again,
was for Beethoven to promote his friend's poetry through
song. Stoll might have offered the poem in recompense for
Beethoven's support; or, perhaps he wrote this little love poem
because he thought it would mean something special to the
composer.

'An die Geliebte' in its first version was for solo voice with
piano or guitar accompaniment. It was fairly common for songs
to be sung to guitar – a portable, relatively quiet instrument
suitable for playing at home – but it was rare for Beethoven to
compose for it. His motivation to do so here might have been
Antonie Brentano, an accomplished guitarist. She wrote in the
top corner of the autograph that it was requested by her from
the composer on 2 March 1812.[13] This first version of the song
was not published until 1836, when it appeared in *Lewald's Europa*
as a 'Reliquie von Beethoven', the commentary claiming that
Beethoven wrote this, 'one of his most passionate songs', in the

album of the Bavarian court singer Regina Lang while she was visiting Vienna, despite there being no records of her having been in the city at that time.[14] Beethoven dedicated several published works to women – including Antonie Brentano – but the gift of a song tends to be taken as a token of affection. Admittedly, he did not inscribe the autograph with any personal message for Brentano, as he had done, warmly but a little stiffly, when he presented her with a copy of the three Goethe songs, op. 83, in 1811; songs that were dedicated to Princess Kinsky. Beethoven's inscription reads: 'to my excellent friend, Toni Brentano, née Edle von Birkenstock, from the author', a formula he repeated for her elsewhere, which mixed intimate knowledge – her nickname, Toni, and not even bothering to sign his name – and perhaps parodic grandeur by citing her maiden name.[15]

Maybe he knew he should not make explicit the strength of his feelings for this married woman. Maybe they were simply friends, enjoying a little flirtatious music-making. It is possible to read too much into such laconic messages.[16] Songs, though, can be immensely personal, and the privacy of this communication – which was not made public in print – has caught the imagination of scholars eager to discover the identity of a woman to whom Beethoven wrote an impassioned letter the summer after he composed 'An die Geliebte': his famous 'Immortal Beloved'.

It took Beethoven two days to complete the letter to his 'Immortal Beloved'. He began 'in the morning' on 6 July, not specifying the year. It was not addressed either. Like the 'Heiligenstadt Testament' of 1802, it was never sent. Between a report of his dreadful journey and his search for lodgings, Beethoven extols his unnamed 'angel, my all, my very self' ('Mein Engel, mein alles, mein Ich').[17] Also like the 'Heiligenstadt Testament',

Beethoven favours dashes over other forms of punctuation, lending the whole a breathless air and a fragmented syntax. He wrote, revealing he was using her pencil:

> can our love endure without sacrifices, without our demanding everything from one another; can you alter the fact that you are not wholly mine, that I am not wholly yours? – Oh God, look at nature in all her beauty and set your heart at rest about what must be – Love demands all, and rightly so, and thus it is <u>for me with you, for you with me</u>. But you forget so easily that I must live <u>for me and for you</u>; if we were completely united you would feel the pain of it as little as I –
>
> . . . We surely shall see each other soon; and today also time fails me to tell you of the thoughts which during these last few days I have had revolving around my life – If our hearts were always closely united, I would certainly entertain no such thoughts. My heart overflows with a longing to tell you so many things – ah – there are moments when I find that speech is quite inadequate – Be cheerful – remain my true, my only treasure, my all, as I am yours. The gods must send us the rest, what for us must and shall be –
>
> Your faithful ludwig.

That evening, Monday 6 July, Beethoven added further pages, apologizing that he had just learned that he had missed the post (the post coach to 'K.' left early on Mondays and Thursdays). Uncharacteristically, he adds multiple exclamation marks to express his frustration:

> You are suffering – Ah, wherever I am, you are with me, I will see to it that where I am, you are also with me . . . What a life!!!! Thus!!!! without you –

Beethoven picks up the letter again the next morning:

Though still in bed, my thoughts rush to you, my Immortal Beloved, now and then joyfully, then again sadly, waiting to learn whether or not fate will hear us – To face life I must live altogether with you or not at all, yes, – I am resolved to wander in distant lands until I can fly to your arms and say that I am really at home with you, and can send my soul enwrapped in you into the land of spirits – yes, unhappily it must be so – you will be the more composed since you know my fidelity to you; no one else can ever possess my heart, never – never – Oh God, why must one be separated from one who is so dear, and yet my life in V.[ienna] is now a wretched life – Your love makes me at once the happiest and the unhappiest of men – at my age I need a steady, quiet life – can that be so in our relationship?

And then he interjects that he has just been told the post coach is about to go so he must rush to send his letter. Then, a final peroration:

Be calm, for only by calmly considering our lives can we achieve our purpose to live together – Be calm – love me – today – yesterday – what tearful longings for you – you – you – my life – my all – farewell. oh continue to love me – never misjudge the most faithful heart of your beloved.

ever thine
ever mine   L.
ever ours.[18]

This long, rambling letter, with its exclamations to fate and God, and its gradual shift from overwhelming passion for the absent woman to resignation to their separation, reveals Beethoven at his most emotionally vulnerable. His fractured prose is comparable to Goethe's Werther:

At times I say to myself: your fate is unique; consider other mortals as happy – none has ever been as tormented as you. – Then I read the work of an ancient poet and it is as if I were contemplating my own heart. I have so much to endure! Ah, have ever men before me been so miserable?[19]

All this is to say that, were it not for the fact that the identity of the 'Immortal Beloved' is unknown, Beethoven's unsent missive might seem like just another love letter, written in the overblown style of the day. With the added mystery, however, there has been endless speculation over to whom it might have been addressed and why it was not delivered, which continues to inspire biographies, academic wrangling, novels and films. Rather than arguing for one name or another, the more interesting question, it seems to me, is why we care. There would probably be scant interest in Beethoven's romantic life had he settled down with a nice wife. His unwanted bachelordom becomes another way to understand or excuse his difficult character, which in turn becomes a way to understand or excuse his difficult music. Scholar Mark Evan Bonds has referred to the 'Beethoven syndrome', whereby autobiography is the dominant mode of interpretation: it is assumed that 'only a personal crisis' could precipitate the outpouring of 'pathos-laden works'.[20] Beethoven's romantic isolation, much like his deafness, is imagined to have sequestered him in his private musical world.

Beethoven's childhood friends Franz Wegeler and Ferdinand Ries both observed that he was always falling in and out of love. Finding a wife, however, proved difficult. Beethoven's preferred women were typically already spoken for, or not interested in someone 'ugly and half crazy' (the judgement of singer Magdalena Willmann, who apparently for that reason had rejected his marriage proposal in 1795), however great his genius.[21] Another problem was the musician's social standing; he may have moved in aristocratic circles as a performer and teacher, but he would not have been considered a suitable match for any of his pupils. Conversely, Beethoven had social aspirations, which meant that lower-class women were not considered appropriate spouses. The forty-one-year-old composer may have been yearning for a 'steady, quiet life', but his search for eternal love was not navigated sensibly.

It becomes clear on examining the multiple names proposed as his 'Immortal Beloved' that there was no shortage of romantic intrigue in Beethoven's life as he searched for someone to settle down with. His assistant-turned-unreliable-biographer Anton Schindler, on publishing the letter to the 'Immortal Beloved' in 1840, asserted that it had been intended for Countess Giulietta Guicciardi, Beethoven's piano pupil and the dedicatee of the 'Moonlight' Sonata. The countess may well have been the 'dear, enchanting girl' Beethoven had hoped to marry in 1801: 'Unfortunately,' the composer conceded, 'she belongs to a different class.'[22] Schindler further claimed that the letter to the 'Immortal Beloved' was written during the summer of 1806, when Beethoven was staying in a Hungarian spa town. To prove his point, he inserted the date '1806' into the letter three times. No matter that on her marriage in 1803 the countess and her husband had immediately left Vienna for Naples. It was not until 1872, in the first, German, edition of Thayer's *Life of Ludwig van Beethoven*, that Schindler's claim was probed, sparking a quest for the 'Immortal Beloved' that continues to this day. Thayer proposed Countess Guicciardi's cousin Therese Brunsvik, who had given Beethoven a copy of her portrait, which he kept until his death (in this she was not alone), and who – along with her sisters – was said to have 'adored' Beethoven (ditto).[23] He, in turn, dedicated his Piano Sonata in F sharp, op. 78, to her. Thayer could not make the dates convincing, however: Beethoven had written 'Monday 6 July' on his letter to the Immortal Beloved, but that date did not fall on a Monday in 1806. While Thayer was right to probe Schindler's version of events, his own argument was undermined. For her part, Therese Brunsvik suggested that if the letter was from 1806, her widowed sister Countess Josephine Deym – who died in 1821 – could have been Beethoven's beloved, a claim that continues to hold sway.

Forged memoirs and other documents did little to clarify matters. Eventually, a more convincing date for the letter was proposed – 1812, the second summer Beethoven spent in Teplitz. He had travelled there via Prague, where his arrival in the city was noted by a local newspaper. Beethoven sent a letter of apology to the writer Karl August Varnhagen von Ense – who had acted as a go-between in negotiations with Prince Kinsky about the unpaid annuity, and with whom Beethoven also met while in Prague – that 'unforeseen circumstances', widely assumed to have been a last-minute tryst, caused him to cancel their evening engagement. He set out for Teplitz at noon on 4 July and the post coach driver decided not to take the mountain route because there had been heavy rain. It was a long, slow journey, on treacherous roads. Beethoven finally arrived at 4 a.m. on 5 July and was properly registered as staying at The Oak in Teplitz two days later. Historical spadework corroborated the timing of the postal services, which made it seem clear that the intended destination of the letter, 'K.', was Karlsbad.

Place and date having been uncovered, the only missing piece in the puzzle was the Immortal Beloved's name. It could have been the young Therese Malfatti, to whom Beethoven seems to have considered proposing in 1810, until he fell out with her family. Singer Amalie Sebald, who met Beethoven in Teplitz in summer 1811, has been put forward as another candidate for immortality. Beethoven asked the poet Christian August Tiedge to send her 'a very ardent kiss, if no one can see us', but that hasn't been taken as anything more than banter, and the flirtation was short-lived. American musicologist Maynard Solomon made a strong case for Antonie Brentano, who met Beethoven through her sister-in-law, the formidable Bettina von Arnim, in 1810. (Arnim was another potential amour – she claimed Beethoven had proposed to her, but then, she claimed lots of things in her memoirs.[24]) Later reminiscences described Antonie Brentano and her banker husband, Franz, as the composer's 'best friends in the world'.[25] On 26 June 1812, shortly before he left for Prague, Beethoven dedicated his Piano Trio in B flat, WoO 39, to one of their five children, their ten-year-old daughter, Maximiliane. The Brentanos arrived in Prague on 3 July and stayed for two nights before travelling on to Karlsbad. By the end of the month, Beethoven had joined them at the same guesthouse; in August, they all moved on to Franzensbad. Despite their company – and indeed, meeting eminent figures such as Goethe – the composer wrote to Varnhagen von Ense on 14 July, 'I am living – alone – alone! alone! alone!'[26] Further corroboration for Beethoven having been intensely in love in 1812 is found on the first page of a *Tagebuch* (diary) he began to keep:

> Submission, deepest submission to your fate, only this can give you the sacrifices - - - for this manner of service. O hard struggle! – Do everything that still has to be done to arrange what is necessary for the long journey. You must - - find everything that your most cherished wish can grant, yet you must bend it to your will. – Maintain an absolutely steady attitude.
>
> You must not be a <u>human being, not for yourself, but only for others</u>: for you there is no longer any happiness except within yourself, in your art. O God! Give me strength to conquer myself, nothing at all must fetter me to life. – In this manner with 'A' everything goes to ruin.[27]

There are shared themes here with the letter to the 'Immortal Beloved': the struggle against fate, the need to give up one's happiness because union with another is impossible and the pleas to God. This does not make it any easier to interpret. There is some disagreement over how to read Beethoven's handwriting as well; the original of the *Tagebuch* has not survived, and what looks like an 'A' in one copy can be read as a different letter elsewhere.

Austrian scholars have cast doubt on the way Solomon dates and reads some of the available evidence. They argue that because Antonie Brentano was married, 'conscience, convention and Catholicism' would have prevented any liaison. They have also noted similarities in language between Beethoven's love letters to Josephine Deym née Brunsvik ('Angel of my heart', 'You – you – you, my all, my bliss') and those to the 'Immortal Beloved', including the aforementioned sign-off: 'ever thine/ ever mine/ever ours'.[28] The Brunsvik sisters had started taking piano lessons from Beethoven in 1799, the year in which Josephine was swept off her feet by Count Joseph Deym von Stritetz. It was only after their marriage that she discovered that the count was enmired in debt. Four years and four children later, the count – who was thirty years her senior – died of consumption. Beethoven had stayed in the Brunsvik sisters' circle, visiting their homes in Hungary and Vienna. After her husband's death, he developed an ardour for Josephine that she partly reciprocated and which it seems from their correspondence peaked in 1805, when he wrote for her a song, 'An die Hoffnung' ('To Hope'), op. 32. She refused the dedication, along with that of the *Andante favori*. She also made it clear to Beethoven that she would not 'satisfy this sensual love', and relations cooled. Josephine married an Estonian nobleman in 1810, from whom she separated five years later. There has been speculation about whether she and Beethoven attempted to rekindle their relationship in 1812, which could make her the 'Immortal Beloved'. It has even been claimed that he fathered her daughter Minona (observed to be almost an anagram of anonym, as in parentage unknown), born the following April. If so, there is no allusion to that relationship in their remaining correspondence.

The only things that seem clear from attempts to uncover the identity of the 'Immortal Beloved' are that Beethoven's encryption was effective and that his plans to marry had been thwarted. The fact that he began to keep a diary around this time has been interpreted as an indication that he felt increasingly estranged from old friends such as Gleichenstein, Breuning and Erdődy.[29] Apparently, from this point onwards he took less care over his appearance – Louis Spohr reported that Beethoven could not leave the house because his boots were in tatters – his drinking increased and his manners roughened. In the first months of 1813, Beethoven made allusions in his letters to his partner-in-crime, Baron Zmeskall, to visiting prostitutes and the attendant risk of venereal disease. It was not uncommon male behaviour. Divorce was forbidden in Catholic Austria. However, the average marriage lasted only five years, reflecting the high mortality rates of the time: if spouses did not succumb to typhoid fever, cholera or syphilis, childbirth could be deadly. Men often married two or three times or resorted to brothels.[30] Diary entries suggest that Beethoven sometimes felt sullied by the experience: 'Sensual gratification without a spiritual union is and remains bestial, afterwards one has no trace of noble feeling but rather remorse.' Nonetheless, he continued to avail himself of 'fortresses', understood to be a codename for brothels – preferably at 'about half past three or four o'clock in the afternoon', he wrote to Zmeskall in the summer of 1817.

Yet Beethoven had not entirely given up on love. To Ferdinand Ries he had explained the previous year: 'Unfortunately I have no wife. I found *only one*, whom no doubt I shall *never possess*.'[31] Unrequited desire was the theme of a new type of song collection he composed in 1816, which again raised the possibility of solving the identity of the 'only one'. Significantly, though, the title was not directly addressed to the beloved, as Stoll's poem had been, but was instead *An die ferne Geliebte* ('To the Distant Beloved'); or, as the autograph had it, *An die entfernte Geliebte*, which means something more deliberate – the *distanced* beloved. Beethoven was evidently drawn to poetry about romantic distance; he set several verses by Reissig on that theme in 1809 (including 'Lied aus der Ferne' ('Song from Afar'), WoO 137 and 'An den fernen Geliebten' ('To the Distant Beloved'), op. 75:5) and it has been suggested that he was sent, chose, or maybe even commissioned the poems by medical student Alois Jeitteles, because of his affinity with their topic.[32]

The six poems of *An die ferne Geliebte* do not tell a story but rather dwell on separation from the beloved. There is no way to send a message other than through song, which will wing its way over the valleys and blue hills, to be whispered on the wind and by babbling streams. What may seem fairly conventional verse is set by Beethoven as a series of, with one exception, varied strophic songs – the kind of simple settings of which, as mentioned earlier, Goethe approved. But the whole is transformed into something greater than the sum of its parts by granting the piano a substantial role. It joins all six songs together through interludes so that the songs run continually. Beethoven further emphasizes the collection's coherence by returning to melodic ideas and to particular harmonies, underscoring the poems' recurring imagery and playing with the idea that the songs can be sung again and again, to remind the beloved of his fidelity. The last song is the only one that is not strophic but through-composed, meaning that it has a continuously developing rather than a repeated melody that here enhances the sense of a wrapping-up or conclusion. At its end, a ghost of the tune heard at the start returns in the piano postlude. *An die ferne Geliebte* is thus not just a collection of songs but a song cycle in which beginning and end are endlessly looped. Beethoven signalled as much when he changed the subtitle from *Sechs Lieder* ('Six Songs') to *Liederkranz* (literally, 'Wreath of Songs') on its second printing. In being a musically coherent song cycle, rather than one unified by a poetic theme or narrative, *An die ferne Geliebte* was the first of its kind. It took some time, though, before it served as an exemplar for subsequent composers.

As mentioned, the published score of *An die ferne Geliebte* was posthumously dedicated to Prince Lobkowitz. Yet it seems that the cycle may have been composed not in commemoration of the prince but of his wife, who died after a brief illness on 24 January 1816. Scholar Birgit Lodes has recently suggested that the songs were intended to console the grieving prince.[33] She points to the emphasis in Jeitteles' poetry on heavenly imagery – clouds and light – and interprets the hope that the separated lovers will be reunited as occurring not in life but in death. Lodes's argument refreshingly shifts the emphasis away from Beethoven's own situation and demonstrates, again, the importance to him of his friends and patrons. However, the more routine assumption has been that the inspiration behind the songs again was the Immortal Beloved – or, at least, a beloved – drawing on a mix of musical analysis and circumstantial biographical evidence. None of the options is particularly convincing. Beethoven may have composed the cycle in reaction to the wedding of Almerie Esterházy on 6 September 1815, another young woman with the initial A, who had moved to Vienna in 1809 and who also summered in Bohemia.[34] In the summer of 1816, Fanny Giannattasio, whose family Beethoven had recently visited in Baden, noted in her diary that she had overheard her father – the headmaster of the school Beethoven's nephew Karl was then attending – talking with the composer about marriage.[35] Apparently, Beethoven admitted that he was still beholden to one he had met five years earlier. There are references in his *Tagebuch* from that year to a 'T . . . her devotion deserves never to be forgotten', but there is no consensus over who T may have been. Beethoven remained in contact with the Brentano family, and T might have stood for Toni, Antonie's nickname. The '*die M*' in his letters, it has been proposed, was her thirteen-year-old daughter, Maximiliane, who could represent an ideal, the notion of which understandably makes some people feel squeamish.[36] The twice-married mother of seven, Josephine Deym, might still have been Beethoven's preference, given the similarity between the main motif of *An die ferne Geliebte* and the *Andante favori*, although she had of course rejected the dedication of that piece, which, anyway, originally had been part of a sonata, op. 53, dedicated to Count Waldstein.[37] The proposal of Beethoven's recently widowed sister-in-law Johanna as his oedipal beloved has been discounted by all bar the makers of the 1994 biopic *Immortal Beloved*, directed by Bernard Rose and starring Gary Oldman.[38]

As long ago as 1927, musicologist Oscar Sonneck conceded of the impossibility of naming the Immortal Beloved that 'many of us will not regret this at all in these days when privacy is fast becoming obsolete and publicity of private affairs a curse'.[39] The situation with regard to an individual's privacy has, of course, only worsened since. Allowing Beethoven's beloved to remain unnamed frees the imagination, much as a composer might be drawn to a poem by the beauty of its imagery or because it lay not within but beyond their own experience.

Songs, an unsent letter, a diary entry. Nothing makes explicit the target of Beethoven's affections, however much they convey deep feelings. The impulse to discover the real Immortal Beloved suggests that commentators have felt less prepared to let the composer reconcile himself to bachelordom than he seems to have been himself. Whatever torment and frustration he may have experienced in the summer of 1812, he apparently enjoyed his stay in Bohemian spa towns with the Brentano family. What's more, he continued to be productive. He gave a concert, with the violinist Giovanni Battista Polledro, to raise funds for the victims of a fire in Baden, and completed the Seventh and Eighth symphonies in quick succession. It is often said that there followed a fallow creative period for Beethoven, marking a divide between his mature middle period and the onset of his late style around 1818. Family business – especially taking care of his nephew Karl – took precedence. However, these years were not wholly inactive.

After his return to Vienna Beethoven accepted commissions to write music to mark current events: the 'Battle Symphony' *Wellingtons Sieg*, commemorating Wellington's victory in Spain on 21 June 1813, and the celebratory cantata for chorus, orchestra and soloists, *Der glorreiche Augenblick* (*The Glorious Moment*). Although it was long considered the nadir of Beethoven's compositional career, recent research has begun to reassess the significance of this period as one of commercial success and public recognition. As will be discussed further in the next chapter, while he might not have composed at the same rate as previously, Beethoven's music was played with greater frequency and approbation than at any other time of his life.

There were two other events during 1812 that had symbolic and practical consequences for Beethoven. First, the Viennese piano-maker Johann Andreas Streicher commissioned a bust of the composer for the music room where he and his wife hosted and often themselves gave concerts. The sculptor, Franz Klein, decided to use a novel technique of making a 'life mask' from which he would then make a cast. Beethoven agreed to have his face first covered in oil and then in a thin layer of plaster, which, when dried, would provide the mould. It was an unpleasant experience, as Beethoven could only breathe through straws in his nostrils, and he broke the first attempt. However, he agreed to try again. The result captures fine details of the composer's complexion – pock marks and a scar on his chin – and, perhaps because of his discomfort, endowed him with a scowl that has been repeated in images of the composer ever since. Both the fragile life mask and Klein's bronze sculpture, which dresses Beethoven in the modish clothes of the day, are agreed to be the best likenesses available (see figs. 5.1 and 5.2). Less often remarked on is Streicher's commission in itself: Beethoven was the only living composer to be celebrated in this way; the other busts were of Mozart and Haydn. (Admittedly, Streicher's own bust was also on display, but presumably that was his prerogative.) At certain moments in performances of Beethoven's music, it was reported, the Streichers would look up lovingly at his likeness.

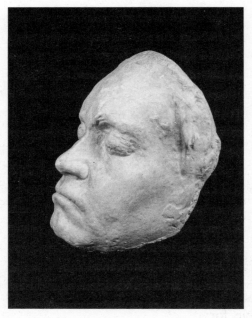

Fig. 5.1 Ludwig van Beethoven's life mask, made in 1812 by Franz Klein.

Fig. 5.2 Ludwig van Beethoven, bronze bust by Franz Klein, 1812 (reproduced 1890).

His elevated status as a member of the pantheon of great Viennese composers was confirmed.

As an aside, in relation to Beethoven's own attitude to his historical standing, another letter of that year bears quoting. On 17 July, ten days after he had completed the letter to the Immortal Beloved, he replied to a note from a 'Miss Emilie M. at H.', a child who had sent him an embroidered pocketbook. He blamed 'business and persistent illness' for his tardy response and urged Emilie 'not to rob Handel, Haydn and Mozart of their laurel wreaths', as he was not yet entitled to one. He recommended that Emilie should not only study piano technique but also consider the meaning of music. Should she ever need his services, he was available, for:

The true artist has no pride. He sees unfortunately that art has no limits. He has a vague awareness of how far he is from reaching his goal; and while others may perhaps admire him, he laments that he has not yet reached the point to which his better genius only lights the way for him like a distant sun. I should probably prefer to visit you and your family than to visit many rich people who betray themselves with the poverty of their inner selves.

The Beethoven of this letter is surprisingly humble and yet confident of the value of his artistic ambition. It is a rare glimpse of a softer side to the composer. The letter he had started to Bettina von Arnim two days earlier, declaring that 'Kings and princes can certainly create professors, privy councillors and titles, and hang on ribbons of various orders, but they cannot create great men, masterminds which tower above the rabble; that is beyond them,' might be feistier in tone but is no contradiction of what he wrote to Emilie or to the Immortal Beloved, simply a reminder that one letter cannot capture the multiple facets of an individual's state of mind.

The second significant development of that year was another technological innovation. The pianist and inventor Johann Nepomuk Mälzel would transform Beethoven's life in various ways – most notably in 1816, through his new device for specifying the tempo of pieces of music: the metronome. In 1812, Mälzel's contribution was more personal. As Goethe had acknowledged when he met Beethoven in Teplitz, the composer's hearing was poor. He was finding it harder to hear conversations and he often spoke too loudly, both of which could cause embarrassment and intensified his sense of social isolation. Mälzel began work on a series of *Höhrrohr* (ear trumpets; the German literally means 'hearing tube', which is a more accurate account of the process). These were essentially inverted

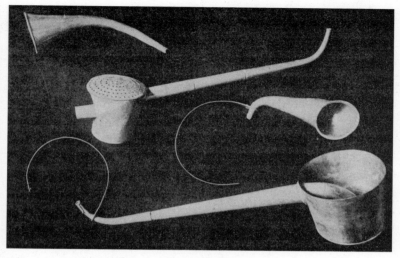

Fig. 5.3. A selection of Beethoven's ear trumpets.

megaphones, funnels that amplified sounds through lengths of tubing, the hollow end of which was inserted into the ear. Sometimes they led to a resonating device that could further amplify the volume (see fig. 5.3). These provided at least a temporary improvement in Beethoven's ability to engage with the world, even if they were fairly crude; he noted in his diary that different-sized trumpets were needed for 'music, speech, and also for halls of various sizes'.[40] Sadly, the ear trumpets could do nothing to counteract Beethoven's increasing deafness: by 1814, his piano-playing was said to have become intolerable to listen to, as he made so many mistakes and could not tell if the instrument was in tune. For a long time his last public performance as a pianist was thought to have been accompanying Franz Wild singing 'Adelaide' on 25 January 1815, around when he began to need an assistant when conducting, but new archival evidence suggests he stopped sooner, with the first performances of the Archduke Trio the previous spring.[41] By 1818, Beethoven had to rely on conversation books to communicate with members of his household and visitors. His rate of composition had slowed considerably but, as will be discussed later, the mammoth scale and profundity of works such as the 'Hammerklavier' Piano Sonata in B flat, op. 106, have been taken to signal a stylistic shift that came to be considered his late period.

The letter to the 'Immortal Beloved' may not have appeared in print for decades, but Stoll's poem 'An die Geliebte', which Beethoven had set to music in 1811, was published in 1814, when it appeared in *Selam. Ein Almanach für Freunde des Mannigfaltigen* and in Erichson's *Musen-Almanach für das Jahr 1814*. An alternative, tighter version of Beethoven's song was published as a supplement to a journal to which Stoll also contributed, the *Friedensblätter. Eine Festschrift für Leben, Literatur und Kunst*, on 12 July that year. The enigmatic titles of the journals illustrate something of the artistic circles in which the poet moved: *mannigfaltig* was used by Kant to evoke multiple sensory experiences, meaning that *Selam* might be described as 'a compendium for friends of aesthetics'. *Friedensblätter* might be translated as 'messenger, or advocate, for peace' (which, interestingly, is also the meaning of the Middle Eastern word *selam*). *Musen-Almanach* is a kind of literary annual.

In Beethoven's revised version of the song, the strumming effect of the guitar was retained, but the piano played more idiomatic, slower figuration, and the underlying anxiety of the new tempo and expression marking *andantino, un poco agitato* (moving on, a little restless) was conveyed by irregular phrasing and subtle dissonances. It is unclear why Beethoven decided to publish 'An die Geliebte' at this point, unless it was again to support Stoll (who died the following year) or, more likely, because it was an opportunity to advertise his music, specifically an upcoming benefit concert. On the page preceding 'An die Geliebte' – described as 'a new composition by the great musical master' ('eine Neue Composition von dem große Meißter der Töne') – there was a reminder to those who claimed that Beethoven wrote only for posterity ('van Beethoven dichte nur für die Nachwelt!') of 'the general enthusiasm aroused by his immortal *Fidelio* ('der allgemeine Begeisterung, welche die unsterbliche Oper *Fidelio* erweckt hat').[42] Beethoven's revised opera *Fidelio* had been performed to acclaim on 23 May 1814. The Immortal Beloved might have grabbed the attention of later biographers. More significant, for Beethoven's immediate reputation, were the claims now being made for the immortality of his music, embodied in the busts being made in his image and the eventual acceptance of the 'unsterbliche Oper *Fidelio*', which he had worked and reworked over the past decade.

6. Liberty: *Fidelio*, op. 72 (1814)

In celebration of the allied armies' very recent victory over Napoleon in France, on 11 April 1814 there was a performance at Vienna's Kärntnertortheater of *Die gute Nachricht* (*The Good News*). Bruno, a local landlord, has promised his daughter Hannchen's hand in marriage to whoever brings the longed-for news that Paris has fallen. Fortunately for Hannchen, her beloved Robert beats his rival by using her father's white dove to deliver the message to the villagers, who break into song: 'Germania! Germania!'

Die gute Nachricht had been hastily devised by playwright Georg Friedrich Treitschke. It is a *Singspiel*, a type of German opera with spoken dialogue, and, appropriately, was a display of Viennese musical talents, with arrangements of numbers by Johann Nepomuk Hummel, Joseph Weigl, Adalbert Gyrowetz, Friedrich August Kanne, and some re-purposed Mozart. The concluding chorus was newly composed by Beethoven.[1] Amid its celebration of German virtues, Treitschke's five verses for 'Germania!' namecheck the newly victorious allied leaders: Russia's Czar Alexander, Friedrich Wilhelm of Prussia and, finally, the Austrian emperor, Franz. The music's popularity is apparent in the decision to publish it immediately in piano arrangement, and the rousing chorus was successful enough to be used in performances of Treitschke's next production, *Die Ehrenpforten* (*The Gates of Glory*), given in honour of the emperor's name day. (This was a Catholic tradition by which children would be named according to the calendar of saints' feasts, which was extended to certain names being celebrated on certain dates. In an era when birth dates could be uncertain – as was the case with Beethoven – name days were reliable party prompts.) On sending a copy of the piano version of the chorus to Archduke Rudolph, Beethoven made the grand claim that 'the song "Germania!" belongs to the whole world'.[2]

As well it might have seemed. Napoleon had finally been forced to abdicate and was exiled to the island of Elba. Statesmen and royalty arrived in Vienna in the autumn of 1814 at the invitation of Emperor Franz. As diplomats negotiated the future of Europe, lavish entertainments were put on for visitors. Sixteen thousand candles illuminated the opening ball at the Imperial Riding School (see fig. 6.1). The next night Austria's Chancellor, Klemens Metternich, hosted a ball for visiting sovereigns. Troops welcomed them to strains of military music and a short play was performed in a copse arranged as an amphitheatre. They were then taken through a reconstructed Russian village, complete with cheering peasants. At the end of a ballet

Fig. 6.1. Ball at the Imperial Riding School during the Congress of Vienna.

danced on a flower-strewn lawn, bouquets were laid at the feet of the royals, accompanied by songs of joy and devotion. Military drills were the final display before the guests entered a newly erected ballroom, decorated with garlands of flowers. After fireworks, the ball began, and supper was served to 150 of the most distinguished guests on a silver service said to be worthy of a king. The following morning, they went hunting – shooting more than one hundred wild boar – and then moved on to a nearby castle and yet another ball. At a public festival at the Augarten there was a parade of four thousand veterans, as well as pony races, athletic competitions, acrobatic displays, archery contests, folk dancing and even a hot-air balloon. But the biggest attraction was seeing foreign sovereignty close up. Everyone was 'gripped by a kind of dancing madness', according to one attendee, and as the entertainments whirled on, gossip about affairs and scandals threatened to overshadow the political ambitions of the Congress.[3] 'The Congress is dancing, but it isn't moving forward,' observed one wit.[4]

Amid the countless balls and receptions, Beethoven was feted as Vienna's most famous composer. 1814 was his most successful year: his music received more performances and he made more money than at any other stage of his career. There is some irony that success happened on the back of the defeat of Napoleon, a man he had once so admired, and the popularity of a work rarely heard today, *Wellingtons Sieg, oder Die Schlacht bei Vittoria* (*Wellington's Victory, or the Battle at Vittoria*). History has not been kind to this particular composition by Beethoven. Until very recently musicians and scholars have not been afraid to dismiss it as jingoistic. For some, it is the low point of his artistic output.[5] Often, they mean that the showmanship and popularity of *Wellingtons Sieg* is unBeethovenian or, at least, not the Beethoven we revere today.[6] Being willing to play to the crowds, according to this view, threatens to undermine his artistic reputation. The political aspect of the piece, meanwhile, roots him as a man of his time rather than allowing him to float free of worldly concerns, a transcendent genius.

Wellingtons Sieg was commissioned by Johann Nepomuk Mälzel in celebration of the British duke's victory over the French in Spain. As mentioned, Mälzel had provided Beethoven with ear trumpets and would in time manufacture a metronome for determining the tempo of music. He had made his name with automata – clockwork models that simulated playing chess, the trumpet, or the flute. Now, he presented the panharmonicon, a mechanical orchestra run on barrel-organ technology. Similar machines had been presented in London, which also played works based on Wellington's recent victory. It's possible that Mälzel had passed off someone else's invention as his own: it would not have been out of character.[7] Beethoven felt it necessary to declare that the idea for a work about Wellington was his, and launched a law suit in an attempt to stop Mälzel from playing *Wellingtons Sieg* in England, even sending a copy of the score to the Prince Regent to claim his authorship.[8]

Beethoven had also devised an orchestral version of *Wellingtons Sieg*, which was premiered in the University Hall on 8 December 1813, at a charity concert in aid of Austrian and Bavarian soldiers wounded in the recent Battle of Hanau. The first half of the programme consisted of marches played by Mälzel's mechanical trumpeter, followed by the premiere of Beethoven's Seventh Symphony. Then came Beethoven's new work. He had fully entered into the commission's spirit. The music's first part represents the two sides of the battle, incorporating the marches 'Rule Britannia' and 'Marlborough' (known now as 'For He's a Jolly Good Fellow'); the second is a 'Victory Symphony' that includes 'God Save the King' amid rousing brass fanfares, stirring strings and rumbustious percussion. *Wellingtons*

Sieg was enthusiastically received and played again and again, including at no fewer than five benefit concerts in which Beethoven participated, on 2 January, 27 February, 29 November, 2 December and 25 December 1814. At the first of these, at the Großer Redoutensaal, Beethoven played up the piece's spectacular potential by having the French and British bands advance towards each other down long corridors on either side of the hall. The hall seated up to a thousand people and the orchestra was unusually large for these concerts, numbering 120 players, an aspect that Beethoven noted with glee in his diaries, listing that there were no fewer than '18 first violins, 18 second violins, 14 violas, 12 violoncellos, 7 contrabasses, 2 contrabassoons' (for comparison, the 'enlarged' orchestra that premiered the Ninth Symphony in 1824 consisted of 24 violins, 10 violas, 12 cellos and double basses).[9] Beethoven attempted to add a further patriotic spin to the January concert, trying to arrange for a statue of the Kaiser, which stood in the hall, to be revealed from behind a curtain on being summoned by Zeus in his incidental music for *Die Ruinen von Athen* (*The Ruins of Athens*). The Russian Emperor Alexander and other leaders were invited to attend his academy on 29 November, which also included the Seventh Symphony and a new cantata, *Der glorreiche Augenblick*, which named the visiting nobles and declared Vienna no longer a city but representative of the whole of Europe ('Europa bin ich, nicht mehr eine Stadt.').

Beethoven's willingness to participate in the pomp and circumstance of the Congress of Vienna might seem surprising to us now. Our image of the composer is of a serious artist, detached from high politics: more revolutionary than reactionary. Yet he and his contemporaries were obliged to play their part in topical entertainments, whether they were employed by a court or court-sponsored theatre, or freelancers, dependent on commercial commissions. There was money to be made by tapping into popular sentiment, especially given the lucrative market for music heard at patriotic events, which was then made available as sheet music to be played at home. Beethoven struggled to persuade publishers to print full scores of his symphonies or opera, but when S. A. Steiner & Co. published *Wellingtons Sieg* in 1816 they did so in no fewer than eight different formats: full score, orchestral parts, and arrangements for string quintet, piano trio, piano solo, piano duet, two pianos, and wind band. In his preface, Beethoven advised potential performers to bear in mind that 'the larger the room, the greater the forces'; advice that might be extended to the performance of his symphonic music more generally.[10]

Beethoven responded robustly to critics who wrote off *Wellingtons Sieg*, writing in the margins of one negative review, 'pitiful scoundrel, my shit is better than [anything] you have ever thought'.[11] Moreover, he was delighted that the multiple benefit concerts finally allowed him to premiere the Seventh and Eighth symphonies, and that it led to an unexpected invitation to revive a work that he had tried out twice before: his opera *Fidelio*. He agreed, on the condition that he would be allowed to revise it, in collaboration with the librettist of *Die gute Nachricht*, Treitschke.

The original libretto for *Fidelio* derived from a German translation of a French play by Jean-Nicolas Bouilly, *Léonore, ou L'amour conjugal*. It had become standard practice for French operas to be translated into German for performance in Vienna after the Treaty of Lunéville of 1801, in which, as a result of the Austrian Army's defeat at the Battle of Marengo, lands west of the Rhine and the Grand Duchy of Tuscany were conceded. Foreign – specifically, French – fare was thereafter tamed, to make it more palatable to the besieged Austrians. *Léonore* had already been made into an opera a few times over – including a version by

Ferdinando Paer, the score of which Beethoven owned and admired (as he had Paer's *Achille*). Like many operas of the revolutionary era, the plot centres on the rescue of someone wrongly imprisoned. It is not a tale of the Bastille being stormed, however, but of an aristocrat having been unfairly treated. In his memoirs, published long after Beethoven's death, Bouilly revealed that the plot of *Léonore* was drawn from a real-life story told during the Terror of an aristocrat from Touraine who was saved from prison by his wife. As the subtitle implies, *Léonore* is also a tale of the strength of married love and may have been chosen to please Marie Theresa, on whose name day Beethoven's opera had initially been due to be performed, and who had a predilection for tales of marital fidelity and for *sotterraneo*, or dungeon scenes.[12]

The first iteration of *Fidelio* had been thwarted initially by the censors; since 1801, they were an office of the Imperial Royal Police who vetted printed and performed materials. Joseph Sonnleithner, who had made the German version of the libretto, had the score returned to him with a message that it was unsuitable for performance. He queried the decision, giving five reasons why it was unjust. First, no less than the empress had admired Bouilly's play 'and assured me that no opera text had ever given her so much pleasure'. Second, Paer's opera, to an Italian text, had already been given in Prague and Dresden – which presumably implied that it could not be that contentious. Third, Beethoven had spent more than eighteen months working on the opera, and 'since there was no fear in the least of a ban', rehearsals were already underway, with a performance planned in celebration of the empress's name day on 15 October. Fourth, Sonnleithner had forgotten to mention on the title page that the action is set in the sixteenth century, 'so there could be no association with current events'. Fifth, there was currently 'a great lack of good opera libretti' and the present one 'features the most touching portrait of wifely virtue, and the malicious Governor exercises only a private revenge'.[13] Sonnleithner's willingness to query the censors' decision probably resulted from his own position – he had recently succeeded the playwright August von Kotzebue as Imperial Royal Court Theatre Secretary and he made his good relationship with the empress clear in his letter. Soon afterwards, Sonnleithner was informed that the opera could be performed if the 'harshest scenes' (*grobsten Scenen*) were changed.[14] The premiere was delayed until 20 November, though this was more likely because of the need for further preparation rather than the censors' intervention.

Unfortunately, by November, Napoleon's troops had occupied Vienna. Beethoven's well-heeled local supporters fled the city, meaning that the audience for the premiere of *Fidelio* consisted primarily of French soldiers, most of whom did not speak German and who were used to lighter and shorter fare. There were only three performances. A second attempt, trimmed from three acts to two, had a couple of more warmly received performances in the spring of 1806. War-worn Vienna was keen for amusement. One English visitor observed that 'the new ballet or play, the dress of the bourgeois, the parade of their emperor's return, etc., is more eagerly talked about than the miserable treaty of peace, the loss of an army, or the overthrow of an empire'.[15]

Beethoven had made an unprecedented deal with the theatre that he would receive a share of the takings. He thought the financial returns were disappointing, though. The ensuing quarrel between the composer and theatre manager Baron von Braun was overheard by one of the singers. French soldiers may not have appreciated the opera, but they had at least filled the cheap seats. For the 1806 production, von Braun pointed out, only the more expensive seats had sold well. He also made an unfavourable comparison to Mozart's willingness to entertain the galleries. 'I do not write for the multitude – I write for the cultured!' Beethoven is supposed to have shouted in response. He withdrew his opera in a huff.

In its early versions, Beethoven's opera focused on the personal relationships between the main characters. Treitschke's revisions reoriented the drama, transforming *Fidelio* from being a tale of private injustice to something that spoke to broader themes of collective peace and freedom. Beethoven told him that he had 'salvaged a few good bits of a ship that was wrecked and stranded'; the maiden voyage of *Fidelio* mark three, at the Kärtnertortheater on 23 May 1814, went well and there were a handful of further performances, on 2, 4, 7 and 21 June; the hiatus was caused by the theatre closing to prepare to celebrate the emperor's return to Vienna on 16 June. Its last outing of the year was the benefit performance Beethoven advertised with his song 'An die Geliebte', mentioned at the end of the previous chapter. Two factors lay behind *Fidelio*'s new-found success. First, the drama had been honed by Treitschke having tightened up the action. Second, the opera's message that tyranny could be overcome by love and courage appealed to Viennese audiences sensing, for the first time in fifteen years, liberation from the Napoleonic Wars.

Whatever parallels might have been drawn between events on stage and contemporary politics, Beethoven and his librettists still had to get around the Viennese censors, who had become far less lenient since the opera's first outing in 1805. As Sonnleithner had then explained, *Fidelio* was set in a safely distant time and place: a sixteenth-century Spanish prison, not far from Seville. The opera begins in the home of the prison guard Rocco. His daughter Marzelline turns down a proposal of marriage from the assistant jailer Jaquino. She only has eyes for the new prison guard, Fidelio. Rocco is happy for Marzelline and Fidelio to be married, as soon as they have enough money to support themselves. Fidelio takes this as a cue to ask for more work, offering to help in the dungeons. There is a prisoner who has been kept there in secret for two years; Rocco explains that he must either be very dangerous or have powerful enemies. Fidelio is not dissuaded. It is revealed to the audience that Fidelio is in fact the prisoner's wife, Leonore. She has disguised herself as a guard in an attempt to infiltrate the prison and free that very inmate, her husband, Don Florestan.

The prison governor, Don Pizarro, learns of an imminent inspection by a minister from the royal court. He does not want Florestan, who is thought to be dead, to be discovered in the dungeon and decides to have him murdered. Rocco refuses to do the deed but agrees to dig a grave. Fidelio, overhearing their discussions, persuades Rocco he should allow the prisoners out into the yard for some sunlight. This angers Pizarro, but he is assuaged by being told that it is in celebration of the king's name day. Moreover, one significant prisoner has been left inside.

Act Two descends into the dungeon. The incarcerated Florestan has a vision of being rescued by his wife. On cue, Fidelio and Rocco appear, but to prepare his grave. Pizarro enters. When he draws his knife to execute the prisoner, Fidelio throws himself between them, pistol in hand, and reveals her true identity: 'First kill his wife!' A trumpet call announces the arrival of the minister. Pizarro and Rocco go to greet him, leaving Florestan and Leonore to celebrate their reunion. In the final scene, townspeople and prisoners assemble in the parade ground to welcome the minister, Don Fernando. He recognizes Florestan as a friend he had presumed dead and orders Pizarro's arrest. Leonore is allowed to release her husband from his chains and all hail her bravery.

★

When it was first performed in 1805, *Fidelio* belonged to a new generation of Viennese operas that forsook comic and magical subjects in favour of stories of individual heroism with realistic settings. Nonetheless, as mentioned, some historical and geographical distance was required so that the drama did not hit too close to home. In its original version, the couple Florestan and Leonore were left in the dungeon, reunited but uncertain of their fate. By 1814, their salvation was assured as soon as the trumpet sounded. Previously, Rocco had taken Leonore's weapon and left the couple metaphorically and literally in the dark. Now he gestured to heaven before heading to meet Don Fernando, indicating to them and the audience that they would be saved. The remainder of the opera becomes a celebration of liberty for all but Pizarro, who is taken away, presumably to be punished.

Beethoven's preferred title for his opera was *Leonore* but, perhaps because there were already operas by that name, he was advised to use *Fidelio* instead. *Leonore* now tends to be used to refer to the 1805 and 1806 versions, which are still sometimes performed, and their overtures (including a third, devised in 1807 for a proposed production in Prague), which are routinely performed in concert. Although it is the 1814 version that is now the standard score, more often than not historical accounts concentrate on Beethoven's initial approach to the opera. It is the composer's situation ten years earlier that thus dominates discussion. The implication is that, with Beethoven, the earliest ideas are always the best, or the most authentic, representations of his inspiration. Opera, however, rarely works like that, as productions are changed to suit different venues, casts and political situations. The same is true of *Fidelio*, and looking at the circumstances in which changes were made in 1814 helps to explain how and why Beethoven and Treitschke reconceived the opera, through its representation of heroism and the use of the chorus, and its ideas about what might constitute freedom.

While, as discussed in Chapter Three, Beethoven's 'Eroica' Symphony was associated with bravery on the battlefield, heroism of a different order is in play in *Fidelio*. Importantly, it is a heroism that goes beyond gender conventions. Cross-dressing had a well-established role in opera. In Italian repertoire, male leads had once been played by castrati, promising singers who had been operated on before puberty to stop their voices breaking. On maturity, the best voices had the power of an adult with an extra-high range. Those roles were now sometimes taken instead by female singers, dressed as men. Commonly called 'trouser roles', they could lend a sexual frisson to romantic duets. Fidelio is not such a part but belongs to a Napoleonic-era celebration of women who disguised themselves as men in order to undertake heroic acts. Leonore may be disguised as a man but the audience, at least, is aware of the deception. Her heroism in deed and voice is feminine; it stems from the valour of the faithful wife. Her husband, Florestan, does not fill the heroic stereotype either. He has something of the Byronic hero about him as he broods over the injustice of being imprisoned; his crime is not specified, but he claims that he has been punished for telling the truth. If the couple are not conventional heroes, neither are they really revolutionaries. Freedom is something they hope for, which is granted to them by the largesse of the governor, who appears as a kind of *deus ex machina*, dispensing liberty earned by loyalty.

The benign rule of the governor, and the duty-bound heroism of Florestan and Leonore, was in keeping with the mass musical declarations of victory and liberty that resounded around Vienna in 1814. Beethoven followed the Franco-Italian precedents of Luigi Cherubini and Paer in his virtuosic solo vocal writing; however, his emphasis on ensembles and the chorus was more in keeping with the city's jubilant soundscape. The importance of the chorus also demonstrates the importance of the opera's visual symbolism. As the prisoners' chorus emerge from their cells into the sunshine, a clear divide is set up between light and dark spaces and, by extension, moral forces.

Beethoven's vocal writing is sometimes criticized for being less suited to singers than instrumentalists. When compared to the French operas that were then popular in Vienna, however, his approach does not seem so unusual. He may also have been writing for a particular type of singer. The first Leonore was soprano Anna Milder, who continued to play the role in 1806 and 1814. A sign of her acclaim in Vienna was that, in between the two early versions of *Fidelio*, she played the female lead in another rescue opera, based on a German translation of a French play: Luigi Cherubini's *Faniska*. Cherubini was widely celebrated and, more importantly, a composer Beethoven admired and even emulated. In this instance he may well also have been envious of him for, in stark contrast to the short run of *Fidelio*, *Faniska* had no fewer than sixty-four performances in its first four years and was published in multiple forms.

On hearing Milder at the start of her career, Haydn had congratulated her on having a voice the size of a house. Critics subsequently compared her sound to woodwind instruments such as the clarinet or likened it to 'the purest metal'. She was praised for her ability to sustain notes, the beauty of her midrange and the consistency of her tone from the lowest to the highest pitches. One review of the revised *Fidelio* described Milder as carving out her own 'new school' of singing; according to Bohemian composer Wenzel Johann Tomaschek, at an 1814 concert of Beethoven's cantata *Der glorreiche Augenblick*, her 'colossal voice' overwhelmed the violin soloist.[16] While these might not seem to be flattering comments or comparisons, their evocation of the strength and resonance of Milder's voice helps explain the unusual way in which Beethoven writes the role of Leonore. It is a challenging part with a large range. At the same time, the singer has to be nimble enough to navigate some fast-moving musical roulades – especially in the 1805 version – and to carry off some pistol-brandishing derring-do.

Take, for instance, the Act I aria in which Leonore reveals that she has come to the prison to try to find her husband, 'Komm, Hoffnung' ('Come, hope'). It was one of the numbers revised in 1814, in this instance by the addition of some preliminary text probably borrowed from the German translation of Paer's *Leonora*, cursing the abominable Pizarro ('Abscheulicher!'). Beethoven set the new words as recitative – speech-like song – with instrumental accompaniment, which allows for more heightened emotions than plain speech (this type of opera still included spoken dialogue). The recitative gradually becomes more song-like as Leonore remembers happy times past. The music is gently illustrative, tracing an arch-shape on mention of a rainbow and staying on one note, lying in Milder's renowned middle range, when referring to being calm and peaceful. The aria proper becomes increasingly florid; repetitions of the verb *erreichen* 'ascend', 'reaching' from the very bottom to the very top of the soprano range. The virtuosic vocal writing intensifies throughout the opera, reaching its high point as Leonore protects Florestan from Pizarro's blade. As she repeats that to kill her husband he would have to pierce her own breast, her melody rises inexorably. It is only at that moment that she sheds her disguise as Fidelio. Pizarro wonders whether he should be scared of a woman.

He should.

Beethoven's attraction to the character of Leonore has been connected to his search for a similarly valiant wife. It need not have been linked so explicitly to his personal situation. The idealization of spousal fidelity was a common theme in revolutionary drama. So, too, was the idea of heroism being somehow androgynous; it could be enacted by women or men. There were plenty of female leaders during the Napoleonic Wars, and stories about female warriors from previous centuries circulated widely. For instance, when the ban on Schiller's works was lifted in Vienna in 1809, Beethoven had rushed to acquire his play about the celebrated cross-dressed martyr Joan of Arc (*Die Jungfrau von Orleans*), who Napoleon had declared a national symbol of France in 1803.[17] It comes as little surprise, then, that Leonore is the active hero of *Fidelio*, rescuing a husband who has resigned himself to enduring his prison term. An illustration of the 1814 performance captures the dynamic well: Leonore pushes herself in front of the dagger-brandishing Pizarro, while Florestan sits in chains, looking on dubiously. Rocco, in the background, might be hoping for intervention from above (fig. 6.2).

If Leonore is supposedly Beethoven's ideal wife, Florestan, locked in the dungeon, has been compared to the composer, kept from the world by his deafness. The audience does not see Florestan until the beginning of Act II. He sits alone, the walls of his cell made more imposing by the pillar-like chords in the orchestra. Something of his inner turmoil amid the gloom is suggested by the repeated plaintive churning motif heard first in the lower strings and then in the woodwind. When Florestan eventually sings it is one long, high note: 'Gott!' The phrase then falls away: 'How dark it is here! What sombre silence!'

Virtuosity is not always fast-moving. That first note is exposed and extended. No one tenor took on the role of Florestan during the course of the opera's revisions in the way that Anna Milder owned Leonore. Austrian tenor Julius Radichi sang for the 1814 performances, having been Florestan in the 1809 Viennese production of Paer's *Leonora*.[18] Comparing the two scores helps to tease out how Beethoven responded to French

Fig. 6.2. Dungeon scene from *Fidelio*, Act II.

models.[19] Paer's scene for Florestan begins with voice alone but is more immediately tuneful. Beethoven places earlier emphasis on the orchestra and begins with recitative. Both Florestans ascend to similar vocal heights in terms of their top notes; Paer's has the kind of build-up towards climaxes audiences would have expected of a leading tenor, while Beethoven's are used to illustrate significant words, such as 'sorrow' (*Leiden*) and 'heavenly' (*himmlische*). It is as if Beethoven's music is encoded with meaning as much as the libretto.

Originally, Beethoven's Florestan was left in the gloom at the end of his aria. Treitschke added a new conclusion that presents a vision no one is sure they can believe. Instead of reminiscing about past happiness and then collapsing in exhaustion, Florestan imagines being saved by Leonore in the form of an angel approaching in a rosy glow. The score describes Florestan behaving as if overtaken by madness. The melodic writing becomes agitated and disconnected, with short repeated phrases. He hopes that they will meet again in heaven.

One of the many peculiarities of opera as a dramatic form is that characters can sing their lines simultaneously. The audience can thus be privy to their inner thoughts and motivations in a way that a spoken play can achieve only in successive lines. Beethoven takes full advantage of this in his ensembles for soloists and in his use of the chorus. There are several ensembles in *Fidelio* that reveal the conflicting preoccupations of all involved, such as the one addition Joseph von Sonnleithner made to his translation of Bouilly's play for the original libretto, the often excerpted Act I quartet 'Mir ist so wunderbar'. The beautifully serene music sounds hopeful, supporting Marzelline's belief that Fidelio loves her too. The other characters pick up her melody, chasing each other in canon. Rocco echoes Marzelline's words, reassuring himself that she and Fidelio are a good match. Fidelio is alarmed by Marzelline's love; the exact words are hard to catch amid everything else, but they recognize the danger and probable hopelessness of their situation. Jaquino's disappointment, while soon put to one side by the plot, was perhaps the most subversively expressed: he can find no solution to his predicament because Rocco seems happy for Marzelline to marry Fidelio. Her father is part of the problem, in other words. Significantly, 'der Vater' was also a name for the emperor. Perhaps through the voice of this minor character there was an attempt to slip past the censors a critique of Vienna's increasingly repressive regimes.[20]

A more obviously fraught situation is captured in the Act II trio in which Leonore, still disguised as Fidelio, has recognized the prisoner as her husband. Rocco is moved by Florestan's plight and is persuaded to allow him to be given some bread. Florestan's noble expression of thanks for the kindness is cut across by a complicated web of asides and conversations between the jailers as each reveals their doubts and anxiety. By the end of the scene they are joined together by music that shows their empathic connection: 'Poor man, it'll soon be over for him,' sings Rocco; 'Oh, that I can give you no reward,' sings Florestan; 'Oh, this is more than I can bear,' sings Fidelio. The arrival of Pizarro, to undertake the execution, makes the trio into a quartet, and the tension increases throughout the scene that leads to the revelation that Fidelio is, in fact, Leonore, intent on saving her husband.

Music, in these ensembles, outwardly deceives even as it reveals inner truths. When the prisoners emerge, blinking, into the yard, they initially exclaim in joy at being able to breathe fresh air again ('O welche Lust, in freier Lust den Atem leicht zu heben!'). One of them hopes that they will soon be free and, while the others excitedly pick up the prospect, another cautions that they are being watched and could be overheard. The need to deceive, to foil the authorities, is evident also in Rocco's quick-thinking explanation to Pizarro that the prisoners have been allowed out in celebration of the king's name day: the power of one tyrant is deflected by paying homage to another. As the prisoners are returned to their cells, Marzelline, Fidelio, Jaquino, Pizarro and Rocco each give their take on what has happened in a quintet, drawing the act to a close with the feeling that they are communicating no better than at the start. Treitschke added a line for Jaquino that encapsulates the situation for the audience as much as his character: 'If only I could understand what everyone is saying!' he complains.

The double-talk of *Fidelio*, typical of a regime lived under censorship, drops away at the end of the opera with the intervention of Don Fernando. He is presented as a benevolent ruler who perhaps was supposed to call to mind similarly noble leaders in an era intent on restoring order to Europe. To be sure, the final choruses of *Fidelio* are emphatically festive: endlessly looped expressions of the here and now that point out towards the real world celebrating liberation from the Napoleonic Wars.[21] Except, of course, that the run of performances of *Fidelio* was over before the Congress proper had begun. Segments of the opera did continue to be heard in concert – particularly the quartet 'Mir ist so wunderbar' – and arrangements for piano and for wind band were widely available. The opera thus entered homes and parade grounds, becoming part of the shared music used to mobilize the masses and to encourage social cohesion during the Napoleonic era.[22] Beethoven may not necessarily have composed *Fidelio* for the multitudes, but it was now being heard by them.

Musical culture in early-nineteenth-century Vienna readily mixed what would now be thought of as high art and more lowly forms of entertainment. For example, there was a fashion, in the years prior to the revision of *Fidelio*, for presenting *tableaux vivants* at venues such as the Kärntnertortheater. These were 'living pictures', paintings or scenes re-created on stage with real people replacing the original figures. Poses were held either in between or for the duration of musical performances or dramatic readings. Thus the Viennese premiere of Beethoven's Fifth

Piano Concerto by Carl Czerny took place on the same programme as three *tableaux vivants* based on paintings by Raphael, Nicolas Poussin and Franz de Troyes.[23] Movements from the Second, Third and Fourth symphonies were used on other occasions. Such tableaux were more than just opportunities for dressing up (although that was admittedly a large part of their appeal for participants, as they often featured men in military attire assisting swooning women in fetching costumes). By adding images to Beethoven's music they guided listeners, much as E. T. A. Hoffmann had used poetic flourishes to explain the power of the Fifth Symphony.

Opera, also, made use of tableaux; indeed, it was a common feature of French revolutionary operas. Cherubini in particular was prone to extended choral conclusions that froze the cast in suspended animation. The action then becomes musical. There are several such moments in *Fidelio*, the libretto of which, commentators have often pointed out, makes repeated reference to the word 'moment' (*Augenblick*).[24] Pizarro relishes the thought of Florestan's demise with the aria 'Ha! Welch' ein Augenblick!' ('Ha! What a moment!'), words that Leonore echoes and subverts as she is given permission to release Florestan from his chains ('O Gott! Welch' ein Augenblick!'). The other characters and the chorus pick up the same phrase and convert it into a musical and dramatic tableaux. For some listeners, the moment is too protracted; it becomes ceremonial.[25] Liberty, long yearned for, defeats the dramatic impulse. Or maybe the problem is that liberty is not here achieved by the people but granted by the state.

News in March 1815 that Napoleon had escaped Elba and was marching towards Paris threw a spoke in the wheels of the lumbering Congress of Vienna. Festivities came to an abrupt halt, giving Beethoven no chance to extend his run of successful premieres and performances by contributing to a grand closing ceremony. With several of his patrons incapacitated financially or by sickness, his extensive plans for further operas, oratorios, piano concertos and symphonies were also shelved. Over the next five years he produced relatively few works. That is not to say, though, that the political upheavals of the period did not leave marks on his music. After completing the *Fidelio* revisions, Beethoven had composed the Piano Sonata, op. 90, which some scholars like to hear as him retreating to the comfort of more familiar musical domains.[26] Yet, for the first time, Beethoven did not use the conventional Italian tempo markings but instead provided expression markings in German: for example, the second movement is headed 'Nicht zu geschwind und sehr singbar vorgetragen' ('Not too quickly and to be performed in a very singing manner'). Its reference to singing perhaps reflected Beethoven's work on *Fidelio* – it shares the same key as Leonore's aria 'Komm, Hoffnung' – or on the song cycle *An die ferne Geliebte*. While he would revert to parallel Italian directions in later sonatas, probably because they were more easily understood internationally, his turn to German was a small but significant demonstration of the intensity of national sentiment.

Beethoven's return to compose for the piano after the excesses of opera and *Wellingtons Sieg* is generally considered a retreat from the world. He read widely on philosophy and spirituality, copying into his diary extracts from Kant's *Universal History of Nature and Theory of the Heavens* and noting down lines from the *Iliad* that he might set to music. At the height of his success during the Congress he had professed to 'prefer the empire of the mind', a statement often taken as an excuse to lift Beethoven and his music out of the quagmire of contemporary politics and the social whirl.[27] It is often overlooked that the letter was to his legal adviser in Prague, Johann Nepomuk Kanka, who was assisting him with the case against the Kinsky family, meaning that the phrase could rather be read as a reminder of the annuity agreement of 1809, with its stipulation that 'the necessities of life should not cause him embarrassment or clog his powerful genius'. Practical matters were pressing: deafness and ill health, financial concerns and family disagreements over care of his nephew Karl all took their toll. Patrons and friends on whom he had once relied were falling away. A fire that started during preparations for a ball at the palace of Count Razumovsky on 31 December 1814, gutting the building and destroying a priceless art collection, had broken the spirit of one of Beethoven's most fervent long-term supporters. The bankrupt Razumovsky, who had represented Russian interests at the Congress of Vienna, retreated from society. Biographer David Wyn Jones points out that Beethoven's life and music had been affected by European conflict for the past twenty-three years but, ironically, it was the end of the Napoleonic Wars that 'initiated a period of tortured rather than liberated creativity'.[28]

The extent of Beethoven's revolutionary tendencies is still debated. The 1814 revision of *Fidelio* has been interpreted as more reactionary than its earlier incarnation for putting its faith in the timely arrival of an enlightened ruler rather than having Florestan and Leonore liberated by an unruly crowd. It had, inevitably, been easier for Beethoven to make grand statements about truth and freedom in previous decades; his views were moderated by age and, importantly, circumstance. Under Metternich's control, Vienna was becoming still more restrictive. Spies were everywhere, and Beethoven, truculent and hard of hearing, was not as careful about what he said as he should have been. Artistic liberty, always at a premium, was under greater threat than ever; better to keep one's head below the parapet.

When *Fidelio* was next heard in Vienna, in 1822, it was no longer the French who dominated operatic repertoire but a newcomer to the city, the Italian, Gioachino Rossini. Very quickly, almost a third of performances at the Kärntnertortheater were of Rossini operas, and thousands of arrangements were made of his music.[29] When the two composers met, Beethoven supposedly told Rossini that he should 'make a lot of Barbers!', referring to the success of his comic opera *Il barbiere di Siviglia*. The veracity of the anecdote has always been doubted, but it was seized on by historians to divide the remaining century into two musical styles: the serious, Germanic tradition of symphonies and chamber music, and the frivolous, tuneful operas of Italy. At the time, it was more a case of the two composers being placed side by side on programmes than them being at loggerheads; soon, though, it was Beethoven vs. Rossini, and it is only recently that the usefulness of the divide has been questioned.

The French roots of Beethoven's *Fidelio* now seemed inappropriate or maybe just quaintly old-fashioned. The revival in 1822, however, was received very warmly in Vienna, in large part because of Wilhelmine Schröder-Devrient as Leonore. Beethoven had been impressed by Schröder-Devrient's physical presence on stage but made no comment on her singing; she recalled that the composer's deafness was evident in his attempts to conduct rehearsals and, in the end, he left that job to someone else. Schröder-Devrient's interpretation of the role of Leonore has been said to have depoliticized the plot through her emphasis on the importance of marital fidelity, transforming what had been revolutionary into something more suited for the politically conservative, economically comfortable and culturally unadventurous so-called Biedermeier era ushered in by the Congress of Vienna.[30] However, Schröder-Devrient took a liberty with the role that both made Beethoven's opera more Italianate, by placing emphasis on the singer over the score, and served to distinguish it from the *bel canto*, or lyrical singing, of Rossini by proposing something more dramatic, maybe more

Germanic, in its place. As she threw herself before Pizarro's blade, Schröder-Devrient shouted, more than sang, the line 'First kill his wife!' Hand pressed to her forehead, she cried out involuntarily, seemingly overwhelmed.[31] The audience erupted in applause. It may not have been Beethoven's preferred interpretation, but the heroism of Leonore once more had saved the day.

7. Family: Piano Sonata no. 29, op. 106, the 'Hammerklavier' (1818)

Beethoven's brother Kaspar Karl died of tuberculosis in November 1815. His will left money for four holy Masses and, to his widow, Johanna, he returned the 2,000 florins in bonds she had given him when they married. Kaspar Karl had originally appointed Johanna and his brother Ludwig to jointly take care of his nine-year-old son, but Beethoven pressured him to make him sole guardian. Kaspar Karl wrote: 'I expect with full confidence and with full trust in his noble heart, that he shall bestow his love and friendship that he often showed me, also upon my son Karl, and do all that is possible to promote the intellectual training and further welfare of my son.'[1] Johanna and Karl were to inherit equal shares of his estate. There was then a codicil, adding that he wanted both Ludwig and Johanna to take over the guardianship of Karl. 'God permit the two of them to be harmonious for the welfare of my child. This is the last wish of the dying husband and brother.' Sadly, for all involved, his request was not honoured.

Two weeks after Kaspar Karl's death, Beethoven filed an appeal to the Imperial and Royal Landrecht, the court of the nobility, to make him the sole guardian of Karl. Apart from the vagaries of the will, he drew to their attention Johanna's conviction for the embezzlement of a pearl necklace, her history of infidelity, and that she had become pregnant with Karl out of wedlock. Widows had few legal rights at the time and, the court having decided Johanna was an unfit mother while Beethoven was assumed to be a nobleman, on 19 January 1816 he was awarded full custody. By the end of the month, he had enrolled Karl in a local boarding school for boys. He asked the master, Cajetan Giannattasio del Rio, to prevent Johanna from seeing her son, complaining that she had already bribed his servant to allow her to do so. Referring to her as 'the Queen of the Night', after the villainous regent from Mozart's *Magic Flute*, he reported that Johanna had been seen cavorting at the Artists' Ball until the small hours, and that she was willing to sell herself for twenty florins. Beethoven, who cast himself in the enlightened Sarastro role of the Mozart opera, claimed the moral high ground; presumably his own brothel visits were none of the court's concern.

High school fees (1,100 florins per month) and Johanna's persistent attempts to see her son prompted Beethoven to consider taking Karl out of school. Illnesses intervened; Karl had a hernia operation and Beethoven struggled with intestinal problems and various infections and fevers. On the anniversary of his father's death, Beethoven wrote to Karl: 'I too mourn for your father, but the best way for us both to honour his memory is for you to pursue your studies with the greatest zeal and to endeavour to become an upright and excellent fellow, and for me to take his place and to be in every way a father to you.'[2] But although Beethoven was certainly invested in being a father figure, his attitude to parenting was strict and could be as brutal as his father reputedly had been to him. He reminded Giannattasio that Karl was used to being beaten into obeisance and admitted to his friend piano-maker Nanette Streicher that he would 'often give him a good shaking, but not without valid reason'. Whether or not Beethoven's behaviour was in keeping with the time, his defensive tone when referring to such punishments suggests that he recognized it would be seen as brutal treatment.

A new financial arrangement to support Karl was agreed in the middle of 1817: Johanna van Beethoven would pay 2,000 florins immediately and from then on give over half her yearly pension payments. The temporary thaw in relations was stymied by the news that Johanna was spreading gossip about Beethoven, and he decided to limit her visits to Karl to twice per year. By the start of the following year, Karl had been removed from school and moved into Beethoven's home. Beethoven was relieved to report that the boy seemed to be in good spirits and affectionate towards him.[3]

By the time Karl moved in with him, Beethoven's hearing had deteriorated to the point that his nephew and servants had to rely on writing messages in chalk on slate to communicate with him at home. He had also begun to carry notebooks to enable him to hold conversations with others, as well as for noting down thoughts and reminders. In his letters to distant friends such as Karl Amenda and Countess Erdődy, Beethoven complained that he lived 'almost entirely alone in this, the largest city of Germany, since I must live practically cut off from all the people whom I love or could love'. It was not a new complaint. He did have a small, supportive social circle of non-aristocratic friends. They were almost all male and – with the exception of Nanette Streicher, whose domestic advice was often sought – seemed to spend most of their time gassing in restaurants and inns.[4] Beethoven would take Karl on walks with him, but his nephew found his scruffy uncle's distracted behaviour embarrassing. His objections were not just those of a child mortified by the eccentricities of an older relation. On one occasion, Beethoven was arrested on suspicion of being a vagrant, having walked further than he intended and lost his way. The police were unconvinced by his claims to be the great composer and it was only when the local music director vouched for him that he was released.

While summering in Mödling in 1818, Beethoven was distressed to find that Johanna was again bribing the servants to give her information about her son and that they had been meeting in secret. Meanwhile, Karl was beginning to rebel. A new village tutor, Parson Frölich, complained that his behaviour was disturbing other students; Karl, in turn, said that the parson had the students whipped. When they returned to Vienna in the autumn the twelve-year-old Karl began studying at the Akademisches Gymnasium, with extra instruction in music, French and drawing. At this point, Johanna submitted a petition to have Karl returned to her, which was rejected. She applied for him to be moved to a boarding school, the Imperial Royal Seminary (Konvikt), where she might have more access to him, but that was rejected too. She stopped paying support. On 3 December, Karl ran away to his mother. She promised Beethoven she would return him and he sent the police round to make sure she did. Karl was sent back to the Giannatasios' and Johanna appealed once more to the Landrecht, claiming that Beethoven was going to send her son far away. All three were summoned to court. Karl equipped himself admirably, saying that he was doing well at school and that he would be happy to live with Beethoven had he someone there with him, 'because his uncle is hard of hearing and he cannot talk with him'. Karl told the court that his mother had not asked him to run away and that his uncle did not treat him cruelly; if he was punished, he deserved it. Johanna was also conciliatory. Her main concern was that Karl could not communicate with Beethoven and that his hygiene was being neglected. Beethoven did less well: he let slip that he would send Karl to a school for the aristocracy, the Theresianium, if he were of noble birth. The judges asked Johanna whether her husband had been of noble birth, and she was unsure. Beethoven then had to admit that he was not: *van*, in Dutch, was not the equivalent of *von* in German. The case was thrown out of the Landrecht and transferred to the civil court, the Magistrat. Everything began again.

By January 1819, no longer shielded by a pretence of nobility, Beethoven lost custody of Karl.

Beethoven and Johanna continued to fight in the courts, each getting better legal advice than they had done previously. For a while, Beethoven's friend Mathias von Tuscher assumed co-guardianship on the composer's behalf, but by June he had resigned, saying he found it 'in every respect burdensome and vexatious', and Johanna was reappointed sole guardian. Karl bounced between schools, eventually ending up at Joseph Blöch-linger's Institute in Vienna, where he would stay for four years. Beethoven spent months preparing another appeal, trying to pull strings through his aristocratic contacts. With the help of expert representation by lawyer Johann Baptist Bach, and Johanna's second pregnancy out of wedlock helping to convince the court of her immoral character, on 8 April 1820 Beethoven

Fig. 7.1 Karl van Beethoven, miniature portrait, 25 June 1825.

was named co-guardian with his friend, amateur painter and tutor to the Lobkowitz family, Karl Peters.

While all this family trauma was taking place, Beethoven continued to work hard. Time was taken up with making arrangements – the Piano Trio, op. 1, no. 3, was converted into a string quintet, op. 104, and he continued to produce dozens of folk-song arrangements for George Thomson in Edinburgh – as well as the usual negotiations over publications and performances. Although the triumphs of 1814 were not repeated, there were dozens of public and private concerts featuring his music. Beethoven often attended the weekly musicales (social gatherings featuring musical entertainment) at the Streicher house – where his bust remained on display – occasionally taking Karl along. His fame was growing elsewhere: he was invited by the Royal Philharmonic Society to visit London at the end of 1818, which did not come to pass but resulted in the commission of the Ninth Symphony.

Beethoven's most substantial compositions from these years were piano sonatas: in A major, op. 101 (November 1816), and in B flat major, op. 106, begun towards the end of 1817; the first two movements were completed by April 1818 and the whole sonata by the beginning of 1819, its relatively long gestation perhaps reflecting, as he explained to Ferdinand Ries, that it had been composed 'in distressing circumstances'. As with the 'Kreutzer' Sonata discussed in Chapter 2, Beethoven's approach to writing for the keyboard was shaped by the instruments to which he had access. In January 1817, he wrote to the publisher Tobias Haslinger, pondering what the instrument for which he had written op. 101 should rightly be called, for he suspected that the fortepiano – or as it was now also called, the pianoforte – was really a German invention.[5] He even consulted a philologist, Wilhelm Hebenstreit, for advice. Eventually, he settled on

'Hammerklavier' and asked Anton Stein to ensure that all his works should use the word in preference to the Italian equivalent from then on. Beethoven's decision to use the term was an extension of the German expression markings he had adopted in a fit of nationalist fervour, mentioned in the previous chapter. As it turned out, only opp. 101 and 106 were published using the word 'Hammerklavier' in their subtitle.[6] There were further inconsistencies in translation: while op. 101 used German expression markings, Beethoven used Italian terms in op. 106. Yet it was the latter sonata that came to be known as the 'Hammerklavier'. The assumption often is that the word *Hammer* somehow reflects the character of the sonata, but while some of its movements can be bludgeoning in performance, the title is not descriptive of anything more than the instrument on which it was to be played.

Towards the end of 1817, Beethoven was delighted to receive news that he was to be sent a piano as a gift by the renowned London makers Broadwood. A sign of the high regard in which he was held across the Channel was that the instrument had been selected from the firm's flagship store by five of the city's most respected musicians, whose names were embossed inside the piano, along with a Latin inscription: *Hoc Instrumentum donum Thomae Broadwood (Londini) propter ingenium illustrissimi Beethoven* ('This Instrument is a gift from Thomas Broadwood (from London) to honour the genius of the most illustrious Beethoven').[7] The piano was then shipped from London to Trieste before being hauled over the Alps to Vienna. The English musician Cipriani Potter helped the Streichers to recondition the instrument after its long journey, after which it was sent on to Mödling, where Beethoven was spending the summer.

An instrument can shape a piece in all manner of ways, and the influence of the newly arrived piano on Beethoven's sonata-in-progress has been much debated. Even at this stage of his

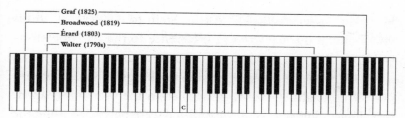

Fig. 7.2 An illustration of the different ranges of the instruments Beethoven owned, shown in comparison to today's standard eighty-eight keys.

career, it turns out, the composer was prepared both to take creative advantage of what was on offer and to make pragmatic compromises. The Broadwood's relatively stiff action and the deeper dip of its keys gave it a heavier touch than Viennese pianos. Its sound has been described as thicker and its articulation 'puffy', with a relatively powerful bass. The treble was weaker, because the heavier wire used by the English firm required the upper strings to be longer. Overall, British instruments were louder; they also had a different range. The standard piano keyboard today consists of eighty-eight keys, stretching just over seven octaves (fig. 7.2). By comparison, in the late 1790s, Beethoven owned a fortepiano by Anton Walter which ranged a mere five octaves. Although Beethoven often hit the top of that range, all his piano music necessarily remained within the five octaves until 1803, when he began to compose for five and a half octaves, as in the 'Waldstein' and 'Kreutzer' sonatas. That year, he had received the Érard piano from Paris, which had a bigger keyboard, in keeping with newer instruments being built in Vienna. By 1808, Beethoven was regularly exploring the lowest notes of the now six-octave span. But it was only with op. 101 that he began to use the bottom notes that were available on British keyboards. So low did it go that Beethoven felt obliged to write a note on the score for the copyist, clarifying which note he meant and confirming that he really was asking for what, on most central European pianos, it would be physically impossible to play for some years to come.

By the time the Broadwood arrived in Mödling, Beethoven had already completed the first three movements of the 'Hammerklavier' Sonata. As mentioned, he explored the limits of Viennese instruments, which might not have gone as low as the Broadwood but had more high notes. For instance, the opening gesture of the 'Hammerklavier' leaps from a bottom B flat up two octaves and then up another two, to hit a high E flat. The gesture is immediately repeated and climbs even higher, to G. The highest note in the movement is a C; the lowest, heard during the rumbling fugue towards the end of the development, is an F sharp. The second movement, a Scherzo, is more contained, until a *prestissimo* run from a bottom F up through all six octaves. As if in acknowledgement of the feat just achieved by the sprinting ascent, there is a moment's silence, followed by trembling chords that seem to wonder what has just happened, before the sprightly Scherzo theme returns. The Adagio repeatedly pushes into the higher register, touching notes the Broadwood did not possess. Towards the end of the fugal finale, by contrast, there is a long *fortissimo* trill that rumbles on a bottom E flat which, when he composed it, only the Broadwood had.

Beethoven very rarely goes beyond the physical boundaries of the instrument available. It should not be assumed that he wrote only for the keyboards he owned; throughout his career he had access to other instruments through his patrons, students, friends and venues. Nonetheless, the piano music he composed after the arrival of the Broadwood stayed within its range, at least until he received his next instrument, a six-and-a-half-octave Conrad Graf piano which encompassed the higher notes that his last sonatas reached for; the C sharp on the last page of op. 109 or the one high E flat in the first movement of op. 111.

Beethoven provided an alternative for that last outlier, making it playable on (slightly) smaller keyboards, demonstrating his constant awareness of the need for his music to not stretch beyond the boundaries of what was sellable. Yet when Beethoven's belongings were auctioned after his death, Gerhard von Breuning recalled that his father refused to buy the Broadwood because it did not have the high notes required by 'music of the modern, that is Beethoven, era'.[8] The conflation of Beethoven with the modern shows how quickly expectations adapt and the assumed extent of the composer's influence. With hindsight, it is easy to assume that an invention is immediately adopted across the board, but five-octave pianos continued to be produced in Vienna into the 1830s; in practice, old technologies continued to be used as well, as Beethoven was aware.

The Streichers may have helped to organize the Broadwood piano for Beethoven because he had recently asked them for a louder instrument. The composer had always been a forceful player and did not look after what were fairly fragile instruments as well as he could have. A visitor who saw the Érard Beethoven had initially been so pleased to receive noted that it was 'completely worn out, out of tune; several strings were in fact missing'.[9] Keyboard instruments, generally, were becoming more powerful. Although it would be some time before the iron-framed, steel-stringed piano became the norm, there were constant improvements being made to increase dynamic range and to enhance tone quality. The Graf piano not only had a large range, it was also quadruple-strung, meaning that the hammers hit four rather than the standard three strings, making it a louder instrument. Whether technical developments reflected creative practice or creative practice responded to new technologies is always hard to determine, but Beethoven's music had some role to play in testing what was possible.

There was a bigger issue: Beethoven's hearing. For several years, Beethoven had been composing away from an instrument, depending primarily on sketchbooks instead. He had, in other words, the ability to imagine sounds regardless of whether he could hear them. Throughout his life, though, he wanted access to the best keyboard instrument available. Once a virtuoso, always a virtuoso. He was resistant to allowing his Broadwood to be tuned, which suggests that by this stage intonation was not his top priority. Trying things out, feeling whether a run or stretch is physically possible, would have been more important. Playing an instrument is a tactile and visual as well as an auditory experience.

The Broadwood was not simply louder than Viennese instruments, it was constructed differently. Its soundboard – in this era, a piece of wood that amplifies the vibrations of the lower strings and cuts off the higher frequencies, balancing the resonance of the instrument – was anchored to its outer frame rather than encased within an internal frame. As a result, the vibrations of the instrument were more evenly distributed and could be felt more directly. The effect was intensified by the use of *una corda*, the left, or 'soft', pedal, which strikes only one string of the three attached to each key, thereby enhancing the note's mutual resonance, meaning that the other strings vibrate in sympathy but do not sound fully themselves. It is a kind of sonic halo effect Beethoven used to musical ends in the slow movements of opp. 101 and 106.

In 1820, Stein made Beethoven a 'hearing machine' (*Gehörmaschine*), a metal cupola which sat on top of the Broadwood, functioning as a basic amplifier. It was one of several devices Beethoven tried out over the next few years and perhaps the most successful.[10] The portrait painter August von Klöber reported seeing the fifteen-year-old Karl practising at the keyboard beneath the contraption, which enabled Beethoven to hear enough to correct him without looking. Beethoven may have used an ear trumpet as well. It was a significant improvement for the composer. Pity Karl, though, encased in his uncle's echo chamber. Since assuming guardianship, Beethoven had decided that Karl would become a virtuoso pianist and enforced a strict practice regime. The impossibility of Karl fulfilling his expectations was clear to everyone except, for the moment, Beethoven.

Beethoven – and, by extension, his music – is often associated with triumph over adversity. As in the case of his battle for the custody of Karl, his victories ultimately seem to isolate him from others, including his family. History often presents that as a price worth paying: Beethoven's achievements are presented as all the greater for his having overcome such difficulties. His own view of art seems in keeping: 'what is difficult also is beautiful, good, great, etc.', he explained.[11] The 'Hammerklavier' Sonata seems to push that view to an extreme. On the surface, it seems fairly conventional. Beethoven reverted to the standard four-movement layout for a piano sonata he had abandoned since op. 31, no. 3, in 1802. Its first three movements – Allegro, Scherzo, Adagio sostenuto – are each self-contained and in classical forms. It is, however, far longer than any other sonata by Beethoven or, indeed, any of his contemporaries. And it is difficult music, to play and to understand. The finale, a huge fugue with introduction, marks the start of a preoccupation with counterpoint – the archaic practice of weaving together independent melodies according to certain formal principles – that Beethoven would explore further in subsequent works such as the *Missa solemnis* and the 'Grosse Fuge'.

As already touched on with regard to the use of register, this is extreme music. It depends on stark contrasts. At the end of the Scherzo, the final two chords that punctuate the main theme

start to take over, alternating between being high, loud and on a
B flat and being lower, softer and on a B natural. It is, as always,
the quiet ones that need to be watched; the B natural is far
removed from the home key and threatens to take over as it is
repeated and accelerates, becoming ever louder. Beethoven suddenly swerves back to the B flat, though, and the main theme
returns, ending as if it was simply beginning again.

The tension between B flat and B natural is present throughout the sonata. Despite the similarity in their letter names in
English, they are far removed from each other harmonically. As
Beethoven slips between keys, new sonorities come to the fore,
rather like when a kaleidoscope is turned and reveals different
colours. In the development of the first movement, the opening
gesture has been fragmented and bounced around the keyboard;
it rises higher step by step until almost all that is left is the
rhythm. Then an arching melody with triplets running underneath, which was first heard towards the end of the exposition,
re-emerges, clad in fresh harmony: B minor. The melody's
appearance is short-lived, but it plants the seed of an idea that is
picked up later in the sonata. The pitch B and its associated harmonies prepare the ground for the unusually distant key of the
Adagio, Beethoven's only movement in F sharp minor, and for
the harmonic adventures of the finale.

Harmonic relationships can seem overly abstract, but they
undergird the structure of the 'Hammerklavier' in significant
ways and help to explain how what might seem on the surface
to be disjointed ideas have connecting threads between them.
The pianist and writer Charles Rosen argued that the melodic
and harmonic structure of the whole sonata is governed by a
falling third. The last two notes of the opening, fanfare-like
motto are a falling third; the Scherzo's first theme constantly
hops down by thirds; the Adagio's main melody sinks by thirds;
finally, the moments when the scurrying fugal theme stops are

drops of a third.[12] On a bigger scale, the main harmonic relationships in the first movement are by third: the first subject is in
B flat major, the second in G. The B flat tonality of the second
movement is related by third to the F sharp minor of the next
movement. And so on. It is questionable, though, whether Beethoven thought those kinds of links were so precious. He asked
Ries to arrange for the 'Hammerklavier' to be published in London simultaneously with its publication by Matthias Artaria in
Vienna. Perhaps in order to expedite the process, he authorized
Ries to present the sonata in one of three ways. He would sanc-
tion omitting the Largo and beginning with the Fugue; or,
giving the first movement, then the Adagio, and then the
Scherzo; or, just taking the first movement and the Scherzo.
Such extreme laxity seems a little out of character, but Beethoven was strapped for cash. Karl's school fees were a significant
expense and the financial situation generally was dire. Even
Archduke Rudolph, his most regular benefactor, could not help
him out. In the end, after much back and forth about corrections
that needed to be made to the proofs (Beethoven apologized that
his loyal copyist, Wenzel Schlemmer, was getting old), the
Viennese edition appeared first. The London version divided
what it describes as the 'Grand Sonata': Part I consisted of the
first three movements, with second and third in reverse order;
Part II was entitled 'Introduction and Fugue'. There was nothing to say that there was a connection between the two parts,
and they had a different dedication, to Antonie Brentano, who
with her husband had given Beethoven advice and support
throughout the court cases over custody of Karl.

The separation of sonata and fugue in the English edition of
the 'Hammerklavier' foreshadows the publication of the 'Grosse
Fugue' divorced from the String Quartet, op. 130, for which it
was originally the finale, discussed in Chapter 9. The composer's openness to different versions may simply have been

commercially pragmatic, as suggested above, or implies that at the time what constituted the final work was not necessarily fixed in the same way that we assume it to be today. As well as the alternative orders Beethoven proposed for the 'Hammerklavier', Ries received a last-minute request from the composer to insert two extra chords at the start of the slow movement; a rising third that introduces the falling third which opens the main theme. Ries admitted that he 'began to wonder if my dear old teacher had really gone daft', as gossip suggested. But the change was made. The two simple chords, if played, as marked, *una corda*, open up the sonority of the instrument, providing a cloud on which the melody can float, divinely.

Unusually, Beethoven didn't use sketchbooks to work on the 'Hammerklavier' but loose leaves that nonetheless, when gathered together, demonstrate how carefully he structured his musical thoughts. Next to some sketches for the finale, he copied out passages from J. S. Bach's *The Art of Fugue* and *Well-Tempered Clavier*, as well as an excerpt from a treatise he had previously used in teaching. He had long held an interest in the intricate music of Bach, whose works were not well known by the public but were valued by aristocratic connoisseurs in Vienna such as Baron van Swieten, whom Beethoven had known for many years. His reference to Bach at this stage of his career seems to emphasize his engagement with abstract musical thought in preference to the world around him. Beethoven, the composer whose theatrical music had been celebrated at the Congress of Vienna just two years earlier, now spent his time alone, working out increasingly elaborate musical puzzles.

Bach was a master of counterpoint, the art of weaving melodic lines together. There were strict rules governing what was considered correct. Fugues are a contrapuntal technique based around imitation. They begin with a subject – one line of melody, referred to as a voice even when played by an instrument – which is then imitated by another voice, the 'answer', starting on a different pitch, in a way that fits together harmonically. A countersubject is added; a melody which complements the subject. And so it goes on, until all the voices have entered. There is then an episode of related but new material before the subject is reintroduced and imitated again, in a different harmonic area. This pattern of fugal entries alternating with episodes can go on indefinitely. Subjects can be turned upside down, reversed, given longer or shorter rhythms or piled on top of each other. There is no set form to a fugue, but the greater the number of voices, the more variations there are and the more adventurous its harmony, the more difficult it is to fit together.

Fugues can seem dry and dusty intellectual exercises, but when handled well they can, as their Latin name *fuga* suggests, take flight. The finale of the 'Hammerklavier' demonstrates Beethoven's virtuosic command of fugal techniques. Unsurprisingly, he was also unafraid to bend the rules. As he acknowledged in the description of the three-voice fugue in the Allegro risoluto, it took some liberties ('Fuga a tre voci, con alcune licenze'). The scurrying subject is unusually long and begins with a leap upwards that perhaps harks back to the opening gesture of the first movement, followed by a trill. All three elements – leap, trill and scurrying – recur in ever more extreme forms, becoming larger, longer and both lower and higher. Beethoven uses dynamics to shift emphasis unexpectedly. There are moments of respite: after a particularly clattering passage of leaps on to trills, a new theme is introduced. Marked 'always sweetly singing' (*sempre dolce cantabile*) and to be played *una corda*, the serene melody looks forward to the 'in nomine Domini' passage of the *Missa solemnis*, which is in the same key of D major. Gradually, the fugal theme encroaches, pulling the music back to B flat and becoming ever more convoluted. The 'Hammerklavier' fugue is noisy and impressive in its scope and scale. It makes a show of the effort involved in its composition and its performance, especially if Beethoven's indication of the speed at which it should be played is taken literally.

The metronome was patented in 1816 by Mälzel, inventor of Beethoven's ear trumpets and the panharmonicon for which *Wellingtons Sieg* was originally commissioned. (As with the panharmonicon, Mälzel based his 'invention' on a similar machine by someone else, in this instance by Dietrich Nikolaus Winkel from Amsterdam that had appeared two years earlier.) Put simply, the device beats out a pulse, the speed of which can be varied. Rather than writing fast or slow, composers could now specify precisely the pace of a piece. Beethoven approved, claiming: 'I have long been thinking of abandoning those absurd descriptive terms, Allegro, Andante, Adagio, Presto; and Maelzel's metronome affords us the best opportunity of doing so. I now give you <u>my word</u> that I shall <u>never again</u> use them in any of my new compositions.'[13] At the end of 1817, the *AmZ* published his metronome markings for all of his extant symphonies and he also provided them for some of his string quartets. On the whole, his metronome markings are thought to be too quick to be practical, and there have been experiments to test the mechanics of his metronome and whether it might have been faulty, none of which have been conclusive. The first movement of the 'Hammerklavier', for instance, was recommended to be taken at 138 beats per minute (in today's electronic dance music, the upper limit for uplifting trance). Mälzel complained that musicians misunderstood the intended purpose of the metronome; it was not a 'Black Forest Clock', to be taken literally, he cautioned, but a way to distinguish what a composer might mean by the same tempo marking: *allegro* in one piece might be slower than in another, and so on.[14] What's more, a movement might not keep strictly to the same tempo throughout, giving heart to those who see the only metronome mark – 144! – for the Allegro risoluto of the 'Hammerklavier' finale.

In a conversation book entry from 1819, Zmeskall told Beethoven that he 'listens to no music apart from op. 106'. The *Wiener Zeitung* followed suit, recognizing that the 'Hammerklavier' signalled 'a new period in Beethoven's keyboard works' not only 'in its richness and greatness of imagination but in its artistic completeness and use of a strict style'.[15] Beethoven was reported to have made various comments around the time of the publication of the 'Hammerklavier' that it was an epochal work. He wrote that in the past 'he did not know how to compose; he knew now' and predicted that it was 'a sonata that will keep the pianists busy when it is played fifty years hence'.[16] He was not far off: there were private performances during the composer's lifetime, by Czerny, Ries and Potter, and the work was championed by Franz Liszt and Ignaz Moscheles in the 1830s.[17] It did not gain a foothold in the piano pantheon, though, until the later nineteenth century and, even then, it was classified as one of the more difficult pieces to conquer.

Despite the acclaim with which Beethoven was heralded by his associates, the works that he produced from 1818 onwards generally were greeted with bafflement, if they were encountered at all. There was no review of the 'Hammerklavier' in the *AmZ*; indeed, that journal, which had always had a complicated relationship with Beethoven, covered very few of his new works from this period. After the composer's death a series of articles evaluating his contribution appeared, none of which were particularly laudatory. The composer's deafness was presented as having prevented him from understanding when he had overstepped the mark, creatively – and probably personally too. 'Ernst Woldemar' condemned Beethoven as having been 'obliged by circumstances to become a composer for the eye' rather than the ear. A work such as the 'Hammerklavier' could only fail in performance because Beethoven had no longer been able to hear its clashes and excesses.

Stylistic turning points are always hard to pinpoint and easy to argue over. Beethoven had declared that he was embarking on a 'new path' in 1803, which has been taken to represent the start of his 'heroic' or 'middle' period; the 'Hammerklavier', recognized by the composer as so challenging it would take decades for performers to master it, then marks the start of his 'late' period. It was only as the decades passed that his more esoteric final works – the piano sonatas and string quartets – began to be re-evaluated. In the process, what had been heard as failures in form and technique began to be appreciated as innovation and even profundity. The 'Hammerklavier' did not become less challenging, but its difficulty became a sign of its greatness. Effort had to be put in not only to play this music but to understand it too. Beethoven's late style, the sense that his music was out of time with its present, made him a prophet of the future. Or, at the very least, of modernist aesthetics, with its privileging of art that is complex, disruptive, and which, on the whole, is appealing to the few, not the many.

While 'late Beethoven' now stands alongside late Rembrandt and late Shakespeare as one of the pinnacles of Western European art, the situation viewed from his own lifetime seemed far messier. Factoring in other aspects of his professional life alongside his compositions illustrates how blurred the boundaries between one stylistic period and another might be. For example, the publishing deal Beethoven struck for the 'Hammerklavier' paired the sonata with the string quintet version of the Piano Trio, op. 1, no. 3, published as his op. 104. The most adventurous number from his first opus thus appeared in what seems now to be the lowly form of an arrangement, alongside his longest and most extreme piano sonata. Indeed, looking at the opus numbers either side of the 'Hammerklavier', there is little sense that he was set on one path: it is flanked by reworked juvenilia and folk songs. His op. 105 was 'Six National Airs with Variations' for flute or violin and piano, and op. 107 was 'Ten National Airs with Variations' for the same instruments; both sets were part of a lucrative deal for arrangements and transcriptions of folk songs made with publisher George Thomson. In the preface to the Quintet, op. 104, Beethoven declared that by reworking an earlier arrangement, by a composer known only as Kaufmann, he had elevated it 'from the greatest wretchedness to some respectability'. Even though the courts stripped him of his pretence to nobility, he clearly had a sense of his own artistic worth. That explains why the 'Hammerklavier' Sonata could appear alongside arrangements in his list of works, and why it would be wrong to label all of his music after a certain date as representing his late style.

Beethoven's attempt to coach his nephew to become a virtuoso pianist came to naught. He had more success with Archduke Rudolph, whom he had taught since 1804. Rudolph was an able musician and became Beethoven's only serious composition student. There were many advantages to Beethoven's friendship with Rudolph: as well as offering financial support several times over – he was the most reliable of the three noblemen who agreed to grant the composer an annuity from 1809 – he had an extensive music library and offered rooms in his palace for rehearsals. He was also genuinely interested in intellectual and cultural pursuits; not something that could be said of all the aristocracy. Rudolph was ordained as a priest and was reputed to be a pleasant and humble man. Beethoven admonished Gleichenstein for missing an opportunity to meet him, because 'you would have met an amiable and talented prince and because you, as the friend of his friend, would not have been made to feel his high rank'.

The *Missa solemnis* was written for Rudolph, who also received from Beethoven the dedications to a dozen major works, including the Fourth and Fifth piano concertos, the Violin Sonata, op. 96, the 'Archduke' Trio, op. 97, the Piano Sonata, op. III, and the 'Grosse Fugue', as well as the 'Hammerklavier' Sonata. There is a sense that Rudolph was always a safe bet for Beethoven when he was unsure who to dedicate a piece to; unlike other members of the nobility, he did not insist on being asked before a piece was dedicated to him and there need not be any particularly personal reason for the use of his name.[18] Nevertheless, Rudolph's presence can be felt a few times in the piece. A sketch for the first movement matched the opening rhythm with the phrase 'Vivat, vivat Rudolphus!', which perhaps was an idea from a cantata in honour of St Rudolph's day that never came to fruition. The fugal finale, like the *Missa solemnis* and the 'Grosse Fugue', might have paid homage to the time the two men had spent together studying counterpoint. But the dedication to Rudolph also signalled an absence at the heart of the 'Hammerklavier' Sonata. Although he was eighteen years Beethoven's junior, so not yet thirty, gout and rheumatism prohibited him from continuing to perform on the piano. Beethoven's impossible piece was thus in honour of a man who no longer could even attempt to play it. The 'Hammerklavier' has been noted as the piece that went beyond the capabilities of amateur musicians; some would say that few professionals really conquer it.[19] The composer had abandoned responsibility to produce music that anyone could truly hear.

8.   Spirit: *Missa solemnis*, op. 123 (1823)

Beethoven was late. He had begun work on a Mass for the installation of Archduke Rudolph as Bishop of Olmütz when news of his election was announced in March 1819 but had not managed to complete the score by the official ceremony a year later. Instead, music by Hummel, Josef Preindl and Haydn was used. There were several reasons for the delay. Ambition was one: it was to be a grand work. In his letter congratulating Rudolph on his elevation, Beethoven declared:

> The day on which a High Mass composed by me will be performed during the ceremonies solemnized for Your Imperial Highness will be the most glorious day of my life; and God will enlighten me so that my poor talents may contribute to the glorification of that solemn day.[1]

This was not just the usual fawning. Given the archduke's long-term support – he was the only patron supplying his annual stipend still alive – Beethoven might still have hoped to be appointed as his Kapellmeister.[2] The composer remained resistant to kowtowing to nobility. 'I never was, still am not, and never will be, a courtier,' he reminded the archduke in the same letter. Yet a steady salary in the musically active Moravian town of Olmütz (now Olomouc in the Czech Republic), just over a hundred miles from Vienna, must have appealed to the composer. His health was poor and he was in the midst of the court battles over the custody of his nephew Karl. Perhaps he hoped that a suitably impressive Mass would seal the deal.

Beethoven was 'late' in other ways too. He enclosed in his

letter some of his recent pieces, including the first two movements of the 'Hammerklavier' Sonata, which would be dedicated to Rudolph. Just as that piece took him an unprecedentedly long time to complete, so did his Mass. Although it has the same layout, it is twice the length of his earlier Mass in C. The music of the *Missa solemnis* may not bear the hallmarks of Beethoven's late style in the same way as do the piano sonatas and string quartets from this period; it subscribes to convention far more than might be expected. However, much as the 'Hammerklavier' exceeded the scale and scope of the sonata, the *Missa solemnis* became so large and complex that it was unsuitable for liturgical use by the time it was finally completed in 1823.

Strictly speaking, a *Missa solemnis* ('solemn Mass') should set all parts of the Mass service, which remembers Jesus's life, the Last Supper and the Crucifixion. The two parts of the Mass are called the Proper and the Ordinary. By the late eighteenth century, it had become common for composers to set only the five sections of the Ordinary but to have more elaborate musical ambitions; something that Beethoven's *Missa solemnis*, with its extended length and large forces, certainly fulfilled. E. T. A Hoffmann explained the Ordinary as 'a guide to devotion':

> In the *Kyrie* God's mercy is invoked; the *Gloria* praises his omnipotence and splendour; the *Credo* expresses the faith that gives the pious soul its firm foundation; in the *Sanctus* and *Benedictus* God's holiness is praised and blessing promised to those who place their full trust in him; and then in the *Agnus Dei* and in the *Dona nobis pacem* the Saviour is implored to grant comfort and peace to the pious, believing, hoping soul.[3]

Beethoven followed the established scheme but took care to understand the nuances of the Mass. He copied out the Latin in full, marking where accents should fall and making a line-by-line German translation with the help of a dictionary. He noted subtle differences between words; for example, between *terra* ('earth') and *mundus* ('the world'). He also made small changes to the text which had implications for his musical setting and for the interpretation of his beliefs. A tiny insertion, which has been taken to indicate the composer's personal investment in the project, is an exclamation, 'o', before the final repetitions of 'miserere nobis' ('have mercy on us') in the Gloria.

Traces of the original impetus behind the composition of the *Missa solemnis* – Archduke Rudolph's installation – might be found in an inscription at the head of the autograph manuscript: 'From the heart – may it again – go to the heart' ('Von Herzen – möge es wieder – zu Herzen gehen!'). The same words were written on a page of sketches for the Gloria. There might be some musical allusions to works dedicated to Rudolph in the score as well.[4] Whether the idea of communicating 'heart to heart' related directly to Rudolph or was a more general statement of intent, though, has been debated. E. T. A. Hoffmann had used a similar phrase in his review of the Fifth Symphony, which states that 'A deeper relationship . . . is often communicated from the heart to the heart.' Read in the context of the symphony, Hoffmann is referring specifically to thematic connections between movements; he might further be suggesting something about the ability of instrumental music to mean more than words. Read in the context of the *Missa solemnis* and its associated religious service, the profound communication seems to be with higher powers. Beethoven's own spirituality, however, was not straightforward and, as much as it can be known, seems caught between Enlightenment humanism and Romantic mysticism.

Beethoven had been raised Catholic and, as an organist in Bonn, would have played regularly at church services. Despite his salutations to the Almighty in letters and diaries, he was not a regular churchgoer as an adult. His diaries and conversations, however, reveal that he was very interested in other cultures, religions and philosophies.[5] Notes in the *Tagebuch* remark on the ancient age of Indian temples ('Nine thousand years!'), their musical scales, tribal polyandry and greater profundities: 'Five years of silence is required of future Brahmans . . . For God, time absolutely does not exist.' Beethoven read translations and interpretations of Hindu scripture – the *Rigveda* and the *Bhagavad Gita* – and *A Code of Gentoo Laws*, which had become popular around Europe as it attempted to understand the mind-set of its Asian colonies. Buddhism also intrigued him. Beethoven was not alone in these interests: from his Illuminati contacts in Bonn, fascinated by ancient Egypt, to writers he admired such as Friedrich Schiller, Enlightenment thinkers avidly explored what could be learned from non-Western religions. While it is difficult to decipher a coherent set of beliefs from the quotations and comments that pepper Beethoven's correspondence, they reveal a more contemplative side to the composer, willing to question dogma and explore alternatives but maintaining a core belief in his own, individually forged relationship with God.

During the year he began work on the *Missa solemnis* Beethoven was in touch with Bavarian orator and theologian Johann Michael Sailer, as were his friends the Brentanos, who had recommended the ex-Jesuit as a potential teacher for Karl. Sailer emphasized the importance of an individual believer's interior experience, defining three forms of religious observance: mechanical and literal; scholastic and conceptual; and, most significant, personal and subjective. Sailer's privileging of the individual's relationship with God was attacked by the Austrian Catholic hierarchy, making him one of several anti-establishment figures in whom Beethoven was interested (others included Redemptorist priest Clemens Maria Hofbauer of the Liguorians and playwright and poet Zacharias Werner). It was a risk, in the Metternich era, to be aligned with such subversive authors. Beethoven rarely held back in expressing his views and was probably saved from police censure by his status. The difficulty of pinning down music's meaning might have helped too. 'Does the censor know what you think while you are composing?' asked the poet and playwright Franz Grillparzer in a conversation book entry. There is no record of Beethoven's response, but it's nice to imagine he might have hummed a nonchalant little tune.

Beethoven's reading around religious topics was matched by an exploration of musical models for the Mass. Contemporary commentators debated the future of Catholic church music, which, according to Hoffmann and others, had become 'insipid and undignified' in the eighteenth century, in comparison to the 'lofty simplicity and dignity' of earlier composers such as Palestrina.[6] Beethoven did not refer as far back as the sixteenth century while working on the *Missa solemnis*, but he did expand his knowledge of the repertoire beyond his familiarity with the Masses of Haydn and Mozart, exploring the music of J. S. Bach, Handel, and copying out parts of Mozart's *Requiem*. There were increasing numbers of Bach and Handel enthusiasts in Vienna, since Baron Gottfried van Swieten had first introduced Mozart – and later Beethoven – to Bach's fugues and founded the Society of Cavaliers, dedicated to performances of Handel's oratorios. Beethoven had borrowed a score of *Messiah* for one of his singing parties in 1809 and in the next decade there were prominent public performances of other Handel oratorios by the Gesellschaft der Musikfreunde (Society of the Friends of Music), including a seven-hundred-strong production of *Samson* during the Congress of Vienna. Bach's music remained more of a minority interest, although there were efforts to publish and perform more of his choral music in Berlin, which, by the end of the 1820s, would result in the 'rediscovery' of the *St Matthew Passion*.[7] An edition of the B minor Mass was rumoured to be underway in 1818 and Beethoven tried to get hold of a score from Breitkopf, explaining with his usual punning charm that he had seen its Crucifixus 'with a basso ostinato as obstinate as you are'. (A *basso ostinato* is a bass line that is repeated over and over.) As with the 'Hammerklavier' Sonata and other works from this period, it was Bach's mastery of counterpoint that attracted Beethoven's attention.

The *Missa solemnis* is full of fugues, as is convention. Convention did not dictate, however, their ubiquity, elaborate architecture and massive length; that was all Beethoven. Along similar lines, the score is replete with routine associations between words and instruments: for example, in the Credo, the trombones symbolize divine power at the word *judicare* ('to judge'), while the flute's trills on reference to the Holy Spirit were recognized as the fluttering wings of the dove, messenger from Heaven.[8] The orchestration is sometimes more inventive and dramatic than is expected for a Mass. The jubilant Sanctus ends, literally, on a high, and then the music sinks straight down to a sparse, slow-moving Praeludium played by the lower strings, woodwind and organ. From above, a solo violin enters, initially accompanied only by flutes. Against the dull backdrop, it is like a shaft of light, announcing the presence of Christ on the altar in the Benedictus. While it was common to use solo instruments for extra colour, and the Benedictus was usually fairly extended in the Austrian tradition, its expansiveness here, and the prominent role given to the violin, which plays nearly continuously throughout the rest of the movement, was unprecedented.

A more dramatic interjection occurs in the Agnus Dei. Despite the music's length, the text is brief: 'Agnus Dei, qui tollis peccata mundi, miserere nobis. Dona nobis pacem' ('Lamb of

God, who takes away the sins of the world, have mercy upon us. Give us peace'). The 'Dona nobis pacem' section is marked as a 'Prayer for inward and outward peace' (*Bitte um innern und äußern Frieden*) and begins gently. It is suddenly interrupted by a solo timpanist, who is soon joined by the trumpets – instruments that wrench the harmony to their own key. War threatens the sense of equilibrium. There are drum rolls, shaking strings, and alarm calls from the woodwind, above which the vocal soloists are directed to anxiously (*ängstlich*) reiterate, in recitative, their prayer to the Lamb of God. It is a moment comparable to the jaunty entry of the tenor soloist in the Ninth Symphony, attempting to alter the course of proceedings. Whereas there the music shifts gear into the 'Ode to Joy', in the *Missa solemnis* peace is gradually restored. The final fugue draws everything to a tranquil close.

Despite Beethoven's attention to the meaning of the liturgy, he also broke up the text into individual words. Their repetition served to unify and characterize sections in a musical fashion. Mass and symphonic forms seemed in this way to be brought closer together. Hoffmann had criticized Haydn's *Creation* for treating the voice too much like an instrument, a criticism that would also be levelled at Beethoven's vocal writing. He not only fragmented the text into single words; especially when composing fugues, he would set one syllable to several notes (known as 'melisma'). This can be heard clearly in the opening Kyrie, where the word *eleison* ('have mercy') is stretched out, imploringly. Musical emphasis such as this to some ears risked introducing too much of the opera house into a work for the Church. To others, it indicated Beethoven's emotional investment, his subjective response 'from heart to heart'. As he completed the score of the *Missa solemnis*, Beethoven wrote to the journalist and librettist Joseph Karl Bernard, 'God *never* left me in this difficult task, I also trust in Him further' ('Gott hat mich *nie* verlaßen in dieser Schweren Aufgabe, ich vertraue auch ferner auf ihn').[9] He subsequently declared it to be his best work. It was a struggle, though, to persuade his contemporaries to perform the complete *Missa solemnis* and, while venerated today, it is not heard often: its scale and solemnity continue to overawe.

Beethoven had not participated in any public concerts in Vienna since 1819 and there seemed, through these years, to be a ring of silence around him. His personal situation is often blamed for his detachment from society. He was deaf, short-sighted and often seriously unwell. Several of his aristocratic supporters had succumbed to death or bankruptcy. He had been revealed through the courts not to be the nobleman everybody had assumed him to be. At the same time, there was a sense that Vienna generally had hunkered down. Metternich's regime following the Congress of Vienna was repressive; censorship and surveillance became the norm, and public life, including the free exchange of ideas in salons, was perilous. Everybody kept a low profile.

The outside world may have heard little from Beethoven, but he was not completely cut off from it. He continued to depend on a close circle of friends and associates, which during this period included the aforementioned Bernard, Karl's piano teacher Joseph Czerny, printer and publisher Tobias Haslinger, composer and writer Friedrich August Kanne (who, incidentally, wrote a history of the Mass), and his long-time copyist Wenzel Schlemmer. Law clerk, violinist and future biographer Anton Schindler became the latest of his unpaid assistants in 1822. Beethoven's routine continued much as usual: he rose early, had his coffee, then composed all morning before lunch at midday. A long walk, sketchbook to hand, took most of the afternoon, after which he might visit a tavern or coffeehouse to read the newspaper. He would have a simple supper at home and be in bed by 10 p.m.

Beethoven was far from inactive, as is evident from his work on the *Missa solemnis*, a further three piano sonatas and other pieces, and commissions he accepted for symphonies, quartets, an opera and an oratorio; the last two projects, he never delivered. He also continued to be a wily negotiator with publishers. In fact, with the *Missa solemnis*, he almost outdid himself. Beethoven had already approached his old friend from Bonn, Nikolaus Simrock, about publishing the as yet unfinished score in March 1820. They agreed a generous fee (100 louis d'or), which was sent in advance. On an enquiry from the Berlin publisher Schlesinger, Beethoven then sold the score again, for the same price. Six months later, he accepted a still more substantial fee for the exclusive rights from a third firm, Carl Friedrich Peters in Leipzig. In Vienna, Steiner was approached, but he was wary of taking on such a large work, especially as he and Beethoven had fallen out over, on the composer's side, long-term debts and, on Steiner's, delayed publications. At a trade fair in Leipzig, Steiner compared notes with Peters, who also discovered that Schlesinger had been offered the Mass. Beethoven denied double-dealing. Brazenly, even for him, he went on to approach the firms of Artaria and of Diabelli in Vienna, and Probst in Leipzig, and eventually signed with Schott in Mainz, who published the full and vocal scores in the spring of 1827, shortly after the composer's death.

Meanwhile, Beethoven invited European heads of state, directors of choral societies and prominent artists (Goethe, Cherubini) to subscribe to receive a handwritten copy of the Mass. Ten invitations were accepted – among them Archduke Rudolph, inevitably, as well as Louis XVIII of France and King Frederick VI of Denmark – and copies were sent out in 1823. At a fee of 50 ducats per copy, Beethoven would have made a tidy sum; he declined the Prussian court's offer of a decoration in lieu, which, according to Schindler, was a sign of his disdain for honours but perhaps is better read as his need for cash. There were further advantages to the scheme. One subscriber, Prince Galitzin, who commissioned the string quartet discussed in the next chapter, organized a performance of the *Missa solemnis* at a benefit concert by the St Petersburg Philharmonic Society. However, the music did not arrive until the month before the concert and the difficulty of the vocal parts was such that it had to be postponed several times, until the premiere finally took place on 7 April 1824. It was advertised as a new work by the 'immortal Beethoven' – that word, 'immortal', again being hung on him while he was still alive. Despite its liturgical origins, the *Missa solemnis* was billed as an oratorio – a choral work that could be performed in the concert hall – destined to attract a 'large and brilliant audience'. As soon as Beethoven had missed the deadline for Rudolph's ceremony, and perhaps even before then, he had begun to market the *Missa solemnis* for secular rather than sacred contexts. In his article on church music, Hoffmann had expressed qualms about presenting Masses in concert because it confused the religious purpose of a piece with the secular associations of the space in which it was heard.

Beethoven had several supporters in Russia, having built up relationships through the dedication of works to members of the royal family.[10] The pianist Wenzel Wilhelm Würfel told Beethoven, presumably with some creative licence, that he had played all of his sonatas to an audience of four thousand people in St Petersburg.[11] Count Razumovsky had sponsored various projects until his bankruptcy following the destruction of his palace during the Congress of Vienna, which also caused the departure for Russia of another important Beethoven collaborator, the violinist Ignaz Schuppanzigh. It might well have seemed to Beethoven that there was a more sympathetic audience for his music abroad than at home. Schuppanzigh had, though, recently returned to Vienna, participating in concerts of Beethoven's music and helping to kick-start a new phase of quartet composition.

Beethoven did not attend the St Petersburg concert of the *Missa solemnis*, which afterwards was lauded as an 'original, sublime masterpiece' in the *Allgemeine musikalische Zeitung*.[12] Prince Galitzin reported back that he had 'never heard anything so sublime . . . The entire work is a treasure of beauty; one can say that your genius has outdistanced the centuries and that, perhaps, there are no listeners sufficiently enlightened to understand the beauty of this music in its entirety. But posterity will render homage to you and will bless your memory, far better than your contemporaries.' Reassuring comments that Beethoven's time would come were common refrains among the composer's admirers.

The complete *Missa solemnis* was never performed in Vienna during Beethoven's lifetime. He had been commissioned by the Gesellschaft der Musikfreunde to compose an oratorio and pocketed the commission, but he rejected the proposed libretto, and no new work emerged. In its place he suggested that they might take on the *Missa solemnis*. After all, he explained, he had really intended the piece for them, and he would be keen to serve the society. His request for a complete performance was refused because costs would be too high and profits too uncertain. In the end, three movements – the Kyrie, Credo and Agnus Dei – were performed at the same concert as the premiere of the Ninth Symphony on 7 May 1824, with which the Society of the Friends of Music were involved.

That was not, though, the first time any of the *Missa solemnis* was heard in Vienna. The Kyrie and Gloria had already featured in the opening concert of the 1821–2 season of the Concerts Spirituels. This was a series organized by one of Beethoven's associates, director of music at the Augustinerkirche (Augustinian Church), Franz Xaver Gebauer. Gebauer, like many of the composer's friends, was the butt of constant puns – most often

'Geh, Bauer' ('Go, peasant') – but that seems not to have deterred him from frequently programming Beethoven's music at the concerts. They took place in the late afternoon and presented sacred music alongside orchestral works; there was much Haydn and Mozart, and all of Beethoven's extant symphonies were played, as well as his Mass in C and *Christus am Ölberge*. As Gebauer explained to Beethoven during a visit in March 1820, recorded in a conversation book, they were 'practice concerts'; run-throughs, rather than polished performances. Gebauer offered to organize a concert of Beethoven's music, saying that people were keen to hear his new pieces. In some ways, the set-up harked back to the opportunities he had been offered earlier in his career, by Prince Lobkowitz and Archduke Rudolph, to try out symphonies in their palaces before their public premieres. This time, though, the new work in the concert attracted the attention of the Vienna *Allgemeine musikalische Zeitung*, a journal founded in 1817 and keen to promote Beethoven's music – unlike its Leipzig namesake. 'The imposing, fantastic compositional power of this master emerges from the deeply felt harmonious choruses,' the reviewer wrote. 'If Beethoven's daring genius occasionally presents its images in too sharp a light, or if some of the features are too strongly characterized, then he repeatedly shows the ability to appease the excited mood of the listener.'[13] The emphasis here on feeling and adventure provides a way of appreciating Beethoven's music even at its most 'daring', a ploy that would be used repeatedly by his supporters to convince detractors of its merits.

Gebauer's death in December 1822 caused a hiatus in the activities of the Concerts Spirituels, which might otherwise have provided Beethoven with further opportunities to try out movements from the *Missa solemnis*. When the Kyrie, Credo, and Agnus Dei appeared on the programme in May 1824, they were listed as 'grand hymns' because, as with the Mass in C almost two decades earlier, liturgical music was not supposed to be performed in the concert hall. To fully pull the wool over the censors' eyes, they were sung in German rather than Latin. The rest of the concert included another fugue-dominated work, the overture to *The Consecration of the House* (*Die Weihe des Hauses*), op. 124, which had been composed for the opening of the Theater in der Josefstadt eighteen months earlier.[14] The other, now much more famous, piece on the programme was Beethoven's last completed symphony, his Ninth.

Of all Beethoven's works, the Ninth Symphony has come to symbolize the composer's isolation from the world through his deafness. The story of how he had to be turned to see the audience's noisy appreciation has been fodder for biographers, novelists, illustrators and film-makers (fig. 8.1). Nonetheless, the story continues, Beethoven's music has been able to speak to

Fig. 8.1 A nineteenth-century illustration of Beethoven at the premiere of the Ninth Symphony.

the hearts of millions, especially in the choral finale, the 'Ode to Joy'. While this chapter is not about the Ninth Symphony, it deserves a digression in part to show how, despite its subsequent reputation, its success was not as immediate as might now be expected and that it depended as much on the people around Beethoven as on his musical genius.

The Ninth Symphony had an even lengthier gestation than the *Missa solemnis*. Beethoven had contemplated composing a D minor symphony to follow the Seventh and Eighth symphonies back in 1812, an idea he returned to several times over the following decade. First thoughts for the striking opening of what became the Ninth Symphony were sketched in the winter of 1815–1816, but work began in earnest at the end of 1822. In July that year, Beethoven had written to Ferdinand Ries in London, asking if the Philharmonic Society would be interested in commissioning a 'grand symphony' for its concert series. A fee of £50 was agreed. Although he had often been invited to London and enjoyed receiving visitors – and of course a Broadwood piano – from there, Beethoven never visited the city; but, then, he did not travel widely. His reputation in the British capital instead had been fostered by musicians who had known him in Vienna, much as had been the case in St Petersburg. In the end, the premiere was not given to the Philharmonic Society – in fact, with some justified disgruntlement, they received the score only some six months after it had been performed in Vienna. The Austrians' determination to secure the Ninth Symphony reveals how cleverly they – and Beethoven, it has to be said – used music as a political tool.

The first three movements of the Ninth Symphony follow something like the usual pattern: an Allegro and then, as he had in the 'Hammerklavier' Sonata and elsewhere, Beethoven swapped the order of the Scherzo and Adagio. Each movement is large and harmonically rich, inventive but scaffolded by traditional forms. With the finale, though, Beethoven broke new ground. He explained to the publishers that he had done something similar to his Choral Fantasy, the hybrid work discussed in Chapter 4, on a grander scale. Initially, the finale cycles through music from the previous movements, each being rejected in turn by instrumental recitatives. Proceedings are interrupted by a solo baritone: 'Oh friends! Not these sounds!' Something more joyous is in order. Here, finally, Beethoven found a place for his long-held plan to set Schiller's 'Ode to Joy' to music.

The origins of the Ninth Symphony thus extend back to the revolutionary era. Beethoven had first toyed with the idea of setting the 'Ode to Joy' in 1793 – a mutual acquaintance told Schiller's wife that he expected 'something perfect, for as far as I know him he is wholly devoted to the great and the sublime'[15] – and made sketches for a setting of the first chorus, 'Muss ein lieber Vater wohnen' ('A dear father must reside') five years later. Schiller revised his 1785 original in 1803, toning down some of its revolutionary fervour in his horror at the execution of Louis XVI and the atrocities of the Terror. The line 'Beggars shall become brothers of Princes' ('Bettler werden Fürstenbrüder') thus became 'All men shall be brothers' ('Alle Menschen werden Brüder') and a final verse hailing 'Salvation from the chains of tyrants' ('Rettung von Tyrannenketten') was dropped. Beethoven knew both versions. He returned to the opening of Schiller's poem in 1812, when as mentioned he contemplated composing a D minor symphony to follow the Seventh and Eighth symphonies, an idea that he returned to several times before embarking on his Ninth Symphony in the early 1820s. Then he worked and reworked the tune to make it seem as artless and singable as possible and freely adapted the 1803 version of Schiller's poem, selecting and reordering a handful of verses and adding his own recitatives. The ode's exhortations in celebration of the spirit of enlightened brotherhood belonged, it might then be argued, to an earlier age. To many Viennese, by this stage of his career, Beethoven seemed out of time.

In November 1823, a portrait of the composer in the popular and influential German arts magazine *Morning Paper for the Educated Classes* (*Morgenblatt für gebildete Stände*) – a title that reveals all you need to know about cultural hierarchies of the time – positioned Beethoven within the world:

> Ludwig von Beethoven belongs among those men whom not only Vienna and Germany, but Europe and our entire age revere. With Mozart and Haydn he makes up the unequalled triumvirate of more recent music. The ingenious depth, the constant originality, the ideal in his compositions that flows from a great soul assures him, despite Italian clangour and modern charlatanism, of the recognition of every true admirer of the divine Polyhymnia.[16]

The aside acknowledging the challenge to Beethoven's German muse (the use of von rather than van was perhaps not accidental) of 'Italian clangour and modern charlatanism' captures the frictions within 1820s Vienna. Dance music was exceptionally popular, with waltzes by Joseph Lanner and Johann Strauss I filling cafés, carnivals and ballrooms. Rossini fever was rife, with Italian opera dominating the city's theatres and street barrel organs. Choral music was also significant, as indicated by series such as the Concerts Spirituels, which had run through some movements of the *Missa solemnis*, and by the activities of the Society of the Friends of Music and the *tableaux vivants* performances held by the Society of Noble Ladies. These last two societies were dedicated to the cultivation and preservation of Austrian musical culture, projects that were both charitable and patriotic. In this they were comparable to national museums and libraries founded during the era to memorialize the multifaceted achievements of the Habsburg Empire. Founder members of the Gesellschaft der Musikfreunde Moritz Dietrichstein and Joseph Sonnleithner, both well known to Beethoven (the latter was the librettist for the 1805 *Fidelio*), were heavily involved in the societies' benefit concerts of choral works. Handel and Haydn featured strongly on their programmes, as did Beethoven's *Christus am Ölberge* and *Der glorreiche Augenblick*, celebrating victory over Napoleon. Indeed, Beethoven's music was heard fairly frequently in Vienna: his quartets, orchestral and choral music appeared in various concert series.

Nonetheless, amid all the other musical activities taking place, Beethoven felt undervalued. He declared that he was disinclined to premiere his new symphony in Vienna, preferring to explore instead his options in Berlin. Two local journals published a letter, signed by prominent musicians and patrons, petitioning him to reconsider. Allusion was made to both the *Missa solemnis* and the Ninth Symphony:

> We know that a grand sacred composition has joined the first one in which you immortalised the emotions of the soul, penetrated and transfigured by the power of faith and super-terrestrial light. We know that a new flower grows in the garland of your glorious, still unequalled symphonies.

They pleaded with him to retain the 'honour of the German muse' against the foreign invader.[17] 'Appear soon among your friends, your admirers, your venerators!' It was a ruse designed to play on his patriotism and vanity that also echoed the campaign to keep him in Vienna when he had considered taking the post in Westphalia back in 1809. It worked. An unofficial committee, of Schindler, Count Moritz Lichnowsky, Schuppanzigh and Beethoven, assisted by Karl, was set up to organize two concerts, the first at the Kärntnertortheater on 7 May and the second, a fortnight later on 23 May, at the Redoutensaal. The musicians would be the same for both: the theatre's regular orchestra and chorus, supplemented by members of the Society of the Friends of Music.

There were two full rehearsals as well as sectional rehearsals for the strings and separate sessions for the chorus. At Beethoven's insistence, Schuppanzigh led the orchestra. The conductor Michael Umlauf, and Beethoven, despite his by then profound deafness, coached the vocal soloists; the composer resisted the singers' pleas to eliminate some of the highest notes. The music seemed to have remained beyond the ken of many: Leopold Sonnleithner, younger brother of Joseph, who was also a lawyer and heavily involved in the Gesellschaft der Musikfreunde, recalled that 'The double-bass players had not the faintest idea what they were supposed to do,' while reviewer Friedrich Kanne noted that weaker violinists simply stopped playing in the more difficult passages. It was reported that some people in the theatre left before the end, but many acknowledged the 'jubilant and heart-felt applause' that broke out, during and after the performance. Beethoven was standing at Umlauf's side, doing his usual interpretative gestures. It may have been during the Scherzo – when the entry of the timpani was apparently greeted with spontaneous applause – that contralto soloist Caroline Unger turned the composer's attention to the audience so that he could see their enthusiastic reaction.

A critic for the *Theater-Zeitung* observed that 'instrumental music is no longer sufficient for the deeply moved artist. He needs to take the word, the human voice, to aid him so that he may express himself adequately. How will he express himself? What shall be his songs? What else but a song of Joy!'[18] Kanne took a similar stance: the world of the symphony was too small to contain all of Beethoven's inspiration; what might seem like random diversity was in fact tightly controlled. Amid the handkerchief-waving ovations and excited reviews, a note of doubt was sounded. Not all were convinced. The finale's recourse to words was thought to show the limits of instrumental music rather than serve as its enhancement. Many found the return of music from previous movements, and the juxtaposed sections of the finale, too chaotic to be comprehensible. On the first performance of the Ninth Symphony in London (when the 'Ode to Joy' was sung in Italian), the *Quarterly Musical Magazine* predicted that the need to engage a chorus and the extra rehearsals required 'may perhaps forbid its ever being done again'. Beethoven himself had qualms about the finale's effectiveness. According to Carl Czerny and Leopold von Sonnleithner, he realized that he had committed a 'blunder' ('Mißgriff') and considered replacing it with an instrumental movement.[19] Critic Ignaz von Seyfried – in an otherwise laudatory review – proposed that like the Quartet, op. 130, there could be two finales, one choral and one instrumental. Although the score was submitted complete to Schott for publication in January 1825, over the next few decades the Ninth was often performed without the 'Ode to Joy'.

The concert of 24 May 1824 had been advertised as a 'celebration among friends of German music': 'France and England will envy us the opportunity of making personal homage to Beethoven, who is acknowledged to be the supreme composer in the entire world.' Afterwards, it was heralded by the journal *Cäcilia* as one of the most important dates in the history of music since the sixteenth century.[20] The *Wiener Allgemeine musikalische Zeitung* published a new engraving of Beethoven and devoted three successive issues to discussion of the concerts. Emphasis was placed on Beethoven as representative of a great musical tradition, standing shoulder to shoulder with Mozart and Haydn.

Through all this hullabaloo, it was not only Beethoven's image at stake. Vienna was curating its own history. On the one hand, this was a commercial venture: *Cäcilia* was the house magazine of the publishers Schott, who published the score of the Ninth Symphony, the *Missa solemnis* and the late quartets. Founded in 1824, the same year as many of these works were premiered, they had a vested interest in the composer; although it should be remembered that other journals, with similar publisher tie-ins, did not necessarily reflect their backers' interests. Leipzig's *Allgemeine musikalische Zeitung*, for instance, was owned by Breitkopf und Härtel; but then, although it reported that concerts of Beethoven's music had happened, it did not review any of his substantial new pieces in the 1820s. The *Wiener Allgemeine musikalische Zeitung*, launched in 1818, compensated for their oversight. It included among its editors two of Beethoven's friends, Kanne and Seyfried. Again, they were not unequivocal in their praise. However, it is clear that the journal's promotion of Beethoven was a self-conscious riposte to the Italian operatic invasion: the Rossini aria included – and applauded – in the second performance of the Ninth Symphony was not mentioned in the press.[21] More broadly, the intellectual and aristocratic circles that had supported the composer and his style of music were ever diminishing. They had been politically and financially weakened by the Napoleonic Wars and their aftermath. They were also threatened socially by the rapidly rising middle classes as well as by the growing, ethnically diverse population extending the city's suburbs. The way in which Beethoven was referred to in correspondence and in the press – 'genius', 'immortal', the creator of 'masterworks', equal of Mozart and Haydn – implied that he already belonged to history, with a capital H. Nobody was going to reveal that the concert was not a financial success: Beethoven had hired the hall, orchestra, chorus and lighting for 400 florins and his request to charge extra for tickets was refused, leaving him with little, if any, profit.

The reference to 'friends of German music' in the concert's

advert illustrates the patriotic urge; although, of course, Austrian identity was distinct from that of the German Confederation. Beethoven, born and raised in Bonn but a lifelong resident in Vienna, straddled both. He served as a symbol of Viennese musical supremacy in an international market – the city would be the envy of France and England – which was stealthily being extended to cover the whole German-speaking world. Beethoven may have preferred the empire of the mind; his compatriots envisioned an empire of music.

Perhaps surprisingly, given its use of the Latin liturgy, the *Missa solemnis* was also caught up in the nation-building project. In April 1828, Italian-born composer and director of the Berlin Opera, Gaspare Spontini, put together a concert programme that included Beethoven's *Coriolan* Overture, Fifth Symphony and the Kyrie and Gloria from the *Missa solemnis*, alongside six parts of the Credo from Bach's B minor Mass and a Sanctus by C. P. E. Bach.[22] Critics noted, disapprovingly, that in so doing he had assembled almost a full Mass within the hybrid programme. More than that, by placing Bach and Beethoven side by side he had presented a concert of great German music, secular and sacred. Since Beethoven's death the previous year, the works were now past masterpieces, around which a musical museum was being made.

9.   Endings: String Quartet, op. 130, and the 'Grosse Fuge', op. 133 (1826)

One August afternoon in 1825, a twelve-year-old boy and his father notice on the streets of Vienna:

> a man walking alone, heading straight towards us . . . He was powerful looking, of medium height, vigorous in his gait and in his lively movements, his clothing far from elegant or conventional; and there was something about him overall that did not fit into any classification . . . He spoke almost without pause, asking how we were . . . My father seldom got a chance to put a word in.[1]

Gerhard von Breuning's recollection of Beethoven limns a familiar image of the unkempt composer on his daily walk. Details can be added from other memoirs: grey hair flew out from underneath his battered hat, which was worn tipped back on his head; his coat was heavily loaded, a handkerchief spilling out from one pocket, while notebooks for musical ideas and conversation, and a thick carpenter's pencil, stretched the seams of another.[2] While many artists drew Beethoven – more often from their imaginations than from an actual encounter – perhaps the most striking aspect of Gerhard von Breuning's account is Beethoven's talkativeness. Granted, his father, Stephan, was a childhood friend, and there seems to have been a rush of excitement for Beethoven as he announced that he would be moving to the same neighbourhood as the von Breuning family. Other memoirs also attest to the composer's sometimes overwhelming

Fig. 9.1 A sketch of Beethoven by Johann Peter Theodor Lyser, originally published in the journal *Cäcilia* in 1833 with the caption: 'Drawn truthfully on the spot as in the last years of his life, he jumped and ran rather than walked through the streets of Vienna.' Although Lyser produced several sketches of Beethoven, it seems he did not visit Vienna until 1845, so they must have been drawn from his imagination.

volubility. But more often Beethoven is described as lost to the world, either through his deafness or being in reverie.

Given the music that was on his mind, Beethoven might well have been lost in his own world. But that was not to say, even in this period, that he lost sight of worldly matters. In the summer of 1825, he was in the midst of working on his third string quartet for Prince Nicolas Galitzin, op. 130 in B flat major. The Russian prince's commission, originally made in November

1822, was for one, two or three quartets, for which he offered to pay 'what you think proper'. Beethoven asked for – and was granted – 50 ducats per piece. Despite the alacrity with which his generous commission had been accepted, Galitzin had to wait for the quartets as Beethoven completed the *Missa solemnis*, the Diabelli Variations and the Ninth Symphony. He then embarked on what became five quartets. The first three, opp. 127, 132 and 130, dedicated to Prince Galitzin as requested, appeared over the course of 1825. There was some overlap between pieces, with Beethoven noting ideas for one while working on another. Two more quartets, which were not commissioned, emerged in the summer and autumn of 1826: opp. 131 and 135. Beethoven then produced his last composition, a movement for string quartet that provided an alternative finale to op. 130, while staying at his brother's in Gneixendorf that winter.

The music of these last five quartets was unlike anything anyone had ever heard. Galitzin had hoped for something akin to Beethoven's earlier works, which stretched but stayed within the confines of established parameters. It was as if ideas from those notebooks that bulged in Beethoven's coat pockets had finally escaped, flying free. There was no restriction to four movements – op. 130 has six, op. 131 seven, op. 132 five – and within those movements, no need to heed routine forms. In the quartets which kept to the standard four movements – opp. 127 and 135 – Beethoven broke down formal conventions of sonata, rondo, variations, fugue and dances, creating massive, multi-part movements. On occasion, words are written on the score – to be read by the performer, not spoken aloud – that seem to reflect the composer's state of mind. For example, at the head of each of the parts for the last movement of op. 135 there is a separate line of music, not to be played, with words written underneath. It is entitled 'Der schwer gefaßte Entschluß'

Fig. 9.2 First edition of the score of the String Quartet in F Major, op. 135

('The Difficult Resolution') and asks 'Muß es sein?' – must it be? 'Es muß sein!' – it must be! – is the answer.

These last quartets seem, then, to be music about music, which, at the same time, is music about life. That life is Beethoven's, coming to an end. This is the paradox of his late style: while his music seems to become more and more abstract, the explanations given for it become more intensely biographical. It is often assumed that an artist's last works bear marks of their awareness of impending mortality. Beethoven had already contemplated death in his 'Heiligenstadt Testament' of 1802, as he set out on his 'new path'. The qualities of his music from the 1820s that make it 'late' are perhaps best explained as a distillation of elements that were already there: experimentation, fragmentation, repetition, unusual sonorities and extended length. Most of his contemporaries thought their exaggeration to be the result of illness and eccentricity, if not madness. Only as the decades passed did his last works begin to be heard as profound, as the start of something new rather than of diminishing powers.

Beethoven's music is never just about his life, of course. Grand claims made for his art can sit at odds with mundane circumstances. Take 'Der schwer gefaßte Entschluß' of op. 135: as the character Tomáš in Milan Kundera's novel *The Unbearable Lightness of Being* recounts, the story goes that Beethoven had reminded a certain Dembscher that he owed him 50 florins; 'Dembscher heaved a mournful sigh and said "Muss es sein?" To which Beethoven replied with a hearty laugh, "Es muss sein!" and immediately jotted down these words and their melody,'

which became a canon for four voices, WoO 196, and, a year
later, a motif in the last movement of op. 135. By then, Beethoven had forgotten about the debt and the words had assumed
a greater magnitude: 'German is a language of heavy words,'
Kundera reminds us, which can turn 'frivolous inspiration into
a serious quartet, a joke into a metaphysical truth'.

There are many variants of the story behind 'Der schwer
gefaßte Entschluß' – Beethoven's amanuensis Karl Holz adds the
detail that Ignaz Demtscher was a musical amateur who had
asked for the parts to play op. 130, but, as he had not attended the
work's premiere, Beethoven refused unless he paid the 50 florins
due for a subscription to the concert series. Schindler thought
the question and answer derived from an exchange between
Beethoven and his housekeeper or with a publisher. Moritz
Schlesinger, who published op. 135, decades later recalled, 'very
clearly', a letter from Beethoven explaining that 'Muss es sein?'
pertained to his misfortune in having to make a fair copy of his
score himself. These everyday explanations from Beethoven's
contemporaries have since been overlain with the heavy meta-
physics Kundera invoked. It is in part a question of how the
words are said; they are not just in German – indeed, without
sight of the score or the help of a programme note, a listener
would not necessarily know that there are words involved – they
are in German music that is now taken very seriously. 'Muss es
sein?' has become a question about fate, life, death and beyond.

This chapter focuses not on the last full quartet, op. 135, but on
op. 130, a work that in the way it was put together thematizes
the idea of ending. As mentioned, it was the third of the five
quartets to be composed and, with the addition of an alternative
finale, the last to be completed. It thus has a claim to be Beethoven's final work; the only music he wrote after its conclusion
was too fragmentary or too irreverent to be granted the mantle.[3]

Yet there has been resistance to granting op. 130 that status. For many people, the notion that Beethoven was willing to change his mind about how a piece should be presented, and that his alternative ending might have been less weighty than the original, is anathema.

Beethoven's own conception of op. 130 seems to have been fairly fluid, and his willingness to provide a different finale, essentially at the behest of his publisher, needs to be understood in the context of performance and publication practices more generally. It was not unusual for individual movements from pieces to be programmed in concerts, and not just popular numbers such as the Minuet of the Septet or the second movement of the Eighth Symphony; the Viennese premiere of op. 127, for instance, was incomplete and, as mentioned earlier, the Ninth Symphony was often performed without the 'Ode to Joy'. Moreover, publishing works in arrangements continued to be the order of the day. Even the 'Grosse Fuge' was produced in versions for two- and four-hand piano, with Beethoven devising his own adaptation, as he was dissatisfied with other efforts. The composer may well have wanted op. 130 to be played in its complete form but evidently did not necessarily expect it to be. Notions of there being a definitive version of a musical work, which should always be honoured, was a concern of later centuries.

Beethoven's formal conception of op. 130 seems to have been freer than usual. He began sketching ideas while still working on op. 132: among them were notes for a 'serious and heavy-going introduction' and for a finale marked 'Fugha'. The quartet was relatively slow to come together, which Beethoven tried to cover up. He had told the British musician Charles Neate, who was always keen to promote performances of Beethoven in London, that the whole thing was almost finished back in March 1825; at the end of August he promised his nephew and Holz that it would be finished in a few days. In fact, it was not ready until November. Unlike with op. 132, the delay was caused not by illness but by ambition. Op. 130 consists of six movements, none of which entirely fits into a conventional mould either singly or in combination. What's more, in this first iteration, the final movement is indeed a great, huge fugue. While Beethoven had composed long, complex fugues before – in the 'Hammerklavier' Piano Sonata and the *Missa solemnis* – the 'Grosse Fuge' was in a different league.

In op. 130, Beethoven plays, over and over, with an idea of ending. The opening bars seem to be as much about closure as they are about setting things in motion. The harmonic figure which conventionally establishes a sense of arrival in a key, known as a cadence, is constantly promised but rarely delivered, making the music seem restless; in search of closure. A slow and ambiguous introduction, Adagio ma non troppo, is followed by an Allegro that presents two ideas: a figure heard initially in the first violin, which constantly scurries up and down, and a very simple fanfare-like motif. Both of these ideas are shared between the instruments, sometimes in conflict with one another, sometimes together. Both ideas are constantly wrongfooted by off-beat accents which throw off a regular sense of metre. Beethoven continues to turn the conventions of sonata form inside out by having the cello slip down to an unexpected secondary key area (G flat). The phrase is marked *sotto voce* – the first marking in the piece associated with a voice – and ushers in a quiet, questioning tone to the end of the exposition: is the music ending here? Or here?

The development section returns to music from the introduction which alternates with the scurrying and fanfare ideas from the Allegro. So, too, begins the coda, but the collision of Adagio and Allegro materials gradually relaxes as the scurrying motif is slurred over and the dynamics dwindle. A similar approach of splicing and softening is taken in the next two movements. The Presto is constantly in motion, until the ever-rising phrases suddenly tumble, in the first violin, down to loud, angry-sounding chords. This interruption seems soon forgotten, though, and the movement ends almost arbitrarily: it could spin around for ever. The opening of the next movement seems mysterious, even overwrought. Beethoven's dynamic and expressive markings are significant: it begins with a *diminuendo*, as if fading away before it's begun. But above that is written *poco scherzoso* ('a little playfully'), and soon a melody marked *dolce* ('sweetly') emerges. This is not a terribly slow slow-movement – with yet more equivocation, it is marked *Andante con moto, ma non troppo* ('at a walking pace with movement, but not too much') – and there is always something moving in the background. Beethoven sets up a tension between the musical material and the detailed instructions about articulation, volume and mood, reversing what Kundera described as 'heavy German' into something lighter.

Beethoven's decision to include another three movements after the Andante, rather than ending with a quick finale, changes the overall structure of the piece and, perhaps most importantly, undermines expectations: the listener now has no map for where the music will go next. This is another way in which op. 130 offers and retracts possible endings. The fourth movement, Alla danza tedesca: Allegro assai, starts as a sweetly spinning dance, with only fluctuating dynamics – suddenly loud, suddenly quiet – suggesting that anything might go awry. Gradually, though, limbs start to flail and, by the end of the movement, the opening melody has been dismembered, stitched back together between the instruments. In the final bar, the viola and cello seem to be about to embark on another return of the theme but instead the music stops.

The next movement, by contrast, seems to have begun already, to be *in media res*, with cello, viola and second violin providing the briefest of preludes to the first violin's long melody. All the instruments, now, are marked *sotto voce* and, together with Beethoven's title for the movement, 'Cavatina' (a short song or operatic aria), an idea of the singing voice comes to the fore. There is a fragility to this music that suggests that the imagined singer is somehow distraught, a feeling intensified in the section marked 'Beklemmt' ('feeling oppressed or uneasy, or anxious'). The violin's melodic line here breaks up into short, erratic phrases, almost as if they have forgotten what they are supposed to be doing. The return of the brief prelude pulls the violin back to its original *sotto voce* melody. The movement ends, again, almost arbitrarily, with the lower strings swelling gently on the final chord.

Holz recalled Beethoven listening to the Cavatina with tears streaming down his cheeks. That it should be this movement that moved him most is understandable: it is beautiful music. In the search for personal meaning in the late quartets, it seems significant that movements that had a more overt biographical meaning – the hymn of thanksgiving in op. 132 or even 'Muss es sein?' in op. 135 – did not elicit the same response (at least, so far as we know). It also seems significant that this music evokes an idea of a singing voice but within instrumental music. And there are no words that can say how much is being expressed, only tears.

Beethoven stipulated that there should not be a pause between the end of the Cavatina and the start of the next movement, which, in its first incarnation, was the 'Grosse Fuge'. The note G in the Cavatina's final chords then acts as a pivot to the stark start of the fugue, when the note G resounds on the open strings of the instruments. Are they tuning up? It is an unusual gesture for the beginning of the last movement of a quartet and, as if in acknowledgement of that, Beethoven gave the opening section of the 'Grosse Fuge' the title 'Overtura'.[4] After the first chord, the four main subjects are introduced, not as exact replicas of what happens later, more like premonitions of what might happen. That they are presented in reverse order and rapidly circle downwards to the home key, B flat major, suggests that this is another movement of op. 130 which is all about ending.

But the 'Grosse Fuge' is more than just an ending to one work: it has often been claimed to be the apotheosis of the fugue as a genre, going beyond J. S. Bach's *The Art of Fugue* (*Die Kunst der Fuge*) and other grand fugues by Beethoven. Earlier chapters have explained how a fugue is constructed from a thematic subject that is imitated by another voice, and then another, and so on, layering up a complex texture of intertwining melodic lines or counterpoint. There are strict rules to how those contrapuntal layers should be constructed, which do not need to be gone into here, apart from to say that Beethoven weaves together a piece that impresses by its command of the rules and its willingness to bend and even break them. Tellingly, above the score's published title is inscribed 'tantôt libre, tantôt recherché' ('partly free, partly learned', the latter meaning in strict counterpoint): a warning as well as an explanation of the score's complexity.

One of the liberties taken by Beethoven is that the 'Grosse Fuge' is not just fugal. Instead, fugues alternate with sections that are lyrical and dance- or march-like and which explore far-flung harmonic areas. Harmonically, the relationships between sections can be distant and the fugues themselves are sometimes dissonant. Such is its scale it seems like it is a multi-movement piece in itself. The extreme aspects of the 'Grosse Fuge' are also highlighted by Beethoven's approach to dynamic markings. Other movements in op. 130 carefully gradate the volume of individual phrases. Here, Beethoven uses block markings, instructing that passages should be one dynamic throughout – very loud, very soft – without nuance. The relentlessness of the

music is perhaps one reason why a psychological study discovered that when played as the finale of op. 130, the first five
movements tended to be played more slowly: subconsciously,
the players were preparing themselves for the onslaught of the
'Grosse Fuge'.[5]

Although Prince Galitzin's commission had spurred on Beethoven to compose string quartets, they had already been on his
mind. He offered the Leipzig publisher C. F. Peters a string
quartet in May 1822, but they baulked at his price (the same 50
ducats) and said they would prefer a piano quartet, 'only on the
condition that it will not be too difficult', because they already
had some excellent quartets in press by Louis Spohr, Bernhard
Romberg and Pierre Rode; names that might be unknown now
but whose chamber works were played far more frequently than
Beethoven's in his lifetime.[6] When he received the Galitzin proposal, Beethoven immediately wrote to Ferdinand Ries in
London, asking him to find a publisher there: he soon agreed
with Neate a fee of 100 guineas for three quartets and continued
to negotiate with Peters in Leipzig and with Schott in Mainz for
publication rights.

   The other impetus for composing quartets was the return of
the violinist Schuppanzigh after seven years in St Petersburg.
He immediately proposed to Beethoven that they should collaborate on a new quartet; they had last done so thirteen years
prior, on op. 95. What's more, Schuppanzigh swiftly established
a subscription concert series, which encouraged consideration of
the string quartet as a genre to be listened to in the concert hall,
as well as played in the home. He further emphasized the need
to take a serious, connoisseur-like attitude to the music by
insisting – at least initially – that tickets could only be purchased
for the whole season, rather than for individual concerts (when
he did begin to sell separate tickets they were at a premium

price). The term that critics used to describe Schuppanzigh's venture was telling: they referred to the music as 'classical', less with reference to a historical period than as a sign of its superior quality and lasting value. The prominent role Beethoven's, Mozart's and Haydn's music was given within the concerts was an early indication of their later veneration. Subsequently, Schuppanzigh made some concessions to the tastes of his audience, who preferred more variety ('especially the ladies', the violinist explained) than just 'classic' string quartets. While Beethoven, Mozart and Haydn still dominated, other living composers featured and there were piano trios and even vocal works programmed.

Schuppanzigh's quartet included violist and composer Franz Weiss, who had played in Schuppanzigh's previous quartets for Prince Lichnowsky in the 1790s and Count Razumovsky in the 1810s, and cellist Joseph Lincke, who had also played in the Razumovsky quartet. The second violinist, Karl Holz, was more than twenty years younger than the others; he made his living as a civil servant but from the summer of 1825 until September 1826 replaced Schindler as Beethoven's unpaid secretary; he was also the composer's regular dinner companion. Beethoven had a string of such helpers from Ferdinand Ries onwards, who copied scores, carried out correspondence and provided company as necessary; they were not servants as such, but they were not quite his equals either. As his hearing worsened he became more dependent on their assistance. That they were willing to work for him unpaid – except in abuse, it sometimes seemed – signalled their appreciation for Beethoven as an artist.

Beethoven's close relationship with his *Leibquartett*, or 'personal quartet' – as he referred to them in the conversation books – is evident in the way they worked together.[7] Schuppanzigh chivvied along composition by asking if the new quartet might be included in his concert series and asking to see his part before organizing a read-through of the whole piece in the New Year. The quartet provided feedback on each new work; in the case of op. 130 they commented on the difficulty of getting their lines precisely together but predicted that all would go easily, except the fugue.[8] Typically, further views were solicited from invited listeners. There is no record of such a meeting for op. 130, but conductor Sir George Smart, visiting from London, remembered going with Ferdinand Ries to the publisher Schlesinger's rooms at the Hotel Wildeman at midday on 9 September 1825, where an 'assembly of professors' had assembled to hear op. 132, which was played twice. Among the fourteen people present were no professors as such, but respected musicians and friends. Beethoven directed the performance, apparently correcting the players' articulation by sight.[9] Despite these preliminary play-throughs and their close relationship with the composer, the Schuppanzigh Quartet's performances were often underprepared, and sometimes disastrous. In the case of op. 127, the premiere went so badly Beethoven handed over the score to rival quartets to see if they could make a better fist of it; cruel treatment of his old friend, perhaps, but a canny way to catch the attention of publishers. Relations between Beethoven and Schuppanzigh remained strained until Holz sought to persuade the composer that the fault had lain with the whole ensemble, not simply the first violin. Still, Schuppanzigh did not premiere any more of the late quartets in his subscription concerts.

Instead, the official premiere of op. 130 took place in a one-off concert, on 21 March 1826. The programme was unlike Schuppanzigh's subscription concerts, which would have prefaced the new piece with a couple of works by Haydn and Mozart. Another model would have been presenting the new piece alone, but playing it twice, as other quartets had done with some success. Schuppanzigh decided, though, to revert to a more conventional mixed programme. He began with variations on a folk song from one of Haydn's quartets, followed by 'Marie', a setting of a poem by Ignaz Castelli with music by the quartet's violist Weiss, sung by Herr Hoffmann (dismissed as 'Nicht bedeutend', 'insignificant', by a reviewer). Then came Beethoven's Trio in B flat (the pianist Anton Halm – who would later attempt to arrange the 'Grosse Fuge' for four-hand piano – apparently had played better on other occasions) and his 'Adelaide', sung by Hoffmann. To end, op. 130. The lengthy and varied programme suggests that Schuppanzigh was hoping to attract a broader audience than just followers of Beethoven; given the scale of op. 130, he must have been hoping that they were quite patient too.

Beethoven decided not to attend the concert. He rarely went to large social gatherings by then, perhaps in frustration at his inability to hear much conversation, not to mention the music. Instead he holed himself up in a local tavern and had Holz report back to him. He was told that the second and fourth movements, the Scherzo and Alla danze tedesca, had been encored (however discerning Vienna audiences were, they still freely applauded between movements and demanded their repetition as they fancied).[10] The fugue, however, had 'passed by uncomprehended'. The *Allgemeine musikalische Zeitung* corroborated Holz's account: the reviewer claimed that they 'did not dare to interpret the sense of the fugal finale' for it was 'incomprehensible to him, like Chinese'. Perhaps the players were unsure of themselves and did not play completely accurately, contributing to the 'Babylonian confusion'. 'Moroccans might possibly enjoy themselves,' the reviewer suggested, in the same way that they had found pleasure only in the orchestra tuning up at the Italian opera.[11] Perhaps if Beethoven had been able to hear his own creation, they concluded, it would have been written differently; 'perhaps the time is yet to come when that which at first glance appeared to us as dismal and confused will be recognised as clear and pleasing in form'. Beethoven was exasperated.

The comparison of the 'Grosse Fuge' to a foreign language or culture returns to the assumption that music – even without words – can carry meaning. Music is not a language, but its conventions are culturally determined. Music from elsewhere that uses unfamiliar patterns or sounds can be as alienating as an unknown language – or, as thrilling. Romantic writers such as Friedrich Schlegel likened instrumental music to Sanskrit: for them, a mysterious script that promised profundities if the code could be cracked. Op. 130 was a similar enigma. Gerhard von Breuning, with the directness of a thirteen-year-old, told Beethoven that his quartet 'didn't go over very well':

> 'It will please them some day' was the laconic answer he gave me; and to that he added fully and firmly aware that he wrote as he thought fit, and was not led astray by the judgements of his contemporaries: 'I know; I am a musician.'

In fact, it would take decades for Beethoven's late quartets to be appreciated by more than a small circle of aficionados. Some friends, in private, expressed a view that those who professed to like the music were simply overawed by the reputation of the composer, rather than actually comprehending his works. Others were more open about their misgivings: the *Allgemeine musikalische Zeitung* described the odd-numbered movements of op. 130 as 'serious, gloomy, mystical, but also at times bizarre, harsh and capricious' ('ernst, duster, mystisch, wohl auch minuter bizarr, schroff und capriciös').[12] There continue to be debates about what this music means and, if it is gloomy or bizarre, whether that is a bad thing. The capacious invention of op. 130 allows for continual reinterpretation, as Beethoven signalled in his response to Holz's claim that it was the greatest of the Galitzin quartets: 'Each in its own way. Art demands of us that we shall not stand still.'[13]

★

One consequence of the bafflement that greeted op. 130 was that neither of Beethoven's next quartets, op. 131 or op. 135, was performed in concert during the composer's lifetime and all five 'late' quartets were rarely heard in the following decades. To make matters worse, Prince Galitzin had paid only for op. 127 and found himself unable to pay for the rest. Some money was recouped through publication.[14] On 11 April 1826, Mathias Artaria broached whether, for an extra 12 ducats, Beethoven would permit him to publish a four-hand arrangement of the 'Grosse Fuge', which would appear simultaneously with the full score and quartet parts.[15] This last element of the offer was a recent innovation that Beethoven had long campaigned for. By having access to the complete score, players and listeners could see how the individual parts of the quartet fitted together, which was all the more necessary with music as idiosyncratic as this. Beethoven agreed and sent the manuscript, with the fugue as the finale, to the engraver. However, Artaria wanted a different, easier last movement. Holz persuaded Beethoven to provide one by arguing that the size and originality of the fugue meant that it should stand alone; moreover, he would be paid an extra 15 ducats for the new movement. The 'Grosse Fuge' for string quartet was published as op. 133, dedicated to Prince Rudolph. The version for four-hand piano as op. 134 was dedicated in 'friendly memory' to the Count of Alberti. Family tragedy intervened before Beethoven produced the next ending to op. 130.

In 1823, Beethoven's nephew Karl, now seventeen, had enrolled as a student at the University of Vienna and moved in with his uncle. Beethoven did not approve of Karl's friends or his lifestyle, suspecting that he was spending too much time carousing and chasing women. The two quarrelled so much that Beethoven's landlady gave them their notice. On the advice of his doctor, Beethoven left Vienna for the village of Baden in May 1824 and remained there until the autumn; it was during this period that he composed op. 127, followed by op. 132, with its 'Hymn of Thanks-giving to God of an Invalid on His Convalescence'. During their separation, Beethoven's suspicions about Karl's behaviour intensi-fied and he tried to monitor and restrict his actions, asking the Schlemmer family, with whom Karl was boarding, to prevent him from leaving their house at night, charging Holz with chaperoning Karl when he did go out, and refusing to give him spending money. Karl declared that he did not want to continue his studies at the university, which had been Beethoven's idea; he wanted, instead, to become a soldier and then decided to transfer to the polytechnic. By the following summer, their relationship was so bad Beethoven decided not to make his usual trip to the country. On 5 August 1826, Karl fled: he pawned his watch and bought two pistols then went to Baden, from where he sent his uncle a suicide note. He then climbed a nearby mountain and shot himself in the head.

The wounds, fortunately, were not life-threatening. Having initially asked to be taken to his mother's, the police then trans-ferred Karl to the General Hospital, where he remained until 15 September. Karl had told the police magistrate that he had attempted suicide because he was 'weary of imprisonment' and that Beethoven 'tormented him too much'; he had also had enough of the constant denigration of his mother. According to Gerhard von Breuning's memoirs, Karl's uncle was 'much more deeply wounded'.[16] The horrific event persuaded Beethoven to relinquish his guardianship and to permit his nephew, once hair had regrown over his scars, to join the army. Stephan von Breuning made arrangements with Field Marshal von Stutter-heim to accept Karl as a cadet in his regiment (Beethoven dedicated op. 131 to Stutterheim in thanks).

For Karl's convalescence, Beethoven finally accepted his brother Johann's long-standing invitation to stay at his country house at Gneixendorf – a name Beethoven said reminded him of a broken axle – some 50 miles north-west of Vienna. They arrived in late September, intending to spend only a couple of weeks there, but they remained for a couple of months, as Karl kept on postponing his departure. Despite his various ailments, Beethoven seemed to find the environment to his liking. The Danube valley reminded him of the Rhineland of his childhood and he spent hours each day walking through the countryside, gaining a reputation among the locals as an eccentric; they said 'der grauperte Musikant' ('scruffy musician') scared the livestock. In the mornings and evenings, Beethoven composed. By the middle of October, he had completed op. 135, copied the parts and sent them to Schlesinger in Paris. He then turned to the new finale for op. 130, which he sent to Artaria – via Schlesinger – in mid-November and which was published the following May.

Beethoven again stipulated that the new finale to op. 130 should follow the Cavatina 'without a long pause'.[17] Like the 'Grosse Fuge', it begins with the sound of an open string, but rather than the whole group crashing in, now the viola quietly sets in motion a ticking pulse over which the first violin introduces a scampering melody that is taken up and developed as the main theme. The whole movement gains energy towards a lively – to my mind, jubilant – conclusion. There are reminders, though, of other possible endings: moments where a fugue is promised but not pursued; a melodic contour that seems reminiscent of passages from elsewhere in the late quartets – the 'Grosse Fuge', the opening of op. 132 and op. 131. Musicologists today are keen to show that, despite the disparity of these sprawling works, they share kernels of thought that make the whole coherent. Whether or not such subtle connections were evident or mattered to Beethoven's contemporaries, when the new finale was rehearsed in late December the musicians found it 'altogether heavenly'.[18]

On 1 December 1826, Beethoven and Karl had begun the return journey to Vienna, arriving back at the composer's lodgings the next day. Beethoven's health worsened. He had already lost his appetite and had swollen feet when they were at Gneixendorf. Now, he caught pneumonia and developed jaundice and ascites, likely the result of underlying cirrhosis of the liver. The fluid filling his peritoneal cavity was tapped by doctors repeatedly, providing some short-term relief, but nineteenth-century medical knowledge was insufficient to cure him. Bed-bound, Beethoven was attended by friends and family. As news of his illness – and rumours of his financial precariousness – spread, he had a stream of visitors and received lavish gifts: wine, cake, stewed fruit, the complete works of Handel, a picture of Haydn's birthplace, money.

Holz, who had worked without pay for Beethoven, attending to all his needs, however trivial or traumatic, detached himself from the household as he prepared to get married. In his place, Schindler returned to the fold. Several of Beethoven's direct contemporaries were themselves unwell, illustrating the shorter life expectancies of those days. Stephan von Breuning was often incapacitated by liver disease, but his young son Gerhard visited each afternoon. Gout-riddled Zmeskall sent greetings from his own sickbed; in his return letter Beethoven thanked him for his sympathy and explained that the most painful thing was not being able to compose. Instead, he read Walter Scott and Homer and dictated correspondence, chasing down publishers to the end. Karl stayed with his uncle until early January, when he left to join his regiment in Moravia. The next day, Beethoven wrote his will, making his nephew his sole heir.

Stephan von Breuning recommended that Beethoven should amend his will so that the irresponsible Karl could not spend his inheritance all at once. Beethoven did so by stipulating that the capital of his estate should fall to Karl's natural or testamentary heirs – meaning that there was a chance it could pass to his mother. Despite his friends' protestations, Beethoven refused to change it. His final days are ringed by myth, each visitor claiming that theirs was the true account. Beethoven was said to have announced to those assembled at his bedside, with characteristic mordant wit, 'Plaudite, amici, comoedia finita est': 'Applaud friends, the comedy is over.' He had written the phrase 'Applaudite amici' over the fugue theme of the Credo in one of his sketches for the *Missa solemnis*. It is said to be a paraphrase of the last words of Augustus Caesar: 'Since the play has been so good, clap your hands.'[19] His very last, more prosaic, words were also typical, apparently expressing disappointment that the wine he had hoped for had only just arrived: 'Pity, pity, too late.' He then fell into a coma. Two days later, in the late afternoon of 26 March 1827, the sky darkened and there was an almighty snowstorm, with thunder and lightning. During it, Beethoven was said to have briefly opened his eyes and lifted his right hand, clenched in a fist, before collapsing: defiant to the end.[20] Or maybe he died in his brother's arms, as Johann claimed. Everybody wanted to make Beethoven's death in the image they thought most fitting.

If Beethoven's last breath could have been bottled, it probably would have been. As was the order of the day, there was a painting of visitors to his sickbed, a death mask was made, and hair was clipped from his head, to be secreted in lockets and even embroidered into miniature landscapes, as if a religious relic.[21] Details of his autopsy were released, remarking on his shrivelled liver and his unusually thick skull. Everybody, it seemed, wanted a piece of the composer. The question was what they would do with it.

Beethoven's funeral took place three days after his death, on 29 March 1827. Crowds lined the streets to watch the cortège on its way from the church to Währing cemetery. Many of Vienna's leading musicians were among the pall- and torch-bearers: Johann Nepomuk Hummel, Carl Czerny, Franz Schubert.

Fig. 9.3 A landscape made out of Beethoven's hair.

Actor Heinrich Anschütz read out an oration by playwright Franz Grillparzer that declared Beethoven to have been 'the last master of resounding song . . . the man who inherited and increased the immortal fame of Handel and Bach, of Haydn and Mozart, has ceased to be; and we stand weeping over the broken strings of an instrument now stilled'. Beethoven may have shunned society, Grillparzer continued, but he 'preserved a human heart for all men, a father's heart for his own people, the whole world'. These three themes: of Beethoven as the culmination of Vienna's musical heritage, of his isolation, and of his universality, continue to permeate celebrations of the composer. Schindler gathered up memorabilia, manuscripts and letters, which he would use – and abuse – for his biography.[22] Stephan von Breuning and Jacob Hotschevar, a lawyer acting on behalf of Karl (after von Breuning's death in June, he became Karl's guardian), took the remaining manuscripts and scores for appraisal. An auction was held that autumn at which Beethoven's sketchbooks, autographs of published works, manuscripts, parts, scores, printed music and books were sold. In an indication of what seems now to be a topsy-turvy assessment of the value of different pieces from his oeuvre, the original manuscript of the *Missa solemnis* went for 7 florins, the Septet for 18. Altogether, the auction raised 1,140 florins. Beethoven's entire estate, including seven bank shares, was valued at just over 10,000 florins. It was a respectable sum. Only 5 per cent of Vienna's citizens left a similar or greater fortune, and 77 per cent left a tenth of that, or less. Among composers, Antonio Salieri left three times as much and Haydn twice the amount, but both had longer and commercially more successful careers.

Among all these papers were the two letters Beethoven seemed never to have sent. One, the 'Heiligenstadt Testament', had been written to his brothers in the autumn of 1802, explaining his deafness, which was published on the front page of the *Allgemeine musikalische Zeitung* under the title 'To Beethoven's friends' on 17 October 1827.[23] The other, pencil-written letter to an unnamed woman, the 'Immortal Beloved', which probably dated from July 1812, was first published by Schindler in the 1840 edition of his biography of the composer.[24] The publication of these two unsent letters fundamentally reshaped perceptions of Beethoven's personality. His eccentricities, and even the rumours and scandals that swirled around him, were mitigated by their insights into how he had suffered. A more sympathetic and romantic portrait slowly began to emerge.

Coda

Beethoven's life has had multiple endings. Founding editor of the *Allgemeine musikalische Zeitung*, Friedrich Rochlitz, was approached to be his biographer but he declined, as did Karl Holz. Anton Schindler slowly began to gather materials for his account and to attempt to discredit anecdotes that he thought besmirched Beethoven's reputation. For similar reasons, he culled papers in his possession and even began to craft stories and forge entries in the conversation books that he thought cast the composer in a more favourable light. While Schindler was not trusted by his contemporaries – the next substantial biography, by Alexander Wheelock Thayer, overturned some of his claims – the falsehoods were not really acknowledged until the 1970s, and aspects of his life continue to be argued over today.

Those nineteenth-century accounts of Beethoven's life contained some compelling stories that still shape the way we understand the composer and his achievements. The allure of trying to solve mysteries about the identity of the 'Immortal Beloved', the precise nature of his political allegiances, the impact of his deafness on his creativity, is undiminished. As I hope this book has illustrated, Beethoven's status as a great composer who dominates music histories, concert programmes and recording catalogues came about through hard work and industry networks, through making mistakes and having occasional good luck, as well as through his music. In the end, perhaps predictably, the tastes of his connoisseur supporters won out: the popular hits of the Septet and *Wellingtons Sieg* were forgotten and Beethoven became known first and foremost as the composer of the Third, Fifth and Ninth Symphonies, of the *Missa solemnis*, late sonatas and quartets; as the man who foresaw the future of music.

Wegeler and von Breuning had difficulty enough identifying Beethoven's birthplace a few decades after his death, as mentioned at the start of this book. The city of Bonn has since made much more of its musical heritage, with the Beethoven-Haus at its centre. Indeed, almost anywhere that can claim to have a connection with the composer in Germany or Austria has become a museum. It is a laudable celebration of an illustrious past and an attempt to foster interest in its future. Wandering around such collections, with their creaky floorboards and glass cases of manuscripts and letters, ear trumpets and spectacles, the audio guides or listening rooms offer excerpts of the music, which in some ways seems more tangible and less archaic. There is always a tension between learning about the history of music and experiencing music in the present; between what we hear in pieces of music and what we can detect from the pieces – the remnants – of a life.

The Europe Beethoven and his family knew was reshaped several times over by war and politics, a process that has continued ever since. Where there were grand palaces, there are now department stores; villages Beethoven summered in are now absorbed into Vienna's suburbs. Perhaps the starkest reminder, for me, of this layering of history comes not from Beethoven himself but from his Belgian grandfather and namesake. This son of a baker is now remembered in his birthplace of Mechelen by a statue of him facing his young grandson, at the end of a street named after him. It's possible he would have kept his place in the town's history without the fame of Ludwig Jr, but it seems unlikely. Then there is St Lambert's Cathedral in Liège, where he sang in the choir as a young man before being appointed to a position at the court in Bonn, paving the way for his descendants to become musicians. The building is no more; it was dismantled under the revolutionary regime of the 1790s and another church became the city's cathedral in the nineteenth century. Liège bore the brunt of both world wars and, like many European cities, has since undergone extensive rebuilding. Where Beethoven's grandfather once sang is now a subterranean multi-storey car park. It's quite a swish car park, but a car park nonetheless; any hope of sensing the spirit of Beethoven's ancestor is overridden by petrol fumes and pop music. The composer's Flemish background does not loom large in his biography, apart from the fatal revelation in the court battle for custody of his nephew that the 'van' of his name did not mean that he belonged to the nobility. The importance of Beethoven's childhood in Bonn is recognized, but this German-born composer, who spent most of his life in Vienna, was claimed by the Austrians. Already during his lifetime Beethoven's fame became international. He was not the first European composer to be known around the world, but he soon became known as the world's foremost composer.

There is some irony in the fact that a man who was unsure of his birth date – in an effort to make his prodigious talents more impressive, Beethoven's father knocked a couple of years off his son's age – has since had his anniversaries celebrated assiduously. Each time, Beethoven and his music have become a vehicle for other projects. The 1870 centenary of his birth coincided with the outbreak of the Franco-Prussian War that led to the unification of Germany. Music's significance for German nationalism was encapsulated in Richard Wagner's long essay on Beethoven, published that same year, which heralded his achievements as a 'Germanic deed, a Germanic art, a Germanic effort towards a Germanic goal'.[1] While many musicians subscribed to similar national sentiment, they did not necessarily agree with Wagner's outlook, and a grand festival of Beethoven's music, planned to take place in Vienna, collapsed because most prominent musicians refused to attend when they learned who else had been invited.[2] Less controversially, but demonstrating the institutionalization of Beethoven worship around Europe, in 1870 the Hungarian music-enthusiast Fanny Linzbauer presented the Royal Philharmonic Society in London with a bust of Beethoven by Johann Nepomuk Schaller, to be placed on the platform of every concert in order that 'England will ever be considered the highest and best friend of that man.'

In 1927, the centenary of Beethoven's death, more of his music than had ever before been available was made so by gramophone companies keen to advertise their new technologies. There was a concomitant outpouring of scholarship and journalism, and those two prongs of the music industry, as well as live concerts, have continued to use anniversaries as an excuse for new releases ever since. For 1970, the Beethoven-Haus in Bonn was renovated, and avant-garde composers such as Mauricio Kagel and Karlheinz Stockhausen attempted to subvert his authority through playfully deconstructing his music and reputation.[3]

Musical works that pay homage to, or question the reputation of, the composer continue to proliferate. Walter Murphy's *A Fifth of Beethoven* (1976) might – just – be considered as an extension of the nineteenth-century practice of arrangements, if with a funkier groove. More recently, recordings of the Ninth Symphony have been compressed to last just a second, by German composer Johannes Kreidler, and 'stretched' by Norwegian conceptual artist Leif Inge to last twenty-four hours.[4] *Fidelio* has been rewritten as *prisoner of the state* by American composer David Lang, while, in British composer Matthew Herbert's *Requiem*, during a rendition of op. 135 a quartet of instruments is sawn apart and set on fire. If these responses to Beethoven's works seem on some level disrespectful, they also prove the resilience of his reputation; moreover, there is a long-held belief that ability to withstand whatever is thrown at it is the mark of a masterpiece.

Beethoven today is a global phenomenon; the 250th anniversary of his birth is being celebrated around the world with yet more recordings and research being released. Concert programmes that failed in Beethoven's day are now being given polished performances in comfortable, heated concert halls. The sketches for Beethoven's Tenth Symphony, from which musicologists have previously attempted to construct a playable piece, are now supposedly being completed by artificial intelligence.[5] Beethoven's revolutionary spirit is praised in armchair rebellions against increasingly repressive, regressive politics, or invoked in lockdown, as orchestra members assemble performances of the Ninth Symphony online.

History is selective, and we carve out an image of the composer for our times. In summer 2019, Ottmar Hörl created an art installation called 'Ode to Joy' in Bonn's Münsterplatz. The Beethoven monument was surrounded by seven hundred waist-high, brightly coloured statues of the composer (fig. C.1).

Fig. C.1 Bonn, Germany. 17 May 2019. Seven hundred Ludwig van Beethoven sculptures stand on Bonn's Münsterplatz in front of the historic Beethoven monument. The sculptures were created by Prof. Dr Ottmar Hörl.

Since the installation, the statues have been distributed around the city and peek out from pharmacy window displays and hotel receptions. The composer would probably have been delighted by the project's success; he certainly would have been impressed by the high number of subscribers to own a statue, in a manner reminiscent of the way he sold his scores. It somehow encapsulates the ubiquity of Beethoven, while celebrating his achievements. At the same time, the statues overturn the standard view: he is shown to be not one man but many and, perhaps most surprisingly, this Beethoven does not scowl but smiles.

Further Reading

There is much more to read about Beethoven and still more being released, from archival discoveries to publishers and record companies taking advantage of new translations, formats and technologies. Below I give an overview of books that expand on points made within this volume. I have concentrated here on English-language publications but have also mentioned some significant German-language books, as there is of course a vast literature in other languages. The Beethoven-Archiv in Bonn in particular has produced an important series of books on all manner of Beethoven-related topics. It is also continuing to work on a complete critical edition (*Gesamtausgabe*) of all the music, a project begun in 1961 to replace the version that the composer himself had envisioned. These editions of Beethoven's music trace the different stages of the creative process from the sketches through to their printed variants.

There has not been a new English translation of Beethoven's correspondence for some time. Emily Anderson's *The Letters of Beethoven* (London, 1961, repr. 1986) remains the most complete, and can be supplemented by Theodore Albrecht's three-volume *Letters to Beethoven and Other Correspondence* (New York, 1996). Michael Hamburger's *Beethoven: Letters, Journals and Conversations* (London, 1984) is a fine and readable selection and superior to *Beethoven's Letters*, edited by Alfred Christlieb Kalischer in 1926, which has been republished by Dover. Three volumes of a new translation by Theodore Albrecht of *Beethoven's Conversation Books* (Woodbridge, 2018–) have been released so far, giving Anglophone readers access to these enigmatic notebooks from the composer's last decade. The three-volume *The Critical Reception of Beethoven's Compositions by His German Contemporaries*, ed. Wayne M. Senner, Robin Wallace and William Meredith (Nebraska, 2001) provides dozens of early-nineteenth-century reviews in translation with helpful explanatory notes.

There are biographies of every size and persuasion: many of the claims made by Anton Schindler's *Biographie von Ludwig van Beethoven* (Münster, 1840) have been discredited, initially by Alexander Wheelock Thayer, whose biography first appeared in German in the late 1860s and then was completed from his notes in the early twentieth century. It is most commonly encountered today in the subsequent two-volume edition by Elliot Forbes: *Thayer's Life of Beethoven* (rev. edn Princeton, 1967). Nineteenth-century memoirs by people who knew Beethoven are always intriguing: Gerhard von Breuning's *Memories of Beethoven: From the House of the Black-Robed Spaniards* (Cambridge, 1997), first published in 1874, is particularly readable. H. C. Robbins Landon gathered together a fascinating range of archival materials into *Beethoven: A Documentary Study* (London, 1970). The influence of Maynard Solomon's *Beethoven*, originally published in 1977 (New York, 2nd rev. edn 2012), continues to be felt in speculation over the composer's psychology. David Wyn Jones's *The Life of Beethoven* (Cambridge, 1998) is compact, interesting and reliable. From more recent years there is Jan Swafford's massive *Beethoven: Anguish and Triumph* (London, 2014) and the Flemish conductor Jan Caeyers's engaging and imaginative take on the composer's life: *Beethoven: Der einsame Revolutionär* (Munich, 2020). Lewis Lockwood's magisterial *Beethoven: The Music and the Life* (New York, 2003) interleaves biography with discussion of the works, as does Barry Cooper's *Beethoven* (Oxford, 2008) and William Kinderman's *Beethoven* (Oxford, 2nd edn 2009). Robin Wallace's *Hearing Beethoven: A Story of Musical Loss and Discovery* (Chicago,

2018), combines an in-depth exploration of the composer's hearing loss with a moving personal narrative. The significance of biography in discussions of nineteenth-century music is critiqued in Mark Evan Bonds's *The Beethoven Syndrome: Hearing Music as Autobiography* (Oxford, 2020); his own, thematic biography is entitled *Beethoven: Variations on a Life* (Oxford, 2020).

Overviews of the symphonies are offered by Lewis Lockwood's *Beethoven's Symphonies: An Artistic Vision* (New York, 2015), and by Martin Geck's *Beethoven's Symphonies: Nine Approaches to Art and Ideas* (Chicago, 2017). Broader introductions to the nineteenth-century symphony are provided in David Wyn Jones, *The Symphony in Beethoven's Vienna* (Cambridge, 2006), and Melanie Lowe's *Pleasure and Meaning in the Classical Symphony* (Indianapolis, 2007). There are many studies of individual works: to give suggestions for further reading on the Third Symphony, focused on in this book, there is Scott Burnham's *Beethoven Hero* (Princeton, 1995), Thomas Sipe's *Beethoven: Eroica Symphony* (Cambridge, 1998) and James Hamilton-Paterson's *Beethoven's Eroica: The First Great Romantic Symphony* (New York, 2017).

There are also useful introductions to individual works in the Cambridge Handbooks series: there are guides to *Fidelio* (by Paul Robinson, 1996), the *Missa solemnis* (by William Drabkin, 1991), and to the Ninth Symphony (by Nicholas Cook, 1993). Charles Rosen remains a helpful guide to understanding the musical intricacies of *The Classical Style* (New York, 2nd edn 1997). Tilman Skowroneck's *Beethoven the Pianist* (Cambridge, 2010) re-examines accounts of Beethoven as a performer. Aspects of the late music are discussed in Maynard Solomon's *Late Beethoven: Music, Thought, Imagination* (Berkeley, 2003). The *Beethoven Quartet Companion*, ed. Robert Winter and Robert Martin (Berkeley, new edn 2009), provides helpful perspectives on the repertoire, while Edward Dusinberre's *Beethoven for a Later Age: The Journey of a String Quartet* (London, 2016) gives a player's insights.

Several books situate Beethoven's achievements in the culture of his time. There are wide-ranging studies of Beethoven and historical and contemporary philosophy, including Hans-Joachim Hinrichsen's *Ludwig van Beethoven: Musik für eine neue Zeit* (Kassel, 2019), Martin Geck's *Beethoven: Der Schöpfer und sein Universum* (New York, 2020), Michael Spitzer's *Music as Philosophy: Adorno and Beethoven's Late Style* (Indianapolis, 2006) and Daniel Chua's *Beethoven and Freedom* (Oxford, 2017). The influences of new technology and theatrical entertainments have attracted the attention of Deirdre Loughridge in *Haydn's Sunrise, Beethoven's Shadow: Audiovisual Culture and the Emergence of Musical Romanticism* (Chicago, 2016). Mark Ferraguto's *Beethoven 1806* (Oxford, 2019) unsettles the conventional divide of the composer's life into early, middle and late periods by demonstrating the importance of the 'unheroic' works; an excellent example of the kind of revisionism that the new generation of Beethoven scholars is undertaking.

Beethoven's political views have been examined more closely in recent years and there continues to be debate over his engagement with revolutionary ideals. Stephen Rumph's *Beethoven after Napoleon: Political Romanticism in the Late Works* (Berkeley, 2004) should be read in dialogue with Nicholas Mathew's *Political Beethoven* (Cambridge, 2012) and John Clubbe's *Beethoven: The Relentless Revolutionary* (London and New York, 2019). The politics of Beethoven's reception since the composer's death have been interrogated in David B. Dennis's *Beethoven in German Politics, 1870–1989* (New Haven, 1996), Esteban Buch's *Beethoven's Ninth: A Political History* (Chicago, 2003) and Alexander Rehding's *Beethoven's Symphony No. 9* (Oxford, 2018).

Historical context on Beethoven's early years in Vienna is offered by John Rice, *Empress Marie Therese and Music at the Viennese Court, 1792–1807* (Cambridge, 2003) and by Tia De-Nora's *Beethoven and the Construction of Genius: Musical Politics in Vienna, 1792–1803* (Berkeley, 1995). Ulrich Schmitt describes concert life in *Revolution im Konzertsaal: Zur Beethoven-Rezeption im 19. Jahrhundert* (Mainz, 1990), and James Johnson tracks the development of attentive listening to music, with reference to Beethoven, in *Listening in Paris: A Cultural History* (Berkeley, 1996). The collection of essays *The Invention of Beethoven and Rossini*, ed. Nicholas Mathew and Benjamin Walton (Cambridge, 2013), explores the relationship between the two artists who were said to have defined the 'two styles' of the nineteenth century, while *Schubert's Vienna*, ed. Raymond Erickson (New Haven, 1997), provides insight into the circles around Beethoven's other famous contemporary, as does John M. Gingerich's *Schubert's Beethoven Project* (Cambridge, 2014), which examines the musical relationships between the two composers. More about the Congress of Vienna can be found in Adam Zamoyski's *Rites of Peace: The Fall of Napoleon and the Congress of Vienna* (London, 2008). Kristina Muxfeldt's essays on Beethoven in *Vanishing Sensibilities: Schubert, Beethoven, Schumann* (Oxford, 2011) give a subtle account of the composer's posthumous reputation.

Acknowledgements

Thanks first and foremost to my editor, Daniel Crewe, for nurturing this book from its early stages through to completion, and to all of the team at Viking for their support. Production started just as Covid-19 hit the UK, and I am indebted to Connor Brown, Chloe Davies, Jessica Barnfield, Ellie Smith, copy-editor Sarah Day, proofreaders Sarah Coward and Pat Rush, and indexer Dave Cruddock, for ensuring everything proceeded as smoothly as possible. A Major Research Fellowship from the Leverhulme Trust enabled me to complete the manuscript. I am also grateful to Oxford's Faculty of Music and St Catherine's College for supporting my research leave.

This book could not have been written without the help of colleagues, friends and family. Erica Buurman, Joe Davies and Roger Parker have read substantial amounts and provided invaluable feedback. Stefanie Arend, Philip Bullock, Lorraine Byrne Bodley, Mark Campbell, Suzie Clark, Barry Cooper, Ian Cull, Julian Davis, Nick Davis, Claire Holden, Daniel Hulme, Gundula Kreuzer, Christian Leitmeir, Saskia Lewis, Birgit Lodes, Natasha Loges, Deirdre Loughridge, Fiona McConnell, Kristina Muxfeldt, Marten Noorduin, Richard Parish, Frankie Perry, Matthew Pilcher, Amanda Power, Susan Rutherford, Emanuele Senici, J. C. Smith, George Strivens, Clare Tunbridge, Christiane Wiesenfeldt and Emily Wuchner, have generously offered advice, ideas, illustrations, information and sometimes simply timely encouragement. As always, thanks and love to my mum, Eileen, and Alec and Clare, for their patience and humour; and, of course, to Richard for, among many other things, being willing to go on Beethovenian wild-goose chases with me.

Notes

Introduction: Beginnings

1 Maynard Solomon, *Beethoven* (New York, 1977, rev. edn 2012), 35.
2 Letter from Joseph Haydn to Maximilian, 23 November 1793, translated by John D. Wilson and quoted in Elisabeth Reisinger, 'The Prince and the Prodigies: On the Relations of Archduke and Elector Maximilian Franz with Mozart, Beethoven, and Haydn', *Acta musicologica* 91:1 (2019), 48–70; 61.
3 See John Clubbe, *Beethoven: The Relentless Revolutionary* (London and New York, 2019); and Hans-Joachim Hinrichsen, *Ludwig van Beethoven: Musik für eine neue Zeit* (Kassel, 2019).
4 'Fürst, was Sie sind, sind Sie durch Zufall und Geburt, was ich bin, bin ich durch mich; Fürsten hat es und wird es noch Tausend geben; Beethoven gibt's nur einen.' Letter from Beethoven to Prince Karl Lichnowsky, Grätz, end of October 1806. Reprinted in Sieghard Brandenburg, ed., *Ludwig van Beethoven. Briefwechsel Gesamtausgabe* [hereafter *BGA*] vol. 1, *1783–1807* (Munich, 1996), 290, which explains that the original source is unknown but it was reproduced in nineteenth-century sources. Translated in David Wyn Jones, *The Life of Beethoven* (Cambridge, 1998), 92.
5 For more on this, see Mark Ferraguto, *Beethoven 1806* (Oxford, 2019).

1. Success: Septet

1 'Middle class public opinion' is the description of Ole Hass in his introduction to the *Allgemeine musikalische Zeitung* for RIPM, the

Retrospective Index to Music Periodicals (1760–1966) [hereafter *AmZ*; figures given denote columns].

2 'Nachrichten', *AmZ* 3 (15 October 1800), 49.

3 Friedrich Schiller, 'Über Matthissons Gedichte' (1794), in his *Werke und Briefe*, ed. Otto Dann et al., 12 vols. (Frankfurt am Main, 1992), 8:1023.

4 Letter to Franz Anton Hoffmeister, 15 January 1801; *BGA*, vol. 1, 63–4; translation from *Beethoven: Letters, Journals and Conversations*, ed., trans. and introduced by Michael Hamburger (London, 1951), 35. The German reads: 'was die Leipziger R.[ezensenten] betrifft, so lassen man sie doch nur reden, sie warden gewiß niemand durch ihr Geschwäz unsterblich machen, so wie sie auch niemand die Unsterblichkeit nehmen warden, dem sie von *Apoll* bestimmt ist'. Emphases in the original.

5 'Ein Septuor von Beethoven ist vielleicht für ein gemischtes Publikum zu lang, aber ein wahres Lieblingswerk für Gebildete, voll Geist, voll neuer, kühner und zarter Ideen, und zugleich mit tiefer Gelehrsamkeit ausgestattet, ohne jedoch im geringsten düster oder kalt und schwerfällig zu werden.' 'Nachrichten', *AmZ* 4 (28 April 1802), 498.

6 From the memoirs of composer Johann Nepomuk Emanuel Doležálek, in H. C. Robbins Landon, *Beethoven: A Documentary Study* (London, 1970), 98.

7 Letter to Zmeskall, *c*.1801, included in Robbins Landon, *Beethoven: A Documentary Study*, 101.

8 *Ludwig van Beethovens Konversationshefte*, ed. Karl-Heinz Köhler and Grita Herre (Leipzig, 1981), 10 vols.; vol. 5, 120; see also Maynard Solomon, *Beethoven* (New York, 1977, rev. edn 2012), 416.

9 Letter from Countess Josephine von Deym to Therese von Brunsvik, 21 December 1801; quoted in Robbins Landon, *Beethoven: A Documentary Study*, 108.

10 John Gingerich, *Schubert's Beethoven Project* (Cambridge, 2014), 139–44.

11 Letters to Franz Anton Hoffmeister in Leipzig, 15 January and 22 or 23 June 1801. *BGA*, vol. 1, 63–4; 76–7.

12 Jordan Musser, 'Carl Czerny's Mechanical Reproductions', *Journal of the American Musicological Society* 72 (2019), 367.

13 For example in Andreas Kretschmer, ed., *Deutsche Volkslieder mit ihren Original-Weisen* (Berlin, 1840), 181–2.

14 'Die Komposition selbst ist bekanntlich eine der schönsten, wenigstens eine der angenehmsten und freundlichsten dieses Meisters, und aus jener Zeit, wo er sich noch nicht jenes besondere Ziel versteckte.' *AmZ* 7:48 (28 August 1805), 769–72; 771.

15 Quoted in Angus Watson, *Beethoven's Chamber Music in Context* (Woodbridge, 2010), 77.

16 Quoted in ibid., 77.

17 Quoted in John Gingerich, *Schubert's Beethoven Project* (Cambridge, 2014), 141.

18 Nicholas Mathew, 'Interesting Haydn: On Attention's Materials', *Journal of the American Musicological Society* 71:3 (2018), 655–701; 669.

19 Discussed in Erica Buurman, *Beethoven's Compositional Approach to Multi-Movement Structures in His Instrumental Works* (PhD Manchester, 2013), 73–4; Douglas Johnson, Alan Tyson and Robert Winter, *The Beethoven Sketchbooks: History, Reconstruction, Inventory* (Oxford, 1985), 79.

20 Letter to Hoffmeister & Kühnel in Leipzig, 8 April 1802. *BGA*, vol. 1, 105–6.

21 For more on this, see Lydia Goehr, *The Imaginary Museum of Musical Works: An Essay in the Philosophy of Music* (Oxford, 1992).

22 'Nachrichten', *AmZ* 4 (28 April 1802), 498.

2. Friends: Violin Sonata no. 9

1 Letter of 16 November 1802 to Franz Gerhard Wegeler in Bonn. The letter is not included in the *BGA* but is held in the Beethoven-Archiv (Beethoven-Haus Bonn, Sammlung Wegeler, W 18).

2 Quoted in Alexander Wheelock Thayer, *The Life of Ludwig van Beethoven*, ed. Henry Edward Krehbiel, 3 vols. (New York: The Beethoven Association, 1921), vol. 1, 182.

3 To Ferdinand Ries, 24 July 1804; *BGA*, vol. 1, 216–17; translation from *Beethoven: Letters, Journals and Conversations*, ed., trans. and introduced by Michael Hamburger (London, 1984), 58.

4 Ulrich Schmitt, *Revolution im Konzertsaal: Zur Beethoven-Rezeption im 19. Jahrhundert* (Mainz, 1990).

5 Donald W. MacArdle and Katherine Schultze, 'Five Unfamiliar Beethoven Letters', *Musical Quarterly* 37 (1951), 491.

6 Translations from Maynard Solomon, 'The Dreams of Beethoven', in *Beethoven Essays* (Cambridge, MA, 1990), 56–76; 63.

7 Letter of November 1802, *BGA*, vol. 1, 136.

8 Sonata op. 23 is a violin sonata but Ries's anecdote does not acknowledge that a violinist was also playing. *Beethoven Remembered: The Biographical Notes of Franz Wegeler and Ferdinand Ries*, foreword by Christopher Hogwood, introduction by Eva Badura-Skoda (Salt Lake City, 1987), 81–2.

9 Else Radant, ed., 'The Diaries of Joseph Carl Rosenbaum, 1770–1829', in *Haydn Yearbook* 5 (1968), 109.

10 Wilhelm von Lenz, *Beethoven: Eine Kunst-Studie*, part 2, *Kritischer Katalog sämmtlicher Werke Ludwig van Beethovens mit Analysen derseleben*, 2nd edn (Hamburg, 1860) 4:258; quoted in Steven M. Whiting, 'Finally Finale, Finely: The Recycled Presto in Beethoven's Opus 47', *Journal of Musicological Research* 32:2–3 (2013), 183–98; 191.

11 Quoted in Owen Jander, 'The "Kreutzer" Sonata as Dialogue', *Early Music* 16 (1988), 34–49; 35.

12 See Maria Rose van Epenhuysen, 'Beethoven and His "French Piano": Proof of Purchase', *Musique-Images-Instruments: Revue française d'organologie et d'iconographie musicale* 7. *Écoles et traditions réginales* 2e partie (Paris, 2005), 111–22.

13 'Es ist ein geistvoller und feuriger Satz, der, von raschen und kraeftigen Spielern vorgetragen, eine treffliche Wirking thut',

'Grande Sonate pour le Pianoforte avec accompagnement de Violon, composée p. R. Kreutzer', *AmZ* 4 *(*August 1802), 778–9.

14 Kai Köpp, 'French or German Bows for Beethoven – A Political Choice' (2015) https://tarisio.com/archet-revolutionnaire/kai-koepp-french-or-german-bows-for-beethoven/; and Maiko Kawabata, 'Virtuoso Codes of Violin Performance: Power, Military Heroism, and Gender (1789–1830)', *19th-Century Music* 28:2 (2004), 89–107.

15 Leo Tolstoy, *The Kreutzer Sonata and Other Stories*, trans. Louise and Aylmer Maude and J. D. McDuff (Oxford, 1997), 145.

3. Heroism: Symphony no. 3

1 See, for example, Scott Burnham, *Beethoven Hero* (Princeton, 1995), 3–28; Martin Geck, *Beethoven's Symphonies: Nine Approaches to Art and Ideas*, trans. Stewart Spencer (Chicago, 2017); James Hamilton-Paterson, *Beethoven's Eroica: The First Great Romantic Symphony* (New York, 2017); and Daniel Chua, *Beethoven and Freedom* (Oxford, 2017).

2 Letter from Ferdinand Ries to Nikolaus Simrock, December 1803, quoted in Thomas Sipe, *Beethoven: Eroica Symphony* (Cambridge, 1998), 48.

3 Letter of 2 August 1794 to Nikolaus Simrock, *BGA*, vol. 1, 26; translation from Emily Anderson, *The Letters of Beethoven* (London, 1961, repr. 1986), vol. 1, 18. *Bier* and *Würstel* are underlined in the letter.

4 Early biographer Anton Schindler is the unreliable source for this story, as well as many others, as discussed by Sipe, *Beethoven: Eroica Symphony*, 31–3.

5 Letter to Wenzel Krumpholz, quoted in Geck, *Beethoven's Symphonies*, 10–11.

6 Letter from Ferdinand Ries to Nikolaus Simrock, 22 October 1803; *BGA*, vol. 1, 190.

7 See the Bill from Anton Wranitsky held in the Lobkowitz archive, reproduced by Geck, *Beethoven's Symphonies*, 79.

8 There were also subsequent private renditions; wholesale merchants and bankers Baron Andreas Fellner and his son-in-law Joseph Würth hosted one at their home, using Lobkowitz's orchestra, on 20 April 1805, and there was another at the Lobkowitz palace three days later.

9 'Vienna, 17 April 1805', *Der Freymüthige* 3 (17 April 1805), 332.

10 'Miscellaneous News. Vienna, 2 May 1805', *Berlinische Musikalische Zeitung* 1 (1805), 174.

11 Sipe, *Beethoven: Eroica Symphony*, 57.

12 'Vienna, 9 April', *AmZ* 7 (1 May 1805), 501–2.

13 'Grosse, heroische Sinfonie, compon. von Beethoven, und zum erstenmale in Leipzig aufgeführt: (1) feuriges, prachtvolles Allegro; (2) erhabener, feyerlicher Trauermarsch; (3) heftiges Scherzando; (4) grosses Finale, zum Theil im strengen Styl.' Republished in Alfred Dörffel, *Geschichte der Gewandhausconcerte zu Leipzig vom 25. November 1781 bis 25.November 1881* (Leipzig, 1884).

14 'News. Leipzig. Instrumental Music', *AmZ* 9 (29 April 1807), 497–8.

15 'On Permanent Concerts in Leipzig during the Previous Semi-annual Winter Season', *Journal des Luxus und der Moden* 23 (1807), 444.

16 The Third Piano Concerto was dedicated to Prince Louis Ferdinand of Prussia, himself a talented composer, who apparently asked for the 'Eroica' Symphony to be played to him three times while he was a guest of Prince Lobkowitz. See Rita Steblin, 'Who Died? The Funeral March in Beethoven's Eroica Symphony', *Musical Quarterly* 89:1 (2006), 62–79.

17 William Meredith, 'The Westerby-Meredith Hypothesis: The History of the "Eroica" Variations and Daniel Steibelt's Fortepiano Quintet, Opus 28, No. 2', *Beethoven Journal* 27:1 (2012), 26–44.

18 Cited in Lewis Lockwood, *Beethoven: The Music and the Life* (New York, 2003), 52.

19 Barry Cooper, *Beethoven* (Oxford, 2008), 120.

20 See Martin Geck and Peter Schleuning, *"Geschrieben auf Bona-parte": Beethovens "Eroica". Revolution, Reaktion, Rezeption* (Reinbek, 1989), which emphasizes the progressive aspects of the French regime.

21 Constantin Floros, *Beethoven's Eroica: Thematic Studies*, trans. Ernest Bernhardt-Kabisch (New York, 2013).

22 Friedrich Rochlitz (probably) in the *AmZ* (18 February 1807).

23 Cited in Sipe, *Beethoven: Eroica Symphony*, 58.

24 See Geck and Schleuning, *"Geschrieben auf Bonaparte"*, 279.

25 Letter of 19 July 1825 to Adolph Martin Schlesinger. *BGA*, vol. 6, 111–12.

26 Karl Nef, *Die neun Sinfonien Beethovens* (Leipzig, 1928), 67; discussed in Geck, *Beethoven's Symphonies*, 51.

27 See Stephen Rumph, *Beethoven after Napoleon: Political Romanticism in the Late Works* (Berkeley, 2004), 72–5.

28 Letter of 18 October 1802, *BGA*, vol. 1, 126.

29 Amended from Michael Hamburger, *Beethoven: Letters, Journals and Conversations* (London, 1984), 48–51.

4. Ambition: Choral Fantasy

1 Johann Friedrich Reichardt, *Vertraute Briefe geschrieben auf eine Reise nach Wien* (Amsterdam, 1809–10), 2 vols.; *Personal Letters Written on a Trip to Vienna*, translated by William Oliver Strunk and Leo Treitler in Wye J. Allanbrook, *Source Readings in Music History* (New York, rev. edn 1998), 1029–43.

2 To Breitkopf und Härtel, December 1809, in Emily Anderson, *The Letters of Beethoven* (London, 1961, rep. 1986), vol. 1, 250.

3 *Der Sammler*, 5 January 1809.

4 See David Wyn Jones, *The Symphony in Beethoven's Vienna* (Cambridge, 2006), 168–9.

5 David Wyn Jones, *Beethoven: Pastoral Symphony* (Cambridge, 1995), 81–8.

6 E. T. A. Hoffmann, 'Review: Beethoven's Symphony No. 5 in C minor', *AmZ* 12 (4 July 1810), trans. Martyn Clarke with David Charlton and Ian Bent, in *Music Analysis in the Nineteenth Century*, vol. 2. *Hermeneutic Approaches*, ed. Ian Bent (Cambridge, 1994), 145–60; 146.

7 Deirdre Loughridge, 'Beethoven's Phantasmagoria', in her *Haydn's Sunrise, Beethoven's Shadow: Audiovisual Culture and the Emergence of Musical Romanticism* (Chicago, 2016).

8 See, for instance, Owen Jander, ' "Let Your Deafness No Longer be a Secret – Even in Art": Self-portraiture and the Third Movement of the C-minor Symphony', *Beethoven Forum* 8 (2000), 25–70; 40. Also Matthew Guerrieri, *The First Four Notes: Beethoven's Fifth Symphony and the Human Imagination* (London, 2012).

9 For more on the Fourth Concerto, see Mark Ferraguto, *Beethoven 1806* (Oxford, 2019).

10 'News. Vienna', *AmZ* 11 (25 January 1809), 267–9.

11 Relayed in Alexander Wheelock Thayer, *The Life of Ludwig van Beethoven*, ed. Henry Edward Krehbiel, 3 vols. (New York, 1921), vol. 1, 448–9, from the Appendix to Ignaz von Seyfried's *Beethoven's Studien* (Leipzig, 2nd edn 1853), 15.

12 *AmZ* 11 23 January 1809 (268).

13 *AmZ* 10 23 June 1808 (623–4).

14 For more on this, see Melanie Lowe, *Pleasure and Meaning in the Classical Symphony* (Indianapolis, 2007).

15 *AmZ* 24 (1822), 320. Clive Brown, 'The Orchestra in Beethoven's Vienna', *Early Music* 16:1 (1988), 4–14; 16–20.

16 Reported in Thayer, *Life of Ludwig van Beethoven*, vol. 2, 371.

17 Reported by Czerny after a Lobkowitz musicale in 1808 or 1810; quoted in Lewis Lockwood, *Beethoven: The Music and the Life* (New York, 2003), 285.

18 Sketch from *c.*1809, quoted in Lockwood, *Beethoven*, 281.

19 Authorities on Beethoven give different names: playwright Georg Friedrich Treitschke is put forward by Gustav Nottebohm, while William Kinderman and Theodore Albrecht support Czerny's proposal that it was Kuffner. Composer and music critic August Kanne has also been proposed.

20 Letter to Breitkopf and Härtel, 21 August 1810. *BGA*, vol. 2, 148–50. In the same letter he admitted that it was composed at top speed.

21 Letter to Bernhard Schott and Sons in Mainz, 10 March 1824, *BGA*, vol. 5, 278; Anderson, *Letters of Beethoven*, vol. 3, 1114–15.

22 Anderson, ibid.

23 Wyn Jones, *Beethoven: Pastoral Symphony*, 41.

24 Letter to Breitkopf und Härtel in Leipzig, 9 October 1811, *BGA*, vol. 2, 214–16.

25 The post had been held by Reichardt, whose winter in Vienna brought the end of his appointment. The *AmZ* reported that Reichardt had been involved in Beethoven being offered the post, but that was refuted.

26 Letter to Breitkopf und Härtel in Leipzig, 7 January 1809, *BGA*, vol. 2, 37–8. Anderson, *Letters of Beethoven*, vol. 2, 211–12.

27 Anderson, ibid.

28 Beethoven's difficult relationship with the Tonkünstler-Societät and Salieri is discussed by Rita Steblin in 'Beethoven Mentions in Documents of the Viennese Tonkünstler-Societät, 1795–1824', *Bonner Beethoven Studien* 10 (2012), 139–88.

29 Otto Biba, 'Beispiele für die Besetzungsverhältnisse bei Auf-führungen von Haydns Oratorien in Wien zwischen 1784 und 1808', *Haydn-Studien* 4:2 (1978), 94–104.

30 Reichardt, *Vertraute Briefe*, 320.

31 Joseph Carl Rosenbaum, 'The Diaries of Joseph Carl Rosenbaum, 1770–1829', trans. Else Radant in *Haydn Yearbook* V (Bryn Mawr, PA, 1968), 145. Haydn's oratorio is discussed in Emily M. Wuchner,

The Tonkünstler-Societät and the Oratorio in Vienna, 1771–1798 (PhD, Urbana-Champaign, IL, 2017), 196.

32 Entry of 27 January 1809, Countess Lulu Thürheim, *Mein Leben: Erinnerung aus Österreichs grosser Welt*, trans. René van Rhyn (Munich, 1913), I, 272.

33 Translation from Thayer, *Life of Ludwig van Beethoven*, vol. 1, 457.

34 From the annuity contract, quoted in Ferraguto, *Beethoven*, 29.

5. Love: 'An die Geliebte'

1 'Ich schreibe nur nicht gern Lieder.' Recounted by Friedrich Rochlitz in 1832, from a conversation that had taken place a decade earlier; quoted in John Reid, *The Beethoven Song Companion* (Manchester, 2008), 1.

2 Goethe, letter to Carl Friedrich Zelter, 2 September 1812, trans. in Kristina Muxfeldt, *Vanishing Sensibilities: Schubert, Beethoven, Schumann* (Oxford, 2011), 149–50.

3 Letter to Breitkopf und Härtel, 9 August 1812, *BGA*, vol. 2, 285–6. Emily Anderson, *The Letters of Beethoven* (London, 1961, repr. 1986), vol. 2, 383–4.

4 *Beethoven Remembered: The Biographical Notes of Franz Wegeler and Ferdinand Ries*, foreword by Christopher Hogwood, introduction by Eva Badura-Skoda (Salt Lake City, 1987), 43.

5 Letter to Breitkopf und Härtel, 26 July 1809, *BGA*, vol. 2, 71–2.

6 Lawrence Kramer, ' "Little Pearl Teardrops": Schubert, Schumann, and the Tremulous Body of Romantic Song', in *Music, Sensation, and Sensuality*, ed. Lynda Phyllis Austen (New York, 2016), 57–76.

7 Translation copyright © by Emily Ezust from the Lieder Net archive: https://www.lieder.net/

8 See Beethoven's postscript to a letter to the firm of Offenheimer, probably from autumn 1811, held by the Beethoven-Haus Bonn (H. C. Bodmer, HCB Br 180).

9 *An die ferne Geliebte* was initially published by Steiner in October 1816 but was so riddled with errors that Beethoven insisted a corrected version was produced before it was sent to Lobkowitz; sadly, it did not appear until the month after Lobkowitz's death on 15 December.

10 Ute Jung-Kaiser offers a detailed account of the settings in 'Wer weiß, was ich leide? – Beethovens Sehnsucht' in *1808 – Ein Jahr mit Beethoven*, ed. Ute Jung-Kaiser and Matthias Kruse (Hildesheim, 2008), 121–75.

11 *Josef Ludwig Stoll's Poetische Schriften* Part 1 (Heidelberg, 1811). Part Two never materialized.

12 Paul Reid, *The Beethoven Song Companion* (Manchester, 2007), 58.

13 Maynard Solomon, 'Antonie Beethoven and Brentano', *Music and Letters* 58:2 (1977), 163–9; 161.

14 Reid, *The Beethoven Song Companion*, 59.

15 Translation from Maynard Solomon, 'The Immortal Beloved', in *Beethoven Essays* (Cambridge, MA, 1990), 182.

16 For more on the problem of interpreting dedications, see Margret Jestremski, 'Biographische Bezüge in Beethovens Liedschaffen. Zueignung – Zuneigung?', in *Der 'männliche' und der 'weibliche' Beethoven. Bericht über den Internationalen musikwissenschaftlichen Kongreß vom 31. Oktober bis 4. November 2001 an der Universität der Künste Berlin*, ed. Cornelia Bartsch, Beatrix Borchard and Rainer Cadenbach (Bonn, 2003), 237–47.

17 Letter of 6 and 7 July 1812, *BGA*, vol. 2, 268–71; the translation is adapted from Anderson *Letters of Beethoven*, vol. 1, 373–6.

18 Solomon's translation may seem archaic, but it mimics the rhyme of the German: 'ewig dein/ewig mein/ewig unß'. Letter of 6 and 7 July 1812, to an unknown address, *BGA*, vol. 2, 268–73.

19 Johann Wolfgang von Goethe, *The Sorrows of Young Werther*, trans. Michael Hulse (London, 1989), 101.

20 Mark Evan Bonds, *The Beethoven Syndrome: Hearing Music as Autobiography* (Oxford, 2020), 11.

21 The story of the proposal was relayed by Thayer, who heard it in 1860 from Willmann's niece. Barry Cooper has questioned its veracity, based on the fact that Beethoven wrote to Wegeler in 1801 that for the first time he was considering marriage; see Barry Cooper, *Beethoven* (Oxford, 2008), 110.

22 Letter to Franz Gerhard Wegeler in Bonn, 16 November 1801, *BGA*, vol. 1, 88–91.

23 Rita Steblin has proposed that the portrait was not of Therese Brunsvik but by her; see 'Three Portraits of Women in Beethoven's Estate: A Re-Examination', *Beethoven Journal* 34 (2019), 4–13.

24 Support for Bettina's case is provided by Edward Walden, *Beethoven's Immortal Beloved: Solving the Mystery* (Lanham, MD, 2011).

25 Letter to Schindler, quoted in Anton Felix Schindler, *Beethoven as I Knew Him* ed. Donald W. MacArdle, trans. Constance S. Jolly (Chapel Hill, 1966), 259; cited by Maynard Solomon, who points out that the original does not survive. See 'Antonie Brentano and Beethoven', *Music and Letters* 58:2 (1977), 153–69; 167.

26 Letter to Karl August Varnhagen von Ense in Prague, 14 July 1812, *BGA*, vol. 2, 272–3.

27 Maynard Solomon, 'Beethoven's *Tagebuch* of 1812–1818', *Beethoven Studies* 3, ed. Alan Tyson (Cambridge, 1982), 212.

28 Virginia Oakley Beahrs, 'The Immortal Beloved Riddle Reconsidered', *Musical Times* 129:1740 (February 1988), 64–70.

29 See Lewis Lockwood, *Beethoven: The Music and the Life* (New York, 2003), 334.

30 Waltraud Heindl, 'People, Class Structure and Society' in *Schubert's Vienna*, ed. Raymond Erickson (New Haven, 1997), 36–54.

31 Letter to Ferdinand Ries in London, 8 May 1816, *BGA*, vol. 2, 256–7.

32 The connection between Beethoven and Jeitteles may have been Ignaz Castelli, the editor of *Salem*. As mentioned, the journal occasionally published songs by Beethoven as well as Jeitteles' poetry – but not *An die ferne Geliebte*. This suggests that Beethoven received the poems directly from Jeitteles and may have commissioned them.

33 Birgit Lodes, 'Zur musikalischen Passgenauigkeit von Beethovens Kompositionen mit Widmungen an Adelige: *An die ferne Geliebte* op. 98 in neuer Deutung', in *Widmungen bei Haydn und Beethoven. Personen – Strategien – Praktiken. Bericht über den Internationalen wissenschaftlichen Kongress Bonn, 29. September bis 1. Oktober 2011*, ed. Bernhard R. Appel (Bonn, 2015), 171–202.

34 William Meredith, 'Miscellanea – Mortal Musings: Testing the Candidacy of Almerie Esterházy against the Antonie Brentano Theory', *Beethoven Journal* 15:1 (2000), 42–7.

35 Fanny's diaries, documenting her own infatuation with the composer, were published by Ludwig Nohl in *Eine stille Liebe zu Beethoven: Nach dem Tagebuch einer jungen Dame* (Leipzig, 1875).

36 Sylvia Bowden, ' "A Union of Souls": Finding Beethoven's "Distant Beloved" ', *Musical Times* 150:1909 (2009), 71–94.

37 Rita Steblin, ' "Auf diese Art mit A geht alles zu Grunde": A New Look at Beethoven's Diary Entry and the "Immortal Beloved" ', in *Bonner Beethoven-Studien* 6 (2007), 147–80.

38 Beethoven's 'obsession' with Johanna is explored at length in Maynard Solomon, *Beethoven* (New York, 1977, rev. edn 2012). On the film's multiple inaccuracies, see Lewis Lockwood, 'Film Biography as Travesty: "Immortal Beloved" and Beethoven', *Musical Quarterly* 81:2 (1997), 190–98.

39 Oscar Sonneck, *The Riddle of the Immortal Beloved* (New York, 1927), 67.

40 Maynard Solomon, 'Beethoven's *Tagebuch* 1812–1818', *Beethoven Essays* (Cambridge, MA, 1990), 260.

41 Klaus Martin Kopitz and Rainer Cadenbach showed that Thayer's date of 25 January 1815 for Wild's performance was wrong and that 23 December 1814 was the correct date in *Beethoven aus der Sicht seiner Zeitgenossen in Tagebüchern, Briefen, Gedichten und Erinnerungen* (Munich, 2009); Rita Steblin added the information that Beethoven was not the accompanist in 'Beethoven in Unpublished Viennese Court Documents from 1814', in R. Bernhard Appel,

Joanna Cobb Biermann, William Kinderman and Julia Ronge, eds., *Beethoven und der Wiener Kongress (1814/15): Bericht über die vierte New Beethoven Research Conference, Bonn, 10. Bis 12. September 2014* (Bonn: Beethoven-Haus, 2016).

42 'Heutige Musikbeylage', *Friedensblätter. Eine Festschrift für Leben, Literatur und Kunst* 1 (1814), 30.

6. *Liberty:* Fidelio

1 The full programme is listed in Nicholas Mathew, *Political Beethoven* (Cambridge, 2012), 9.

2 Ibid., 169–70.

3 Adam Zamoyski, *Rites of Peace: The Fall of Napoleon and the Congress of Vienna* (London, 2008), 287–9.

4 Charles-Joseph, Prince de Lignes, quoted in Mathew, *Political Beethoven*, 68.

5 Maynard Solomon, *Beethoven* (New York, 1977, rev. edn 2012), 222.

6 Mathew, *Political Beethoven*, 3.

7 Emily I. Dolan, *The Orchestral Revolution: Haydn and the Technologies of Timbre* (Cambridge, 2013), 191–3.

8 See Nicholas Cook, 'The Other Beethoven: Heroism, the Canon, and the Works of 1813–14', *19th-Century Music* 27:1 (summer, 2003), 3–24; 6.

9 Maynard Solomon, 'Beethoven's Tagebuch of 1812–1818', *Beethoven Studies* 3, ed. Alan Tyson (Cambridge, 1982), 222.

10 David Wyn Jones, *The Symphony in Beethoven's Vienna* (Cambridge, 2006), 179.

11 Quoted in Cook, 'The Other Beethoven', 3–24; 9.

12 Letter from Joseph Sonnleithner to the Imperial Royal Police Director, 2 October 1805, Letter 109 in *Letters to Beethoven and Other Correspondence*, ed. Theodore Albrecht (Nebraska, 1996), 169.

13 Robin Wallace, 'The Curious Incident of *Fidelio* and the Censors', in *The Oxford Handbook of Music Censorship*, ed. Patricia Hall (Oxford, 2015).

14 Quoted in Jan Swafford, *Beethoven: Anguish and Triumph* (London, 2014), 421–2.

15 On the influence of Marie Therese, see John Rice, *Empress Marie Therese and Music at the Viennese Court, 1792–1807* (Cambridge, 2003).

16 18 July 1814 performance of *Fidelio* reviewed in *Der Sammler* 6: 118 (24 July 1814), 471. Tomaschek's autobiography was first published in the Prague periodical *Libussa* 5 (1846), 357–61, and is reproduced in Klaus Martin Kopitz and Rainer Cadenbach, eds., *Beethoven aus der Sicht seiner Zeitgenossen*, vol. 2 (Munich, 2009), 994.

17 Matthew Head, 'Beethoven Heroine: A Female Allegory of Music and Authorship in *Egmont*', *19th-Century Music* 30:2 (2006), 97–132.

18 Rocco sung by Johann Michael Vogl – who later championed Schubert's songs – and Rocco sung by bass Carl Friedrich Weinmüller, who had first sung 'Germania!'.

19 Lobkowitz had hosted a performance of Paer's *Leonora* at his palace between the first and second versions of *Fidelio*. The production of 1809 was in German rather than the original Italian.

20 Kristina Muxfeldt, *Vanishing Sensibilities: Schubert, Beethoven, Schumann* (Oxford, 2011), 5–6.

21 Mathew, *Political Beethoven*, 68.

22 Ibid., 194.

23 11 February 1812; the event was called 'Concert und Vorstellung drei berühmter Gemälde' and was reviewed in *Thalia* 15 (19 February 1812), 57–78, and the *AmZ* (March 1812), 210–11. It was given under the auspices of the Society of Noble Women to Promote the Good and the Useful (*Gesellschaft adeliger Frauen zur Beförderung des Guten und Nützlichen*).

24 See Mathew, *Political Beethoven*, 63–4.

25 Daniel Chua, *Beethoven and Freedom* (Oxford, 2017), 158–72.

26 See Lewis Lockwood, *Beethoven: The Music and the Life* (New York, 2003), 342.

27 Letter to Beethoven's legal adviser, Johann Nepomuk Kanka, in Prague; autumn 1814, *BGA*, vol. 3, 64–5.

28 David Wyn Jones, *The Life of Beethoven* (Cambridge, 1998), 126.

29 Benjamin Walton, '"More German than Beethoven": Rossini's *Zelmira* and Italian Style', in *The Invention of Beethoven and Rossini*, ed. Nicholas Mathew and Benjamin Walton (Cambridge, 2013), 162.

30 Paul Robinson, *Beethoven: Fidelio* (Cambridge, 1996), 150.

31 Claire von Glümer, *Recollections of Wilhelmine Schröder-Devrient* (1862); translated in Thomas S. Grey, ed., *Richard Wagner and His World* (Princeton, 2009), 207–13.

7. Family: Piano Sonata no. 29

1 Kaspar Karl van Beethoven, Will and Codicil, 14 November 1815, *Letters to Beethoven and Other Correspondence*, trans. and ed. Theodore Albrecht (Lincoln, NE, 1996), vol. 2: 1813–23, 82–5.

2 Letter to Kaspar Karl von Beethoven, 15 November 1816, *BGA*, vol. 3, 322.

3 Letter to Nanette Streicher, 24 January 1818, *BGA*, vol. 4, 159–60.

4 Letter to Karl Amenda, 12 April 1815, *BGA*, vol. 3, 137.

5 Beethoven's initial thoughts were 'Tastenflügel', 'Hammerflügel' or 'Federflügelklavier'; see letter from Beethoven to Tobias Haslinger, between 9 and 23 January 1817, *BGA*, vol. 4, 11–12.

6 Op. 109 used the word 'Hammerklavier' on its autograph and the word appeared on a fair copy of op. 110, but the published edition reverted to 'pianoforte'.

7 The musicians were Frederick Kalkbrenner, Ferdinand Ries, John Baptist Cramer, Jacques-Godefroi Ferrari and Charles Knyvett.

8 Gerhard von Breuning, *Memories of Beethoven: From the House of the Black-Robed Spaniards* (Cambridge, 1997; first published in 1874), ed. Maynard Solomon, trans. Henry Mins and Maynard Solomon, 113.

9 Peter Josef Simrock, quoted in Friedrich Kerst, *Die Erinnerungen an Beethoven* (Stuttgart, 1913), 2 vols., vol. 1, 204. By 1810, Beethoven had declared the Érard unusable and it was overhauled by Matthäus Andreas Stein in the spring of 1813. In 1824, Beethoven gave the Érard to his brother Johann; in 1845, it was passed on to the *Oberösterreichisches Landesmuseum* in Linz.

10 They are discussed in detail by Robin Wallace, *Hearing Beethoven: A Story of Musical Loss and Discovery* (Chicago, 2018).

11 Letter to Sigmund Anton Steiner, around 9 January 1817, in connection with op. 101: 'denn das was schwer ist, ist auch schön, gut, gross usw', *BGA*, vol. 4, 8.

12 Charles Rosen, *The Classical Style* (New York, 2nd edn 1997), 403–21.

13 Letter to Ignaz Franz Edler von Mosel, November 1817, *BGA*, vol. 4, 130–31.

14 Johann Nepomuk Mälzel, 'Anzeige', *AmZ* 23, Intelligenz Blatt no. 8 (September 1821), 53–5; cited in Marten Noorduin, 'Czerny's "Impossible" Metronome Marks', *Musical Times* 154 (2013), 24.

15 Cited in Lewis Lockwood, *Beethoven: The Music and the Life* (New York, 2003), 377–8.

16 Alexander Wheelock Thayer, *The Life of Ludwig van Beethoven*, ed. Henry Edward Krehbiel, 3 vols. (New York, 1921), vol. 2, 381.

17 Marten Noorduin, 'Early Performances of Beethoven's "Hammerklavier" Sonata op. 106 in France and England'; https://www.ripm.org/cnc/?p=592, posted 4 April 2017.

18 It is on this basis that Poundie Burstein argues that the notion that the dedication of the 'Lebewohl' Sonata marked Beethoven's sadness at Rudolph's departure from Vienna is unlikely. There may also have been a more personal farewell in Beethoven's mind, to

the young wife of Stephan von Breuning, who had died suddenly that year. '"Lebe wohl tönt überall" and a "Reunion after So Much Sorrow": Beethoven's Op. 81a and the Journeys of 1809', *Musical Quarterly* 93:3–4 (2010), 366–413.

19 Rosen, *The Classical Style*, 404.

8. *Spirit:* Missa solemnis

1 Letter to the Archduke Rudolph, end of April/early May 1819, *BGA*, vol. 4, 269–70.

2 Johann Friedrich Reichardt reported in 1809 that Beethoven hoped to be appointed as Rudolph's Kapellmeister when he was made Cardinal.

3 E. T. A. Hoffmann, 'Review of Beethoven's Mass in C', *AmZ* 15 (16 and 23 June 1813), 389–97, 409–24; trans. in *E. T. A. Hoffmann's Musical Writings: Kreisleriana, The Poet and Composer, Music Criticism*, ed. David Charlton (Cambridge, new edn 2008), 234–51.

4 The leaps at the start of the Credo are reminiscent of the 'Viva Rudolphus' motto from the 'Hammerklavier' Sonata, and the 'Qui tollis' section may allude to 'Das Lebewohl' Sonata, op. 81a, written for Rudolph in 1809–10. Birgit Lodes, *Das Gloria in Beethovens 'Missa solemnis'* (Tutzing, 1997).

5 See Maynard Solomon, 'The Quest for Faith', in *Beethoven Essays* (Cambridge, MA, 1990), 216–32.

6 All quotations from E. T. A. Hoffmann, 'Old and New Church Music', *AmZ* 16 (31 August, 7 and 14 September 1814), 577–84; 593–603; 611–19; trans. in Charlton, ed., *E. T. A. Hoffmann's Musical Writings*, 352–75.

7 Celia Applegate, *Bach in Berlin: Nation and Culture in Mendelssohn's Revival of the 'St Matthew Passion'* (Ithaca, NY, 2005).

8 Warren Kirkendale, 'New Roads to Old Ideas in Beethoven's "Missa Solemnis"', *Musical Quarterly* 56:4 (1970), 665–701.

9 Letter to Joseph Karl Bernard, 26 January 1823, *BGA*, vol. 6, 16. The implication that the process of composition had confirmed his religious beliefs is strengthened by a letter to the harpist Stumpff on his inspiration from God.

10 The Violin Sonatas, op. 30, were dedicated to Czar Alexander I, and other manuscripts were sent to Maria Feodorovna, widow of Czar Paul I, in 1805. Beethoven had presented the Polonaise, op. 89, to Czarina Elizabeth during her visit to Vienna in 1815.

11 Conversation book entry BKh 8:42, John Gingerich, *Schubert, Beethoven* Project (Cambridge, 2014), 24n. 26.

12 'Nachrichten', *AmZ* 26 (27 May 1824): 'Der Eindruck, den dieses originelle, erhabene Meisterwerk auf die anwesenden Verehrer Beethovens machte, war gross.'

13 [*Wiener*] *AmZ* 5 (1821), 706, cited in David Wyn Jones, 'The *Missa Solemnis* Premiere: First Rites', *Musical Times* 139:1864 (1998), 25–6; 28; 25.

14 Then it had prefaced a performance of a paraphrase of the recently assassinated August von Kotzebue's play *The Ruins of Athens* (*Die Ruinen von Athen*) with Beethoven's incidental music from a production for the opening of a new theatre in Pest by Emperor Franz II back in 1811. Like the *Missa solemnis*, *The Consecration of the House* bears the marks of Beethoven's recent engagement with the music of J. S. Bach and Handel in its central fugue.

15 Bartholomaeus Fischenich, quoted in Lewis Lockwood, *Beethoven's Symphonies: An Artistic Vision* (New York, 2015), 201.

16 S . . . i 'Beethoven', *Morgenblatt für gebildete Stande* 17:265 (5 November 1823), 1057–8. Translated in *The Critical Reception of Beethoven by His Contemporaries*, ed. Wayne M. Senner, Robin Wallace and William Meredith (Nebraska, 2001), 3 vols.; vol. 3, 245.

17 The letter is reproduced and discussed in Nicholas Mathew, *Political Beethoven* (Cambridge, 2012), 178–80.

18 Quoted in Nicholas Cook, *Beethoven, Symphony no. 9* (Cambridge, 1993), 37–8.

19 Quoted in Maynard Solomon, *Late Beethoven: Music, Thought, Imagination* (Berkeley, 2003), 216–17. There are sketches for a finale, which eventually found its way into the String Quartet, op. 132, that may have been intended for the Ninth Symphony.

20 Volume 8 (1828) of *Cäcilia* included two reviews, the first a near-unprecedented twenty-six pages long.

21 See Nicholas Mathew, 'On Being There in 1824', in *The Invention of Beethoven and Rossini*, ed. Nicholas Mathew and Benjamin Walton (Cambridge, 2013), 178–94.

22 See Efthycia Panapikolaou, 'Spontini and the City: Bach and Musical Politics in Berlin', *German Quarterly* 92 (2018), 389–99.

9. Endings: String Quartet

1 Gerhard von Breuning, *Memories of Beethoven: From the House of the Black-Robed Spaniards* (Cambridge, 1997; first published in 1874), ed. Maynard Solomon, trans. Henry Mins and Maynard Solomon, 19.

2 Ludwig Rellstab, quoted in *Beethoven: A Documentary Study*, H. C. Robbins Landon (London, 1970), 323.

3 There was an introduction to a string quintet, published by Diabelli – in two- and four-hand piano arrangements – as 'Ludwig van Beethoven's Last Musical Thoughts, after the Original Manuscript of November 1826', and a canon Beethoven sent to Holz asking for payment for the alternative finale to op. 130.

4 He used the French spelling, *Ouverture*, on the manuscript, but it was given in Italian in the first edition. Its use may be a nod to the French baroque tradition often reflected in overtures by Handel and Bach.

5 Manfred Clines and Janice Walker, 'Music as Time's Measure', *Music Perception* 4 (1986), 85–120.

6 Letters to Beethoven 3 and 12 July, 1822, cited in Maynard Solomon, *Beethoven* (New York, 1977, rev. edn 2012), 413.

7 On misreadings of the term, see Theodore Albrecht, 'Beethoven's So-Called Leibquartett, Op. 130: A Case of Mistaken Identity', *Journal of Musicology* 16:3, *New Perspectives on Beethoven Sources and Style* (1998), 410–19.

8 See *Ludwig van Beethovens Konversationshefte*, ed. Karl-Heinz Köhler and Grita Herre (Leipzig, 1981), 10 vols., vol. 8, 243; 250.

9 Op. 127 was heard in private, and then the prince arranged its premiere in St Petersburg on 7 April 1824, a month before its partial performance in Vienna. The Schuppanzigh Quartet's performance of some movements from op. 127 in May 1824 was not wholly successful; it was thought to have been done better by Böhm and Mayseder.

10 The *AmZ* described the second and fourth movements as 'full of mischief, good cheer, and roguishness [*Müthwillen, Frohsinn und Schalkhaftigkeit*] . . . The repetition of both movements was demanded with stormy applause.'

11 'Nachrichten. Wien', *AmZ* 28 (10 May 1826), 310–11.

12 *AmZ* 28:19 (May 1826), 310–11.

13 The translation comes from Elliot Forbes, ed., *Thayer's Life of Beethoven* (rev. edn, Princeton, 1967), 982. The original German text is first given in Wilhelm Von Lenz, *Beethoven: Eine Kunst–Studie, part 2, Kritischer Katalog sämmtlicher Werke Ludwig van Beethovens mit Analysen derselben*, 2nd edn (Hamburg, 1860), 4: 217: 'Jedes in seiner Art! die Kunst will es von uns, dass wir nicht stehen bleiben.' It is quoted in Bathia Churgin, 'The Andante con moto in Beethoven's String Quartet Op. 130: The Final Version and Changes on the Autograph', *Journal of Musicology* 16:2 (spring 1998), 227–53; 253.

14 Schott in Mainz published op. 127 in June 1826. The remaining quartets were all published posthumously: op. 131 by Schott, and opp. 132 and 135 by Schlesinger in Berlin.

15 The meeting with Beethoven and Holz took place at Artaria's office, as is documented in Conversation Book no. 108. Mathias

was not part of the Artaria company with whom Beethoven had published earlier in his career but a scion of the Mannheim branch of the family who had set up his own music publishing house in Vienna in 1822. Originally, Anton Halm was commissioned to make the arrangement, but it was not to Beethoven's satisfaction and so he produced his own for publication.

16 Gerhard von Breuning, *Memories of Beethoven: From the House of the Black-Robed Spaniards*, ed. Maynard Solomon, trans. Henry Mins and Maynard Solomon (Cambridge, 1997; first published in 1874), 85.

17 Lenz, *Beethoven: Eine Kunst-Studie* 5:216; quoted in Solomon, *Beethoven*, 134.

18 DSB, Heft 126, fol. 13v (unpublished); quoted in Solomon, *Beethoven*, 69.

19 Jan Swafford, *Beethoven: Anguish and Triumph* (London, 2014), 898.

20 According to Anselm Hüttenbrenner, cited Robbins Landon, *Beethoven*, 392–3.

21 Abigail Fine, *Objects of Veneration: Music and Materiality in the Composer-Cults of Germany and Austria, 1870–1930* (PhD, Chicago, 2017).

22 Daniel Brenner, *Anton Schindler und sein Einfluss auf die Beethoven-Biographik* (Bonn, 2013).

23 'Den Freunden Beethovens', *AmZ* 42 (17 October 1827), 705–10.

24 Anton Schindler, *Biographie von Ludwig van Beethoven* (Münster, 1840), 97–8.

Coda

1 Roger Allen, *Richard Wagner's 'Beethoven' (1870): A New Translation* (Woodbridge, 2014); and David B. Dennis, *Beethoven in German Politics, 1870–1989* (New Haven, 1996).

2 Scott Messing, 'The Vienna Beethoven Centennial Festival of 1870', *Beethoven Newsletter* 6:3 (1991), 57–63.

3 Beate Kutschke, 'The Celebration of Beethoven's Bicentennial in 1970: The Antiauthoritarian Movement and Its Impact on Radical Avant-garde and Postmodern Music in West Germany', *Musical Quarterly* 93:3/4 (2010), 560–615.

4 Johannes Kreidler's *Compression Sound Art* series (2009) and Leif Inge's *9 Beet Stretch* (2012) are discussed in Alexander Rehding, *Beethoven's Symphony No. 9* (Oxford, 2018).

5 Barry Cooper produced a score of the Tenth Symphony which was first performed in 1988; a new edition was published by Universal Edition in 2013. Matthias Röder of the Herbert von Karajan Stiftung is responsible for the completion of the Tenth Symphony by machine learning.

Index

Page references in *italic* indicate illustrations.

Adam, Jean-Louis 64, 65
Alberti, Count of 219
Alexander I of Russia 142
Allgemeine musikalische Zeitung (AmZ)
    Berliner *AmZ* 83
    Leipziger *AmZ* 20, 21, 22, 36–7,
        65, 77, 95, 96, 104, 178, 179,
        193, 202, 217, 218, 225
    Wiener *AmZ* 194, 201, 202
Amenda, Karl 164
Anschütz, Heinrich 224
Arnim, Bettina von 49, 134
Artaria, Mathias 175, 219, 221
Artaria (publishing company)
    8, 9, 191
Auernhammer, Josepha 27
Austerlitz, Battle of 79
Austrian currencies viii

Bach, Carl Philipp Emanuel 22, 203
Bach, Johann Baptist 166
Bach, Johann Christian 40–41
Bach, Johann Sebastian 16, 41, 187–8
    Art of Fugue 176
    B minor Mass 188, 203
    and Beethoven's
        'Hammerklavier' 176
    St Matthew Passion 188
    Well-Tempered Clavier 176

Baden 49, 219–20
Bähr, Joseph 29
Beethoven, Johann van (father) 3, 228
Beethoven, Johanna van
    (sister-in-law) 130, 162–6, 222
Beethoven, Karl van (nephew) 10,
        16, 162–6, *166*, 167, 172–3, 175,
        181, 183, 186, 199, 209–10, 219,
        220–22, 225
    and Beethoven's will 222–3
    suicide attempt 220
Beethoven, Kaspar Karl van
    (brother) 6–7, 36, 74–5, 131,
        159, 162
Beethoven, Ludwig van:
    correspondence/letters
    apologetic, in over-the-top
        fashion 45
    to Bettina von Arnim 134
    with a 'Barbarian Friend' 51
    to Bernard 189
    with Breitkopf und Härtel 77
    and Stephan von Breuning 45–6
    with brothers 88 *see also (below)*
        'Heiligenstadt Testament'
        (unsent)
    complaining about isolation 164
    contemplative themes 186
    over corrections to editions 41

Beethoven, Ludwig van – *cont'd*
  to Gleichenstein 110
  'Heiligenstadt Testament'
    (unsent) 15, 88–9, 207, 225
  to Hoffmeister 22, 32–3
  to the 'Immortal Beloved'
    (unsent) 15, 119–22, 123–7,
    129–30, 225
  to Kanka 158–9
  with 'Miss Emilie M. at H.' 133–4
  to publishers in final days of his
    life 222
  quotations peppering letters
    113–14
  to Ries 127, 196, 214
  to Archduke Rudolph 183–4
  to Schlesinger 208
  to Varnhagen von Ense 125
  to Wegeler 44–5, 47–8
  to Wetzler 55
  to/concerning Zmeskall 127
Beethoven, Ludwig van: the man
    and his life
  appearance 127, 132, 204 *see also*
    (below) busts; Horneman
    portrait *46*; Lyser sketch *205*
  arrest on suspicion of vagrancy
    164
  baptism 1
  birth: 250th anniversary 229–30;
    centenary 1, 228; date,
    uncertain 139, 228
  and brothels 127, 163
  busts 137; by Klein 131–2, *132–3*;
    by Schaller 229
  character: heroism 14–15, 80–81,
    87–8; jest-making and sense of
    humour 51–2; nationalist/

  patriotic tendencies xi, 158,
    167–8, 199; perceptions
    reshaped by discovery of
    unsent letters 225;
    rebelliousness 11–12, 230; and
    tussles concerning Johanna and
    guardianship of Karl 162–6
  and Cherubini 150
  and coffee vii, 50–51, 190
  as conductor 99
  daily routine 190
  deafness *see (below)* hearing loss
  death 223; 1927 centenary 229;
    and monument in Bonn 1, *2*,
    17, 230–31, *230*
  diary (*Tagebuch*) entries 125–6,
    129–30, 158, 186
  distaste for business dealings 32
  early biographical accounts 226
  early court employment (from
    age 13) 4
  education 3
  and electoral orchestra 4
  and Enlightenment ideals 3
  family background 1–3, 227–8
  family relationships 44
  final illness 222–3
  finances viii–ix, 175; annuity ix,
    108, 109–10, 117–18, 181; and
    auction of his estate 225; and
    catering to popular sentiment
    142–3; income from
    commissions 7, 196, 206, 214;
    income from handwritten
    copies of works 191; income
    from performances 7, 8;
    income from publishing 8, 9,
    63–4, 191; income from

teaching 7; income from
temporary ownership of a
work 75; with national
inflation and currency
devaluation viii, 108, 116–17;
and patrons ix, 7, 17, 25, 33,
181 *see also* Beethoven, Ludwig
van: the man and his life:
patronage; pricing schemes for
compositions 31; school
expenses for nephew, Karl
175; support from admirers in
Vienna 8
Flemish background 227–8
friendship circles 43–55, 129–31,
190; and growing isolation 15,
16, 43, 127, 134, 164, 173, 190,
195; and nicknames 51, 53, 58,
119
funeral 223–4
and Goethe 112–13, 125, 191
guardianship of nephew, Karl
10, 162–6, 219, 220; and
coaching to become a virtuoso
173, 181; court cases and
tussles with Karl's mother 10,
162–6, 183; relinquished 220;
school expenses 175
and Haydn 4, 11–12, 26
hearing loss 89, 110, 135, 152,
164, 165, 171–2, 179; and
Broadwood piano 171–2; and
ear trumpets 134–5, *135*, 141,
172; and inability to
communicate with nephew,
Karl 164, 165; and reliance on
helpers 215; and social
isolation 15, 43, 134, 135, 164,

165, 190, 217; and Stein's
'hearing machine' 172
'heroic', 'new way' of composing
58, 179–80
image 13, 17, 71, 94, 132, 142,
201, 204, 230–31
interests: classical literature
113–14, 158, 222; philosophy
114, 158, 186; religious/
mystical 114, 158, 186
international fame during
lifetime 201, 203, 228
Kapellmeister offer in Kassel
104, 108, 110
landscape made out of his hair *224*
and *Lesegesellschaft* (Reading
Society) 4, 46–7
Morgenblatt für gebildete Stände on
his standing 198
and Mozart 4
and Napoleon 67, 72–4, 86, 87,
140, 199; and Third Symphony
73–4
and Napoleonic Wars *see*
Napoleonic Wars
Neefe's influence 3
own attitude to historical
standing 133–4
patronage: in Bonn 3, 4; and
independence 17; in Vienna
ix, 7, 17, 25, 33, 49, 55, 75,
108–9, 117, 159, 181
as pianist 15, 19, 81, 112; when
deaf 135; improvisatory skills
4, 19, 20, 81, 100–101
as piano teacher 30, 181
pianos *see* pianoforte and
fortepiano

Beethoven, Ludwig van – *cont'd*
portrait by Horneman 45–6, *46*
romance and search for a wife
48–9, 54, 110, 113, 122–30, 151;
disappointment 15, 127
and Rossini 160
social isolation 15, 16, 43, 122,
127, 134, 164, 173, 190, 195,
217, 224
spirituality and faith 185–6
and Vienna *see also* Vienna: 1800
Akademie at Burgtheater 19, 23,
24, 25, *26*; 1808 *Akademie* at
Theater an der Wien 90–103,
105, 106; apartments 49–50;
Augarten concerts 56–7;
campaigns to keep him in 108,
199–200; concert of 24 May
1824 201–3; early visits 4;
feeling undervalued in 199;
financial support from
admirers 8; highlights of
success and status 20, 31, 132,
140, 146, 158; and his funeral
223–4; and his reputation 15,
201, 202, 215, 224; as Imperial
Music Director 108; as an
instrument-building centre 10;
Liebhaber Concerte 105–6;
move to 5–6; patronage ix, 7,
17, 25, 33, 49, 55, 75, 108–9, 117,
159, 181; publishers 8–9;
regular performances of his
work during his lifetime in 31;
and Royal Court Theatre 108;
Schwarzenberg palace venue
24, 28; as symbol of Viennese
musical supremacy 203;

Tonkünstler-Societät concerts
25, 105; and Viennese currency
viii, 32, 108, 117
Wagner's essay on 228
will 222–3
Beethoven, Ludwig van: works
'Adelaide', op. 46 for solo voice
and piano 217
'Ah! Perfido', op. 65 91–2, 95
'An den fernen Geliebten', op. 75
no. 5 128
An die ferne Geliebte, op. 98 117,
127–30
'An die Geliebte', WoO 140 15,
115–16, 118–19, 136, 146
'An die Hoffnung', op. 94 117, 126
canon for four voice, 'Es muss
sein', WoO196 208
cantata, op. 136, *Der glorreiche
Augenblick* (*The Glorious
Moment*) 131, 142, 150, 199
Cello Sonata, op. 69 in A major
103, 109
Choral Fantasy, op. 80 in C
minor 15, 92, 99–103, 104–5;
dedication 104; and 'Ode to
Joy' 15, 94, 102; premier 94,
95–7, 99–100, 104, 109
chorus used for *Die gute Nachricht*
and *Die Ehrenpforten* 138–9
Christus am Ölberge, op. 85 (*Christ
on the Mount of Olives*) 27, 28,
194, 199
Clarinet Trio, op. 11 in B-flat
major 81
composed in 'heroic', 'new way'
58, 179–80
for Congress of Vienna 15

Consecration of the House overture, op. 124 (Die Weihe des Hauses) 195

Coriolan overture, op. 62 106, 109, 203

counterpoint *see* counterpoint

Fidelio, op. 72 13, 15, 70, 95, 137, 143–56, 199; censorship issues 144, 146; double-talk 155–6; dungeon scene 147, 152, *153*; early versions 146; and heroism 149, 152, 161; and Lang's *prisoner of the state* 229; *Leonore* and *Fidelio* titles 148; libretto 143, 157; and Marie Theresa 144; and Paer's *Leonora* 152–3; plot summary 146–7; premiere 145, 148; reactionary aspects of 1814 revision 159; and Treitschke's revisions 146, 148–9, 154; Viennese performance of 1822 159–61

French in front pages of first editions 6, 7

French musical influence 73–4

fugues *see* fugues

with German expression markings xi, 158, 167–8

Geschöpfe des Prometheus, op. 43 (*Creatures of Prometheus*) 29, 82

hierarchy established by composer 36

Horn Sonata, op. 17 in F major 21, 27

humour in 12

immortality claims 137

and improvisation's importance in musical imagination 81

incidental music, op. 113, for *Die Ruinen von Athen* 142

instructions to performers 41

'Leonore Prohaska', WoO 96 73

'Lied aus der Ferne', WoO137 128

'Lob auf den Dicken' (WoO 100) 53

Mass in C, op. 86 92, 103, 109, 194, 195

metronome markings 178

Missa solemnis, op. 123 in D major 13, 16, 103, 173, 177, 182, 183–95, 199, 203, 227; declared by composer to be his best work 190; dedication 183, 185; handwritten copies for prominent people 191–2; inscription on autograph manuscript 185; manuscript auction price 225; publishing negotiations 191; St Petersburg premier 192–3

piano arrangement for four hands, op. 134, of 'Grosse Fuge' 219

PIANO CONCERTOS

First, op. 15 19, 21, 31; cadenza sketch 40

Second, op. 19 33

Third, op. 37 27, 105

Fourth, op. 58 92, 94, 181

Fifth, op. 73 75, 181; Viennese premiere 156–7

PIANO SONATAS

and capabilities of instruments 168–71

op. 2 set 12

op. 13, 'Pathétique' in C minor 12

op. 14 set 27; No. 1 40

Beethoven, Ludwig van – *cont'd*
  op. 22 in B flat major 31, 33
  op. 26 in A flat major 73
  op. 27 no. 2, 'Moonlight' in C
    sharp minor 54, 123
  op. 49, no. 2 in G major 36
  op. 53, 'Waldstein' in C major
    63, 130, 169
  op. 57, 'Appassionata' in F
    minor 63
  op. 78 in F sharp major 123
  op. 90 in E minor 158
  op. 101 in A major 63, 167, 168
  op. 106, 'Hammerklavier' in B
    flat major 16, 136, 167–8, 170,
    173–81, 182, 184; dedication
    181–2, 184; separation of
    sonata and fugue in English
    edition 175; sketches 176, 182;
    title 167–8
  op. 109 in E major 170
  op. 111 in C minor 170, 181
  PIANO TRIOS
  op. 1 set 7, 9, 11; no. 3 in C
    minor 11–13, 167
  op. 70 set 103
  op. 97 in B flat major, 'Archduke'
    135, 181, 217
  WoO 39 in B flat major 125
  Quintet for Piano and Winds,
    op. 16 in E flat major 51
  and rights 34
  romanticism 78, 93
  'Schuppanzigh ist ein Lump'
    (WoO 184) 53
  sensibility 22, 37
  Septet, op. 20 in E flat major 13,
    14, 19, 21–4, 31–41, 52, 226;

  Beethoven's own
    arrangements 33–4, 35, 36;
    dedication 29–30; manuscript
    auction price 225;
    orchestration 24; sketches
    40; success 21, 22–4, 28, 29,
    30, 37; unauthorized/later
    arrangements 34–5, 37;
    versatility 24, 33–4
  'Seufzer eines Ungeliebten
    – Gegenliebe', WoO 118 100
  and significance of numbers
    three and nine 14
  'Six National Airs with
    Variations', op. 105 for flute/
    violin and piano 180–81
  sketches 38–40; 'An die Geliebte'
    118; auctioned 225; string
    quartet in C sharp minor *39*;
    Third Symphony 81–2
  songs of diverse forms 111–12, 114
  STRING QUARTETS
  op. 18 set 24, 28, 41; sketches
    39, 40
  op. 59 'Razumovsky' set 109
  op. 95 in F minor 214
  op. 127 in E flat major 206, 209,
    220; premier 216
  op. 130 in B flat major 16, 205–6,
    208–12, 213, 215–16, 217, 218;
    Beethoven listening in tears to
    Cavatina 212; and 'Der
    schwer gefaßte Entschluß'
    206–8, *207*; new, alternative
    ending 208, 219, 221; original
    ending *see (below)* op. 133,
    'Grosse Fuge' in B flat major;
    premier and reception 216–19

op. 131 in C sharp minor 206;
sketch *39*

op. 132 in A minor 206, 220

op. 133, 'Grosse Fuge' in B flat
major 16, 173, 182, 210, 212–14;
dedication 219; dynamic
markings 213; four-hand piano
arrangement, op. 134, by
composer 219; Halm's
arrangement attempt 217;
premier and reception 217–18

op. 135 in F major 206–8, *207*, 221;
and Herbert's *Requiem* 229

STRING QUINTETS

op. 29 in C major 64

op. 104 in C minor 167, 180, 181

string trios, op. 9 set 33

SYMPHONIES

First, op. 21 19, 106, 157

Second, op. 36 27, 31, 33, 106, 157

Third, 'Eroica', op. 55 13, 14, 37,
58, 69–89, 106, 149, 157, 227;
critical responses 82–3;
dedication 78; first
performance at Lobkowitz's
palace (1804) 75; first public
performance (1805) 76–7; and
'Kreutzer' Sonata 70, 75;
Leipzig premiere programme
(1807) 78–9; and Napoleon
73–4, 79–80, 87; and political
situation 70–74; and Rizzi's
*Beethoven: 'Sinfonia Eroica II
Tempo'* 86, *87*; sketches 81–2;
subtitle of Cianchettini and
Sperati 1809 edition 86; title
74; title page 78, 79–80, *80*

Fourth, op. 60 75, 98, 109

Fifth, op. 67 12, 13, 92–4, 103–4,
157, 185, 203, 227

Sixth, op. 68 91, 92, 103–4, 230

Seventh, op. 92 98, 131, 141, 142,
143

Eighth, op. 93 98, 131, 143

Ninth, op. 125 13, 14, 98, 167,
195–8, 199–201, 209, 227;
London premier 201; 'Ode to
Joy' 13, 15, 45, 94, 102, 196,
197–8, 201; recordings 229;
Vienna premier 193, *195*

Tenth sketches 230

Concert Spirituels performances
194

'Ten National Airs with
Variations', op. 107 for flute/
violin and piano 180–81

Three Songs, op. 83 (Goethe) 119

Triple Concerto, op. 56 in C
major 96

Twelve Contredanses, WoO 14 82

unauthorized arrangements 34–5

Variations (6) on an original
theme for piano, op. 34 in F
major 103

Variations and Fugue for Piano,
op. 35 in E flat major 70, 103

Variations for Mechanical Organ
(*Flötenuhr*) 35

Variations on Mozart's 'Là ci
darem la mano', WoO 28 105

Variations on Mozart's 'Se vuol
ballare' 8, 9

and Vienna: Concerts Spirituels
193–5; Eroica-Saal, Palais
Lobkowitz 75

and Viennese classical style 10–11

Beethoven, Ludwig van – *cont'd*
Violin Concerto, op. 61 76, 109
VIOLIN SONATAS
op. 23 52
op. 30, no. 1, in A major 58
op. 47, 'Kreutzer' 14, 56–68, 169;
dedication 57–8, 63, 64–5, 70;
and the 'Eroica' 70, 75; gender
relations upset by 68; premier
57; subtitle/title page 58–9;
violin–piano relationship 60–61
op. 96 in G major 181
Wellingtons Sieg, op. 91 ('Battle
Symphony') 13, 131, 140–43,
226
Beethoven, Ludwig van the Elder
(grandfather) 1, 3, 227
Beethoven, Maria van (mother) 3, 4
Beethoven, (Nikolaus) Johann van
(brother) 220–21, 223
Beethoven Archive 2
Beethoven House Association 2
Beethoven-Haus 2, 227, 229
*Berliner Allgemeine musikalische
Zeitung* 83
Bernadotte, Jean Baptiste Jules 65,
72–3
Bernard, Joseph Karl 189, 190
Bolla, Maria 26
Bonaparte, Jérôme 104
Bonaparte, Napoleon *see* Napoleon I
Bonds, Mark Evan 122
Bonn
Beethovenfest of 1845 1
Beethoven-Haus 2, 227, 229
Beethoven's centenary in 1
Beethoven's patrons in 3, 4
electoral orchestra 4

and Electorate of Cologne 5
fall to Napoleon 5
Lesegesellschaft 4, 46–7
monument to Beethoven 1, 2,
17; and Hörl's sculptures
230–31, *230*
Münsterplatz 230–31, *230*
musical life/heritage 3, 227
refugees in 71
Bouilly, Jean-Nicolas 29, 143, 144
Léonore, ou L'amour conjugal 143
bowing techniques 66
bows, violin 65–7, *66*
Braun, Josephine 27
Braun, Peter von, Baron 27, 145
Breitkopf und Härtel 20, 74–5, 77,
103–4, 188, 202
Brentano, Antonie 119, 124–6,
130, 175
Brentano, Franz 125
Brentano, Maximiliane 125, 130
Brentano family 130, 131, 186
Breuning, Eleanor von 44
Breuning, Gerhard von 171, 204,
218, 220, 222, 227
Breuning, Helene von 44
Breuning, Stephan von 44, 45–6,
127, 204, 220, 222, 224–5
Bridgetower, George Polgreen
53–5, 56, 57–8, 65
Broadwood, Thomas 168
Broadwood piano 168–9, 170, 171–2
brothels 127, 163
Browne, Anna Margarete von,
Countess 9, 33
Browne, Johann Georg von, Count
9, 33
Brunsvik, Franz von 30

Brunsvik, Josephine von 30, 35
  as Countess Deym 124, 126
Brunsvik, Therese von 30, 123–4, 126
Buddhism 186
Bürger, Gottfried August:
  'Gegenliebe' 100
Byron, Lord 20

Cäcilia 201, 202, *205*
Campo Formio 72
Cavaliers, Society of 187
censorship 15–16, 72, 144, 146, 159,
  187, 190
Cherubini, Luigi 73, 149, 150, 157,
  191
  Faniska 150
Chopin, Frédéric 1
Cianchettini and Sperati 86
Clement, Franz 76, 95
Clementi, Muzio 109
coffee ix, 50–51, 190
coffeehouses 50, 116
concertmasters 98–9
Concerts Spirituels, Vienna 193–5,
  198
conducting 98–9
Conti, Giacomo 21
copyright laws 40–41
counterpoint 173, 176–7, 182, 188,
  213 *see also* fugues
Czerny, Carl 35, 36, 37, 95, 157, 179,
  190, 201, 223
  'Anekdoten und Notizen über
    Beethoven' 102

Demscher, Ignaz 208
Deym, Josephine, Countess
  (née Brunsvik) 124, 126,
  130 *see also* Brunsvik,
    Josephine von
  and daughter Minona 126–7
Deym von Stritetz, Joseph, Count
  126
Diabelli (publisher) 191
Dietrichstein, Moritz, Count 54, 199
Dietzel, Johann 29
Doležálek, Johann Emanuel 95–6
Dresden 53, 86, 144
Duncker, Johann Friedrich 73
Dušek, Josefa 26

ear trumpets 134–5, *135*, 141, 172
Enlightenment humanism/thinking
  185, 186
Érard pianos 62–3, 64, 169, 171
Erdődy, Anna Marie, Countess 48,
  108, 109, 127, 164
Erdődy, Péter, Count 9
Esterházy, Almerie 129
Esterházy, Nikolaus 9, 57
Esterházy family 7, 57
Euripides 114

Finanzpatent 117
fortepiano *see* pianoforte and
  fortepiano
France
  and court culture of Vienna 6
  Franco–Prussian War 228
  French in front pages of
    Beethoven's first editions 6, 7
  French occupation of Vienna
    107, 114, 116, 145
  French operas translated into
    German for Vienna 143
  French Revolutionary Army 72

France – *cont'd*
  Napoleonic Wars *see* Napoleonic
    Wars
  vogue for French operas in
    Vienna 73
Franz I of Austria 139
Frederick VI of Denmark 191
Freemasons 47
  Illuminati 3–4, 47, 186
Freymüthige 37, 76
Friedensblätter. Eine Festschrift für
  Leben, Literatur und Kunst 136
Fries, Maria Theresia von,
  née Princess Hohenlohe-
  Waldenburg-Schillingsfürst 48
Fries, Moritz Johann Christian,
  Count 48
Frölich, Parson 165
fugues 70, 170, 173, 176–7, 188,
  189, 213
  separated from original works
    of Beethoven 175 *see also*
    Beethoven, Ludwig van:
    works: string quartets: op. 133,
    'Grosse Fuge' in B flat major

Galitzin, Nicolas, Prince 192, 193,
  205–6, 214, 219
Gallenberg, Wenzel Robert,
  Count 54
Gebauer, Franz Xaver 193–4
George, Prince of Wales (later
  George IV) 54
German nationalism 228
Gesellschaft der Musikfreunde,
  Vienna 187, 193
Giannattasio del Rio, Cajetan 163
Giannattasio del Rio, Fanny 129

Gleichenstein, Ignaz von, Baron
  109, 110, 127, 181
Gluck, Christoph 7–8
Gneixendorf 220–21, 222
Goethe, Johann Wolfgang von 10,
  22, 111, 128
  and Beethoven 112–13, 125, 191;
  op. 83 songs 119
  The Sorrows of Young Werther 113
Gossec, François-Joseph 73
Graf, Conrad, piano 170, 171
Grasnick sketchbooks 39–40
Grillparzer, Franz 187, 224
Guicciardi, Giulietta, Countess 48,
  54, 123
Gyrowetz, Adalbert 138

Habsburg Empire 5–6, 6, 71
Halm, Anton 217
Handel, George Frideric 187
Härtel, Gottfried Christoph 103–4,
  114 *see also* Breitkopf und
  Härtel
Haslinger, Tobias 51, 167, 190
Haydn, Joseph 8, 9, 29, 41–2, 57,
  64, 75, 111, 132, 183, 215, 225
  and Beethoven 4, 11–12, 26
  Creation (Die Schöpfung) 24, 189
  and Esterházy family 7
  'Joke' Quartet 12
  Mass in B flat major
    (*Theresienmesse*) 29
  and Maximilian 5
  and Milder 150
  Ritorno di Tobia 90, 106
  and Viennese classical style 11
  witticism 12
Hebenstreit, Wilhelm 167

Heiligenstadt 49, 87–8
'Heiligenstadt Testament' (unsent
    letter of Beethoven) 15, 88–9,
    207
Held, Johann Thomas 54
Herbert, Matthew: *Requiem* 229
Hermann, Heinrich 83
heroism 14–15, 80–81, 87–8, 148,
    149, 152, 161
    as androgynous 152
    Beethoven's 'heroic', 'new way'
        of composing 58, 179–80
Hinduism 186
Hoche, Lazare 73
Hofbauer, Clemens Maria 186
Hoffmann, E. T. A. 93, 157, 184,
    185, 187, 189, 192
Hoffmeister, Franz Anton 22, 31,
    32–3
Holz, Karl 37, 51, 208, 209–10, 212,
    215, 216, 217, 218, 219, 220, 222,
    226
Homer 74, 82, 114, 222
    Iliad 158
Hörl, Ottmar, 'Ode to Joy'
    installation 230–31, *230*
Horneman, Christian, portrait of
    Beethoven 45–6, *46*
Hotschevar, Jacob 224–5
Hummel, Johann Nepomuk 35,
    138, 183, 223

Illuminati 3–4, 47, 186
Immortal Beloved (Rose film) 130
Imperial Royal Police 144
improvisation 4, 19, 100–101
Inge, Leif 229
intellectual property 41

Jacobin sympathizers 72
Janáček, Leoš 68
Jedlesee 49
Jeitteles, Alois 128
Jones, David Wyn 159
Joseph II, Holy Roman Emperor
    26, 50, 56
Joubert, Barthélemy Catherine 73

Kagel, Mauricio 229
Kanka, Johann Nepomuk 158–9
Kanne, Friedrich August 138, 190,
    200, 202
Kant, Immanuel 3, 38, 45, 136
    *Universal History of Nature and
    Theory of the Heavens* 158
Kassel 104, 108, 110
Kerner, Justinus 116
Killitzky, Josephine 95
Kinsky, Caroline, Princess 117,
    119
Kinsky, Ferdinand, 5th Prince
    Kinsky of Wchinitz and
    Tettau 108, 109, 117, 124
Kinsky family 159
Klein, Franz, life mask and bust
    of Beethoven 131–2,
    132–3
Klöber, August von 172
Klopstock, Friedrich 114
Kneisel, Carl Moritz 1, 2
Körner, Christian Gottfried 45
Kotzebue, August von 145
Kreidler, Johannes 229
Kreutzer, Rodolphe 64, 66, 70
    42 Études 65
    Grande Sonate in A minor 65
Kuffner, Christoph 101

Kundera, Milan: *The Unbearable Lightness of Being* 207–8
Kunst-und Industrie-Comptoir 77–8

Lang, David 229
Lang, Regina 119
Lanner, Joseph 198
Lenz, Wilhelm von 60, 83
Leopold II, Holy Roman Emperor 71
Lesegesellschaft (Reading Society) 4, 46–7
Lewald's Europa 118–19
Lichnowsky, Karl, Prince ix, 9, 17, 27–8, 47–8, 108, 215
Lichnowsky, Moritz, Count 47, 54, 199
Liège, St Lambert's Cathedral 227–8
Lincke, Joseph 215
Linzbauer, Fanny 229
Liszt, Franz 1, 179
Lobkowitz, Joseph Franz von 9, 75, 78, 90, 104, 108, 109, 117, 129
Lodes, Birgit 129
Louis XVI 71–2
Louis XVIII 191
Lunéville, Treaty of 143
Lyser, Johann Peter, sketch of Beethoven *205*

Maecenus 33
Mähler, Willibrod Joseph 81
Malfatti, Therese 124
Mälzel, Johann Nepomuk 134–5, 141, 178
Marengo, Battle of 143
Maria Theresa, Empress 29, 33, 74, 146

Maria Theresia Hohenlohe-Waldenburg-Schillingsfürst, Princess 48
Marie Antoinette 71–2
Marx, Adolf Bernhard 83
Matauschek, Johann 29
Maximilian Franz of Austria 4–5, 33, 71, 72
Maximilian Joseph of Bavaria 104
Mechelen 227
melisma 189
metronome 134, 141, 178
Metternich, Klemens von 15–16, 139, 159, 190
Milder, Anna 95, 150–51
Mirabeau, Honoré Gabriel Riqueti, Count of 73
Mödling 164, 168, 170
Montez, Lola 1
Monti, Vincenzo: *Il Prometeo* 82
Morgenblatt für gebildete Stände 83, 198
Moscheles, Ignaz 96, 179
Mozart, Constanze 26
Mozart, Wolfgang Amadeus 4, 7–8, 9, 27, 40, 41–2, 75, 132, 215
  and *Die gute Nachricht* 138
  entertaining the galleries 145
  Requiem 187
  and Viennese classical style 11
Munich opera house 86
Murphy, Walter: *A Fifth of Beethoven* 229
Musen-Almanach für das Jahr 1814 136

Napoleon I 5, 15, 87, 116, 152
  abdication 139
  and Beethoven 67, 72–4, 79–80, 86, 140, 199

escape from Elba 157
exile to Elba 139
Napoleonic Wars viii, 5, 14, 71–4,
    106–7, 138, 146, 152, 156, 159, 202
    and Fifth Coalition 107
    French occupation of Vienna
        107, 114, 116, 145
    and Third Coalition 107
Neate, Charles 209, 214
Neefe, Christian Gottlob 3, 111
Nickel, Mathias 29
Nickelsberg, Karl Nickl von 33

Oldman, Gary 130
Oliva, Franz 116
Olmütz (now Olomouc) 183
Oppersdorff, Franz von, Count 17,
    104
Ossian (James Macpherson) 114

Paer, Ferdinando 144, 149
    Achille 74, 144
    Leonore 152–3
panharmonicon 141
Paris 1, 6, 70
Peters, Carl Friedrich 191, 214
Peters, Karl 166
Pezzl, Johann ix
pianoforte and fortepiano 9–10,
    167–8
    Broadwood 168–9, 170, 171–2
    Érard 62–3, 64, 169, 171
    ranges of Beethoven's
        instruments 169–71, *169*
    Anton Walter 169
Pleyel, Ignaz 100
Polledro, Giovanni Battista 131
Potter, Cipriani 37, 168, 179

Prague 124, 125, 144, 148
Preindl, Josef 183
Prichowsky of Prague, Count 54
Prometheus journal 118
Prussia 5, 71
    Franco–Prussian War 228
Punto, Giovanni 21

Radichi, Julius 152
Razumovsky, Andreas, Count 9,
    57, 159, 192, 215
Razumovsky, Maria Elisabeth,
    Countess 9
Reicha, Anton 63
Reichardt, Johann Friedrich
    90–91, 101, 108
Reissig, Christian Ludwig 114, 128
Richardson, Samuel 22
Ries, Ferdinand 52, 56–7, 63–4,
    73–4, 75, 79, 122, 127, 167, 196,
    214, 215, 216
    and the 'Hammerklavier' 175–6,
        179
    as Illuminati member 3
Ries, Franz 3
Rizzi, Antonio: *Beethoven: 'Sinfonia
    Eroica II Tempo'* 86, 87
Rochlitz, Friedrich 20, 226
Rode, Pierre 214
Romberg, Bernhard 214
Rose, Bernard: *Immortal Beloved*
    130
Rosen, Charles 174
Rosenbaum, Joseph Carl 57
Rossini, Gioachino 160, 198
Rousseau, Jean-Jacques 22
Royal Philharmonic Society,
    London 167, 196, 229

Rudolph, Archduke of Austria 108,
109, 118, 139, 175, 181–2, 183,
191, 219

S. A. Steiner & Co. 143
Sailer, Johann Michael 186
St Petersburg Philharmonic Society
192
Salieri, Anton 31, 105, 108, 225
Salomon, Johann Peter 32, 34
Sammler 91
Schaller, Johann Nepomuk, bust of
Beethoven 229
Schikaneder, Emanuel 26, 27
Schiller, Friedrich 22, 45, 72,
114, 186
Die Jungfrau von Orleans 152
'Ode to Joy' 45, 102, 197–8
Schindler, Anton 51, 94, 123, 190,
191–2, 199, 208, 222, 224,
225, 226
Schindlöcker, Philipp 29
Schlegel, Friedrich 116, 218
Schlemmer, Wenzel 175, 190
Schlemmer family 220
Schlesinger, Moritz 208, 221
Schlesinger (Berlin publishing
company) 191
Schmidt, Johann Adam 48
Schönbrunn, Treaty of 107
Schönfeld, Therese 55
Schott (publisher) 191, 201, 202, 214
Schreiber, Anton 29
Schröder-Devrient, Wilhelmine
160–61
Schubert, Franz 40, 114, 223
'Erlkönig' 54
Schulz, Johann Abraham Peter 100

Schuppanzigh, Ignaz 21, 28–9,
30–31, 52–3, 56, 192–3, 199,
200, 214
caricature 53
and his quartet 215–17
subscription concert series
214–16
Schwarzenberg, Joseph Johann zu,
Prince 24
Scott, Walter 222
Sebald, Amalie 124
*Selam. Ein Almanach für Freunde des
Mannigfaltigen* 136
sensibility 22, 37
Seyfried, Ignaz von 95, 201, 202
Simrock, Nikolaus 3, 63–4, 72,
75, 191
Smart, Sir George 216
Society of Noble Ladies, Vienna
198–9
Society of the Friends of Music
(Gesellschaft der
Musikfreunde), Vienna 187,
193, 198–9, 200
Solomon, Maynard 3, 124–6
Sonneck, Oscar 130
Sonnleithner, Joseph 77, 144, 145,
146, 154, 199
Sonnleithner, Leopold 200, 201
Spohr, Louis 99, 127, 214
Spontini, Gaspare 203
Milton 104–5
Steibelt, Daniel 21, 31, 81, 101
Stein, Anton 168
'hearing machine' 172
Stein, Carl Friedrich 105
Stein, Johann 48
Steiner, Sigmund Anton 51, 191

Stockhausen, Karlheinz 229
Stoll, Joseph Ludwig 116, 118, 136
    'An die Geliebte' 118, 136
Strauss, Johann I 198
Strauss, Richard: *Metamorphosen*
    86–7
Streicher, Anton 48
Streicher, Johann Andreas 131, 132
Streicher, Nanette 48–9, 163, 164
Streicher family 167, 168, 171
stringed instruments 97 *see also*
    bowing techniques; bows,
    violin
Stutterheim, Joseph von 220
Swieten, Gottfried van, Baron 9,
    41, 187

Teplitz (now Teplice, Czech
    Republic) 112, 124
Thayer, Alexander Wheelock 95,
    226
    Life of Beethoven 123–4
Theater-Zeitung 200
Thomson, George 114, 167, 180–81
Thun, Maria Wilhelmine von,
    Countess 9
Thürheim, Lulu, Countess 108
Tiedge, Christian August 124
Tolstoy, Leo: *The Kreutzer Sonata*
    67, 68
Tomaschek, Wenzel Johann 150
Tonkünstler Societät (Society of
    Musicians, Vienna) 25, 90, 105
Tourte bow 65–7, *66*
Treitschke, Georg Friedrich
    Die Ehrenpforten 138–9
    Die gute Nachricht 138
    and *Fidelio* 143, 146, 148, 154

tuning 97
Tuscher, Mathias von 166

Uhland, Ludwig 116
Umlauf, Michael 200
Unger, Caroline 200

Varnhagen von Ense, Karl August
    124, 125
Vienna
    Akademisches Gymnasium 165
    Augarten hall 56–7
    Augarten park 140
    and Beethoven *see* Beethoven,
        Ludwig van: the man and his
        life: and Vienna
    Burgtheater 19, 27, 90, 105, 116;
        Beethoven's 1800 Akademie
        19, 23, 24, 25, *26*
    café culture 51
    Café Frauenhuber 51
    celebrations after Napoleon's
        abdication 139–40
    and censorship 15–16, 72, 144,
        146, 159, 187, 190
    centenary of Beethoven's birth
        (1827) 228
    coffeehouses 50, 116
    Concerts Spirituels 193–5, 198
    Congress of viii, 15, 140, 142,
        157, 159; ball at Imperial
        Riding School during 139,
        139; and Biedermeier era 160
    court culture 6
    currency viii, 32, 108, 117
    dance music 198
    French occupation 107, 114,
        116, 145

Vienna – *cont'd*
French operas translated into
German 143
Gesellschaft der Musikfreunde
187, 193, 198–9, 200
Großer Redoutensaal *139*, 142
as a hierarchical society 47
as an instrument-building centre
8, 10
Italian opera's popularity 198
Joseph Blöchlinger's Institute
166
Kärntnertortheater 27, 74,
104–5, 138, 146, 156, 160, 199
location and character 6
map 50
Mehlgrube 98
under Metternich 15–16, 139,
159, 187, 190
musical factions of 1820s 198
musical heritage and cultural
kudos 7–8, 41–2; and
mixture of 'high' and 'low'
art 156
nobility 17; practising 'soft
power' 25
Palais Lobkowitz, Eroica-Saal 75
population growth 49
publishers 8–9
Redoutensaal 98, 199
reputation 8, 17, 203
Schwarzenberg palace 24, 28
Society of Noble Ladies 198–9
Theater an der Wien 26–7, 70,
91, 108; Beethoven's 1808
Akademie 90–103, 105, 106;
orchestra 95, 98
Theater in der Leopoldstadt 26

Tonkünstler-Societät concerts
25, 90, 105
Viennese classical style 10–11
vogue for French operas 73
women in 48–9
Viotti bow 65
Voltaire 3, 73

Wagner, Richard 228
Waldstein, Ferdinand, Count 4,
130
Walter, Anton, fortepiano 169
Wegeler, Franz Gerhard 1, 2, 44–5,
113, 122, 227
Beethoven's letters to 44–5,
47–8
Weigl, Joseph 138
L'amor marinaro ossia Il corsaro 81
Weiss, Franz 215, 217
Werner, Zacharias 187
Wetzler, Alexander 55
Wieland, Christoph Martin 114
*Wiener Allgemeine musikalische
Zeitung* 194, 201, 202
Wiener Zeitung 179
Wild, Franz 135
Willmann, Magdalena 122
Winkel, Dietrich Nikolaus 178
Woldemar, Ernst (Heinrich
Hermann) 83, 179
Wranitzky, Paul 21
*Grande Sinfonie caractéristique pour
la paix avec la République
Françoise* 72, 92
Würfel, Wenzel Wilhelm 192

Zmeskall, Nikolaus, Baron 28, 47,
51, 63, 127, 179, 222